**PENGUIN BOOKS**

# DAYS LIKE THIS

Phyllis Gillis is president of Entrepreneurial Communications Inc., a midsize public relations firm specializing in communications programs and marketing
strategies for privately owned companies, and the
publisher of *Entrepreneurial Communications,* a newslet-
ter offering strategies, tactics, and techniques for the
small-business owner. She is also the author of *Entrepreneurial Mothers,* co-author of *The New Pregnancy,* and
has written many magazine articles on the changing
roles of the family in America today.

D1044529

# DAYS
# LIKE THIS

## PHYLLIS GILLIS

Penguin Books

**PENGUIN BOOKS**

Viking Penguin Inc., 40 West 23rd Street,
New York, New York 10010, U.S.A.
Penguin Books Ltd, Harmondsworth,
Middlesex, England
Penguin Books Australia Ltd, Ringwood,
Victoria, Australia
Penguin Books Canada Limited, 2801 John Street,
Markham, Ontario, Canada L3R 1B4
Penguin Books (N.Z.) Ltd, 182–190 Wairau Road,
Auckland 10, New Zealand

First published in the United States of America by
McGraw-Hill Book Company 1986
Reprinted by arrangement with McGraw-Hill, Inc.
Published in Penguin Books 1987

LIBRARY OF CONGRESS CATALOGING IN PUBLICATION DATA
Gillis, Phyllis L., 1945–
Days like this.
1.  Divorce—United States—Case studies.
2.  Equitable distribution of marital property—
United States—Popular works.    3.  Divorce—Law
and legislation—United States—Popular works.
I.  Title.
[HQ834.G49    1987]      346.7301'66      86-30663
ISBN 0 14 01.0156 X        347.306166

Printed in the United States of America by
Offset Paperback Mfrs., Inc., Dallas, Pennsylvania
Set in Baskerville

*For "Nathaniel"*

# PREFACE

Almost four years ago I became an unmarried woman. I thought I'd be just like Erica, the character played by Jill Clayburgh in the movie *An Unmarried Woman*. I'd be hurt, but I'd be okay. I'd get along financially. I'd have my child. I'd fall into a good job. And I'd find a lover like Alan Bates. Unfortunately, nothing could have been farther from the truth.

For eleven years I thought I was one-half of the picture-perfect, dual-career marriage. I thought of myself as financially aware, emotionally sound, and easily able to cope with both the expected and unexpected shifts in our life plans. Here, too, nothing could have been farther from the truth. Our perfectly modern, dual-career marriage left me completely unprepared for the realities of modern-day divorce.

What divorce 1980s-style actually entailed was something of a long, drawn-out horror show. I was ill-prepared for it both emotionally and financially, and, to top it all off, I was woefully ignorant legally. Looking back on those early months of our separation, I suppose I expected to be "taken care of" in some way. Perhaps I expected that after an initial period of dickering, my estranged spouse and I would strike a modern "no-fault" deal and we would both go on with our respective lives, living happily ever after.

But it took two long and sometimes emotionally brutal years before our version of this very grim fairy tale would end, and another before each of us could regain a sense of equilibrium and order in our lives. Ultimately, we would learn more about each other and ourselves during the process of divorce than we ever had in marriage.

I wish I could outline in black and white why the process of divorce took so long or cite causes for the interminable delays, hang-ups, and hold-outs. I wish it were possible to point the finger of guilt at someone or something and name outright who or what was to blame. I can't. There were times that I was so angry at my ex-husband, so emotionally distraught, that I lost all semblance of rational thought. It was if my brain had suddenly taken a vacation. In my confused struggle to come to terms with the breakup of our marriage, I am certain there were instances when I was unfair to him—just as he might have been unfair to me.

The issue of whether or not we were "fair" with each other is history. In divorce there is no "right" and no "wrong." I don't even know what right is. For us, resolving our differences meant hammering out a settlement we both could live with. We are fortunate as humans that, just as our feelings ebb and flow, so too are they tempered with the passage of time.

What is *not* history is the question of whether divorce eighties-style is "fair." During the period when my marriage was coming unglued, a wave of divorce reforms were sweeping the country. "No-fault" divorce codes, "equitable distribution" provisions, and "joint custody" laws were becoming part of the language of family law. These were the end result of a massive effort to correct an outmoded legal code that was degrading and humiliating to all parties in the process and often unfair to one party in the outcome.

These "reforms" may have made divorce easier, but in no way have they made it any fairer. *Days Like This* is a personal story written to demonstrate the effect of these reforms on one unmarried woman, and thereby to help those undergoing divorce understand the laws today and just how inequitably the "equitable" distribution provisions can work out. Especially for women.

As *Days Like This* goes to press, a great deal of research is beginning to surface that provides overwhelming evidence of how these "reforms" have backfired. In an effort to make divorce less traumatic, these very reforms have had dramatic negative economic and social consequences for women. The "no-fault" laws which treat men and women "equally" at divorce ignore the very real economic inequalities that marriage creates. They also ignore the economic inequalities between men and women in society at large. "Joint custody" statutes ignore the practical considerations of just *who* is raising the children in favor of some theoretical ideal of dual child-rearing. The main result of this is that the child suffers.

The most startling statistic to emerge from this new body of research is that divorced women and their children are rapidly becoming a new underclass, suffering a decline of 73 percent in their standard of living after divorce. At the same time, divorced men are experiencing an increase of 42 percent in theirs. The sharpest drop and most severe deprivation are suffered by older homemakers and women with young children.

Divorce settlements are often handed down under the (mistaken) assumption that women can swiftly become self-sufficient, putting their lives on "go" at the precise moment when they become single again. While self-sufficiency is a desirable goal, for the woman who has chosen to remain home with her children, or has never worked, or has entered the workforce later in life and is capable of finding a "job" but not of recapturing lost career opportunities of her younger years, the assumption of equal financial footing with an ex-spouse who has never left the workforce is a cruel joke.

If anyone could have been expected to sail through divorce and spring back to self-sufficiency, I would have been the ideal candidate. I had a professional track record and was (I thought) emotionally stable. And I completely fell apart.

In an effort to avert the inequitable results of equitable distribution, many states have now started judicial divorce education programs for the very judges who will be deciding the financial and custodial fates of the newly unmarried. These programs involve outside experts from a broad variety of fields (psychology, sociology, economics, etc.). In time, this may result in a better situation for divorced women. It may also result in some new divorce legislation.

But, as much as the new divorce laws have created a lopsided environment for marital dissolution, there is another, often overlooked factor that works in favor of men. Men tend to approach divorce from an economic perspective. This may be one reason why men seem to be better able to treat divorce as a business deal, and to weather the long and often unpleasant process of negotiation with a bit of self-protecting distance. For women, on the other hand, divorce is an overwhelmingly emotional issue. Ill-prepared psychologically to undergo divorce, women are often their own worst enemies. Instead of marshaling her resources to confront a system that has gone haywire, an unmarried woman often caves in under the first bit of intimidation. "I don't want to make waves," "There's nothing I can do," or "He wouldn't treat me like this if I hadn't done something to make him angry," are all comments I have heard repeatedly from other women undergoing divorce. I've heard some of them from myself. Women, socialized to be nurturing and giving, often give in and give up. In the end, settlements may have been quicker, but by giving up in spirit, many of today's unmarried women are giving up their financial futures and giving away the lives of their children.

My case was one of the luckier ones because I was able to apply some of my business training to the negotiation and settlement process. I also had two crackerjack attorneys working with me on the financial and custody aspects of my case. Still, I often fell prey to severe and prolonged bouts of depression, anxiety, and insecurity over whether I would be able to "tough it out" and establish some kind of an adequate future for myself and my child. In the process of "toughing it out," I was castigated for doing so by more people than I care to admit, not only men but women as well. Virtually everyone's assumption seemed to be that what had been an acceptable standard of living and behavior for me while I was married automatically evaporated in divorce. To fight for my rights, I learned, was somehow not the way a "lady" should act.

But acting like a "lady" is not what divorce is all about. Divorce is a complex game, an extended business negotiation. And just as women today have had to learn new games and new rules of behavior in business, in relationships, and in child rearing, so too we have to learn the new game of divorce. After all, we all know people who are going through it, and fully 50 percent of us will go through it ourselves. While some of the new research findings now surfacing may help to change the divorce laws so that women get a better break, women should still learn to treat the divorce process as a business negotiation and, however difficult it may be, to park their emotions outside the courtroom door and stand up for what is rightfully theirs.

I have told my story to the best of my knowledge. Much of it is based upon extensive notes taken by me during the divorce process. At the behest of my attorney, I took notes on every meeting and every telephone conversation with my ex-spouse. My attorney wanted nothing left to memory. Perhaps as my ex-husband was talking with me, he was doing likewise. On one occasion, I taped a conversation

with him over dinner in a restaurant, with his permission.
The intent of this was not to spy, but to obtain a running
log of conversations, commitments, and comments so that
my lawyer and I might obtain a clear insight into what
really was being offered in the negotiation process. Based
on two years of notebooks filled with dates, times, places,
and conversations, I was able to reconstruct my story. Extensive court documents provided backup data when my
memory failed or when gaps in my notebooks appeared.
I have, however, taken the liberty of changing names, places,
and descriptions in order to protect my child, whose care
and feeding, emotional well-being, and custody was, and
is, the most major of all my concerns.

*Days Like This* is very much a personal history. It is told
in the hope that other women undergoing the trauma of
divorce within the no-fault environment will gain solace,
support, and insight into the emotional and financial fallout affecting so many unmarried women in the aftermath
of the divorce revolution. It is a story also for the vast
numbers of those who are not unmarried as well as those
who intend to marry some day. I can't think of anything
better than to find and be married to one's "own true love"
and live "happily ever after." It's what I wish for myself
and for all my friends. And it *does* happen. I've seen it.
Unfortunately, it also *doesn't* happen . . . .

# ACKNOWLEDGMENTS

With flourish but not favoritism I gratefully acknowledge the unending support of the following special friends: Marion and Joseph Chiesa, Marc Leotta, John Kalbach, Marcelle Bijou, Virginia and Orley Ashenfelter, Rebecca Shaw, Luisa and Robert Fernholz. To my assistants who never balked at repeatedly retyping the same words in different fashion, I acknowledge Martha Capps, Sandra Karp, and Barbara Reeder. To my agent, Ellen Levine, who has provided a decade of encouragement, I express gratitude. To my editor and friend, Elisabeth Jakab, who helped mold "days like those" into *Days Like This*, I express my warmest appreciation and deepest gratitude. Special thanks to my longtime friend Faith Grill and her family for their love and support over the years.

# CONTENTS

*Momma said there'd be*
*days like this,*
*there'd be days like this,*
*Momma said. . . .*
*—from the song, "Momma Said,"*

# CHAPTER 1

# MY NIGHTS AT ARTURO'S

"Who will take care of us, Mommy?" The words ricocheted through my mind. It was my child's question. The words of a frightened six-year-old. Now that Daddy has left, who will take care of us?

"I will, Nathaniel. Mom's not leaving. I'll take care of you."

Easy to say, not so easy to do.

It was midnight. My back and legs ached. I could barely move my arms. My head was swimming. I was standing before a hot stove in a stifling restaurant kitchen. Through my daze I mechanically checked a set of orders. Three chicken Parmesans. Two steak sandwiches—one plain, one loaded with onions, peppers, and mushrooms. A curried chicken, cranberry duck, and veggie sandwich. Two fries, two French onion soups.

Who would order French onion soup in ninety-degree weather? I wondered as I pushed the waitress call buzzer. Two more hours until I could go home. My son's words kept coming back to me as an avalanche of food orders continued to be posted.

"Who will take care of us, Mommy?"

"I will, honey."

It was my first night at Arturo's "working the line" as a short order cook.

I stared at the row of orders hanging before me like an orderly line of clothing drying in the sunshine on a hot sunny day. How could people eat full meals at midnight? When did they sleep? How could they sleep on full stomachs? The very thought nauseated me. The heat and the noise nauseated me. I leaned against the butcher-block counter in front of me, my hands clutching at its sides. I was so woozy, I was certain I was going to faint. The unfamiliar surroundings, heat, and kitchen tumult were really getting to me.

Every time the swinging doors to the bar and dining room opened, the muffled din of the outer areas collided with the clatter of the kitchen. In, out, in, out. Whoosh, whoosh. The traffic through the doors was unending. Waitresses with orders, bartenders pulling back-up beer and wine from the walk-in cooler, busboys bringing in overflowing tubs of dirty dishes. When would it slow down? Didn't those lounge lizards ever want to go home?

I told myself to concentrate. My job was to feed people, not question their eating habits. Only two more hours. Don't screw up. You need this job. You'll get used to it.

How far away the frenetic pace of the kitchen was, I thought, from the controlled white-collar world to which I was accustomed.

The orders kept coming. I couldn't keep up. I felt like Mickey Mouse in "The Sorcerer's Apprentice." One day when the sorcerer is away the lazy mouse apprentice disobeys orders and casts a spell over the sorcerer's water buckets. The buckets keep bringing him water, too much water. But he cannot control them, nor stop the flow of the water, and the water rises step by step, threatening to drown him. Here at Arturo's, as each new order was posted, another wave of panic struck. I saw myself being drowned by a pile of restaurant checks. I envisioned the food flying out of the refrigerators and ovens and off the plates. I would be buried alive.

No one would miss me. No one on the kitchen staff had even asked my name when I arrived. I would be swept away by chicken Parmesans, cranberry ducks, and veggie sandwiches, boiled to death by French onion soup in ninety-degree weather.

"Who will take care of us, Mommy?"

"I will, honey. I will."

"Jesse," I shouted to my dishwasher. "Pans! I need fry pans."

I had run out of pans. The dishwashers couldn't keep up either. Jesse, a Guatemalan immigrant, was scrubbing hard at the mountain of pans stacked in the triple sink, a kitchen radio next to him turned up so loud that he couldn't hear me.

"Pans!" I screamed again, as I rescued a batch of shrimp tempura about to burn in oil in the deep fryer. I pressed the call button. Two buzzes. Waitress in, another order out.

Then I marched the ten steps over to the sink and pulled a sauté pan from a clean pile of cookware left to drain before being hung on the hooks within arm's reach of the cooks' station next to the ovens.

"Jesse!" I shouted. "I need sauté pans!"

He picked his head up from his scrubbing, looked me straight in the eye, then turned his gaze to my breasts. Still saying nothing he opened his mouth, licked his lips with his tongue, and tried to wrest the pan away from me. I had stepped into his territory, the delivery of fresh pans, and he was warning me.

My spine prickled with fear. Was my fear justified, I wondered, or was I simply a new dish to be tested? I knew I couldn't let him see I was afraid. Defiantly, I grabbed the pan away from him, pretended to wipe the sweat from my brow, and retreated to my stove.

It was the third time that evening Jesse had come on to me.

The first time he had scored a direct hit. I had been removing a cumbersome container of partially cooked spareribs from the bottom shelf of a walk-in refrigeration unit.

"I want to get to know you," he had hissed, pressing his body against mine.

"*Basta!* Enough!" I commanded, using the only bit of school Spanish I could remember.

"A woman of *your* age needs a man of *my* age," he said threateningly in half Spanish, half English. His toothless smile widened and his eyes sparkled as I pushed him away. He was acting as if he thought I was flirting.

I could see he wasn't deterred. I decided to focus my attention on the food. He focused his attention on me. As I was bent over, carefully removing the steaming crocks of onion soup from the 500-degree oven, I felt a set of hands on my behind.

"So beautiful, like fresh melons," a hoarse voice whispered in my ear. "Sometimes you just have to touch them."

By the time I was able to place the crocks on serving platters and release the kitchen tongs, Jesse was gone.

Had I been employed in an office, or, for that matter, any other job, I would have been bellowing to the boss about sexual harassment. I knew all about it, having published dozens of articles about sexual shakedowns, employer-employee confrontations, low pay, and a host of other workplace concerns during a twenty-year career as a journalist.

But here I was virtually powerless. I needed this job desperately. The former Ms. Success, the managerial woman, now financially and emotionally bankrupt, was riding herd over an unruly kitchen staff, trying to feed 200 hungry and impatient customers on a sultry summer evening in a singles joint.

I didn't have time to worry about Jesse and whether he would be trouble or something I could handle. That would have to come later. As closing time neared, I rushed to complete the food orders. One more cheese sandwich and the kitchen was closed.

Now we could break down and clean up. The day shift was scheduled to arrive a few hours later and food had to be stored properly to avoid spoilage. Equipment had to be cleaned and ready for use. As the "line" chef, in charge of the actual cooking, I was also responsible for preparing extensive notes for my daytime counterpart that detailed what had been sold, what supplies or ingredients needed to be reordered, and which sauces or menu items needed to be prepped or replenished.

I could barely remember my name at this point, let alone all the cleanup details. How would I ever survive this, I thought? Office work was so much easier, but there were no offices in this area which would have me. I was overqualified for every available job. But I needed work. I was willing to take anything to support my son and survive. Anything meant this job as a cook—working the line at Arturo's.

I finished my notes, hung them on the "dupe" rack above the food preparation area (where duplicate table checks were placed for easy visual access by both cook and server), and began to scrub the oven burners with a steel wool pad dredged up from the bottom of a soap-filled bucket. I was entitled to $5 worth of food from the menu per shift, but I was too exhausted to eat.

The night manager entered the kitchen carrying a glass of white wine for me. I hadn't requested it, but I accepted the wine gratefully. He had iced the glass and the cool liquid tasted like a fine French vintage as it passed through my parched lips.

I had earned $42 for my night's work, and I was thrilled to have it.

I untied my apron, which by now was caked with grease, marinara sauce, dishwater, parsley, and onion bits, tossed it into the linen bin, and dragged myself out to my car. I had made it, toughed it out physically. Emotionally I wasn't so sure. I wanted to cry, to scream, to talk to someone, anyone. I couldn't. I couldn't even get my thoughts together. I was simply exhausted. I wanted to leave Arturo's behind me, go home, and sleep.

I reached my home a few minutes later, considered a shower, but reconsidered when I realized that I did not even have the strength to turn on the faucets. I threw myself across the top of my bed, and, still dressed in my filthy clothing, slept until 3:30 the next afternoon. When I arose, I showered and telephoned my son, who was visiting his father for a few days.

An hour later, I was back at the restaurant, on the line.

My nights at Arturo's had their beginnings unexpectedly on an autumn night eight months earlier. I was reflecting on how all the problems in my marriage were finally being ironed out. It had taken a long time, but I was sure that now I had finally found the perfect solution to combining motherhood and career in a small town. I was about to open my own business (with three partners, one of whom was my husband): a restaurant which was to serve as the cornerstone for my eventual conversion of an antiquated hotel into a fashionable tourist bed-and-breakfast.

I felt good; for the first time in months I was free of the bone-crushing headaches which had plagued me daily from the moment I rose to the moment I drifted off to sleep. I was relaxed. Curtis and I weren't fighting so much anymore. Things were really coming together. My life, my family, my business.

Maybe now we could even finish furnishing our home. After eleven years of marriage the house was still largely unfurnished. It never struck me as odd. Curtis and I had just never got around to it.

Now, as I lay stretched out on a newly purchased beige modular couch, watching the season premier of "Hill Street Blues," I thought how nice it would be to keep going after this initial purchase, how nice it would be to turn our beautiful contemporary house into a warm and livable home.

Tomorrow would be October 1, the first day of my most favorite month. I had always loved October because to me it signaled the start of a new year. As a schoolgirl I had relished the promise of the fall semester, which brought with it a new class, new friends, and new activities. Each job in my checkered career path had had its inception in October. Even my son had been conceived during this month.

I *was* looking forward to my new venture. After a year of preparation and setup I would witness the flowering of every homemaker's fantasy—a boutique restaurant. I was pleased that I was carving out a niche of my own in my community and, more importantly, that my business venture was one around which the demands of my family could easily be met. I would do lunch, another chef would run the dinner service. We would collaborate on catering and special events. Perfect, the venture was simply perfect. Curtis would see. He'd been against it for the longest time but I'd finally brought him around.

The floor-to-ceiling windows in the family room were open and an occasional breeze darted in from the early fall night air, teasing the nape of my neck. It felt so good to be free from pain. Dozens of hours of medical tests and hundreds of dollars for physician consultations had yielded no organic reason for the excruciating headaches. Tension, the professionals decreed, was the reason for the nausea, vomiting, and viselike head pain which had haunted me every day, morning, noon, and night, for so long.

I was trying to do too much, these wise men and women had told me repeatedly. I was on overload. I couldn't be everything to everyone. Superwoman was shorting out.

I had heard the same story from my husband. Constantly.

I couldn't do it all, he told me. I was compromising all areas of our life together. Something had to give.

"You must choose," he would say, standing at the foot of our bed as he loosened his tie after a dinner meeting or upon returning from a business trip. No matter what time he came home from one of these meetings or trips, nine P.M. or one A.M., he would wake me. I was usually asleep early, exhausted after a day of mothering and work. He saw my sleep-time habits and headaches as evidence of overload. I saw them as a normal response to an active day with a small child and the standard tensions attendant on the start-up of a business.

"C'mon," I mumbled. "Give me a break. I'm exhausted."

It was easier to ignore his complaints than argue. Maybe they would go away. I wanted so to show him I could manage, prove to him that I *could* succeed.

"I can see you're exhausted," he went on. "You must unclutter your life, cut out the nonessentials, pare down the extraneous activities," he lectured. I sighed resignedly. I had heard this speech so much that sometimes I believed it. Besides, though I didn't like to admit it, Curtis was usually right about most things.

But his rationale for my headaches just didn't make sense. I had uncluttered my life until it was practically vacant. Since the birth of my son six years earlier, I had worked only in part-time or free-lance positions. I had left my well-paying full-time job, given up commuting. I was currently spending two days a week attending restaurant management school. My remaining hours were split between tennis and carpooling.

The "burnout" or "excessive-stress" syndrome didn't make any sense as an explanation for the never-ending pain in my head. I was tired, sure, but I wasn't *that* tired.

I attributed the way we viewed my headaches as just another one of our differences in the way we looked at our dual-career life. Curtis thought I was working too hard; I thought I wasn't working enough.

I was insensitive, noncommunicative, he said, and that was the reason for any marital discord we experienced. He had a point, I thought. It was hard for me to speak up. And when I did, I tended to get a little overemotional. That never sat well with Curtis, who always argued clearly, rationally, and objectively. I argued like a wild woman storming through the house, my voice pitched about two octaves higher than normal. Still, it seemed to me that our arguments were no more profound than those experienced by any other dual-career couple with multiple work and family responsibilities.

So what if we argued a bit? Every other couple I knew trying to combine work and family did too. That was the difference between dating and being married. Married was "for better or for worse." When you married it was time to grow up. Married people worked things out. One of the things being worked out, it seemed to me, was some kind of fallout from the women's movement, which had made clear to me that I not only wanted to work, I *needed* to work. Curtis had grown up with very traditional views about women working. I knew he was trying to accommodate me, but I also knew he'd rather I didn't work at all. He'd have to adjust, I thought—or rather, *hoped*.

I excused the constant undercurrent of friction that had hovered lately within the household as a temporary interlude in the education of the American male—from macho, all powerful, all controlling, to nurturing and supportive. He simply needed to learn the new marital rules. He'd change, sooner or later.

"He means well," I justified to my more feminist friends when they asked why I did all the errands, household chores, business entertaining, child-care arrangements. It was small stuff. Why sweat it? So he doesn't want to help clean, so what? So he doesn't want to help me out so that I can wrap up a free-lance article, so what? I'll get help. Curtis works hard, bringing in the money to support us. So what if an assignment had to be turned down because Curtis had a convention to attend and needed his wife along? Or a social evening with business associates? Or a company party or picnic? I went because I was his wife, his partner.

His job meant *I* didn't have to work, I could free-lance, dabble in the things that interested me. My personal time wasn't all that important since I had given up a full-time career, and I could easily fit in my business activities around the edges of our life together.

Our life together. Actually, it could be better. My favorite way of spending an evening was having a few friends over for an informal meal. His favorite way of spending an evening was going out—as a couple alone. Every couple of weeks I entertained his business associates at our house and we went out alone together. I loved to travel, each time visiting a different place. He returned like a homing pigeon to the same beach year after year. We compromised. I took a European cooking holiday. We went as a family to the beach.

We were different personalities, but I thought that was what made our marriage work. We were complementary partners, not identical twins. I was impulsive, intense, and easily excited. He was stable, structured, and correct, everything I was not, and I loved him for his strength. I depended on it more, perhaps, than I liked to admit, even to myself. Thanks to him I had become calmer, more organized. I could see how he approved of that when I serenely hostessed gatherings of his business associates, sometimes two, three, four times a month. When I still commuted to a full-time job, I would often leave in midday to cook and prepare for his guests, then arrive at my job late the next morning after a long evening. These days, working at home, it was easy to interrupt my writing schedule to accept deliveries from the local butcher, baker, or laundry.

When we did argue he could usually bring me around to his point of view. Since my way of arguing was volatile, emotional, all over the place, and his was articulate, logical, carefully prepared, he could usually convince me of anything. I hadn't mastered his measured approach to life, but maybe someday I would. In the meantime I didn't worry much about it.

Take, for instance, our most recent blowup. Just a few days ago we had been discussing my financial projections for the restaurant. I had carefully stashed away several months' worth of payments I had received for baking breads and desserts for a local store. These funds would be the initial capital for my business.

"Oh, but we're not going to set it up as a profit-making venture," Curtis said as I laid out my plans. "We can use the restaurant as a tax shelter. We'll run the funds through Red Top Leasing."

I couldn't believe my ears. He had just started a small leasing company as a sideline to his main job and planned to run *my* restaurant as a subsidiary of this new operation. He had never mentioned this to me. My business would lose money from the start.

We argued back and forth over the merits of saving money by sheltering income or paying taxes on my profits. Of course there would be profits, I said heatedly. I was certain of that.

I couldn't prevail against his financial acumen. He had a fine sense of money, how to make it and keep it, how to work the tax codes to their best advantage. What he was suggesting was not illegal. It made very good business sense and I knew it.

"What's such a big deal, Phyllis?" he asked after we had both calmed down. "We're married. The money comes out of our joint funds. If you lose money in your business, we'll save money that we would ordinarily have paid out in taxes."

The next day I accompanied Curtis to the bank where the checkbook for my business was ordered. The bank officer sat behind his desk facing both of us, listening to Curtis explain the necessity of changing the form of my business and our need for new checks. The officer occasionally glanced at me, his eyes questioning my understanding of this transaction, but he asked me no questions and I volunteered no opinion. I was uncomfortable, acquiescing as I had. I felt rather like a doormat for having done so. But I *had* agreed, and now I wanted to get it over with and get out of the bank.

Curtis handled all the banking requirements. Change of address cards. Initial deposit. Joint signature cards. Both of our signatures were now required to cash checks. I had become a subsidiary of his operation.

"Where do I sign?" was the only question I asked. And even though I knew what we had done was all for the best, I was terribly upset for the next two days. I had *so* wanted the business to be a success.

Tonight Curtis was out for the evening, attending what he said was a dinner meeting with business associates. It had been a week of irregular schedules and meetings. Curtis worked for a large contractor and this was contract negotiating time. He liked wheeling and dealing. He was good at it and he got his way a lot. In past years, labor-management bargaining sessions had continued well into the morning hours, and I expected nothing new or different from this round.

He was on management's side of the table, and every three years he played out the same scenario. The union demanded; management denied. Eventually contract terms which dissatisfied everyone were agreed upon and business continued as usual.

I heard the car turn into the driveway and listened as the tires crushed the gravel which blanketed the steep, nearly vertical climb to our home.

I glanced up from the TV screen as Curtis opened the door and came into the room. He strode silently across the floor to the television set and pressed the off button. The picture faded from the tube.

I remember thinking at the time that the contract negotiations must have been particularly difficult that evening. He looked perturbed and disheveled. He was wearing a lightweight navy blue pinstriped suit, a white shirt, and a patterned maroon tie. The shirt was unbuttoned at the neck, the tie loosened, the pants and jacket wrinkled. Even when he was rumpled, his superb taste in clothing was evident. Everything he owned matched perfectly. He would not even purchase a shirt if a suitable tie wasn't available to complete the outfit. For years he had selected my ward-robe as well as his.

He faced me, his arms rigid at his sides, and began to talk at me:

"Phyllis, I'm leaving you. I've taken an apartment and I will be moving in the morning."

I just looked at him. I didn't quite realize what he was saying.

"Jackie is coming with me," he continued. "She's break-ing the news to Stan right now."

I was bewildered. Jackie was a friend, my next-door neighbor. We played tennis together, alternated car pools.

I waited for an explanation. He offered none. This had to be a bad joke. He couldn't be serious.

His face registered just how serious he was. I could think of nothing to say. I was stunned. I didn't know how Curtis expected me to act. I didn't know what to say, what to do, so I said nothing, showed nothing. I searched my feelings—I didn't seem to have any: no pain, no emotion, nothing. I just sat and looked at him, trying to figure out why or when it had happened. Somewhere far away from me, feelings of sadness and regret began to stir. Rather than growing together, we had grown apart. Why? When? How long had this been going on? Why hadn't I noticed anything? My mind began racing. Suddenly, eleven years of marriage were compressed into a moment. Hundreds of memories flashed by. Only one locked into vivid focus.

He and she were walking home after a tennis match at a neighbor's court. I was returning home with my son from a friend's birthday party. We converged near the base of our driveways. I slowed the car and asked if they wanted a lift for the remaining quarter mile. They declined; they preferred to walk the distance in the early fall air.

The tennis date itself was not unusual. A cadre of neighborhood hackers frequently shared partners when court time was available. The image locked in my memory was their faces. Flushed, exuberant, and glowing, they looked totally fulfilled. At the time I attributed the look to the excitement of a well-played, fast-moving tennis match. Now I knew that what I had seen was a relationship. He had been looking at her in a way he had never looked at me. His gaze had been one of desire, possession, and peace.

She was the woman he had always wanted—the woman I could never be: a professional wife, mother of two boys, school-board member, contented businessman's helpmate.

"She's perfect for you, Curtis," I said.

The words blurted from my mouth without rancor or bitterness.

"She's the woman with whom you've always wanted to share your life. She's your perfect mate."

Whether my reaction was based upon an honest assessment of a marriage gone wrong, or the realization that this was a challenge I could not meet, I do not know. Years of being an ostrich, my head firmly implanted in the sand, had ended in minutes. I couldn't hide any longer, nor could I push away the brutal recognition that my marriage was over.

The shrill ring of the telephone provided a welcome interruption. As I picked it up, I knew it would be Stan, the other spouse.

"What are you going to do about this, Phyllis?" he demanded. "Did you know anything?"

His voice, angry, anxious, and hurt, told me that he too had been caught completely unaware. And here I always thought his marriage had been a good one. So, obviously, had he. I had no idea what to say to him. I fumbled for words, wanting to help him in his pain, but I was numb, *anesthetized*. I fell back on the mechanics of a competent professional, a nurse soothing a sick patient. You'll be fine, I said with a sort of wooden kindness. It's for the best, I'm sure. Everything will work out. *Cluck-cluck*, I was the efficient mother hen.

As I spoke I was struck by the absurdity of our little domestic drama. The scenario was straight out of the day time soaps. The woman next door, the unsuspecting spouses the children asleep in their beds.

"Let me speak to Jackie," Curtis said, looking at me as if I were a secretary answering a call on his line. I told Stan to put his wife on and handed the phone to my husband.

"Hang in there, honey," he said softly. "I love you."

This had to be a dream, a bad dream. I shook my head, unable to believe what I was hearing. My head was spinning, I was dizzy. While my emotions seemed to be hidden away somewhere, my body was reacting like gangbusters. From my stomach to my head to my ears and neck—everything ached, my legs, my back, every part of me felt on fire.

By now it was midnight. This is enough, I thought, more than enough. I decided I would retire for the evening. I had a vague thought that by morning maybe everything would fall back into place. I would wake up and discover that I had just had a nightmare. This couldn't be real.

But Curtis had other plans for me.

"Since you are taking the news like a lady," he said, hanging up the phone, "we can go over a few details in preparation for the separation."

He took off his suit jacket, pulled his tie through his collar, and placed them both carefully on the kitchen table. He rolled up his shirt sleeves, walked across the expansive space which made up our combined kitchen-family-perfect-for-entertaining area, hitched up his pant legs to avoid further creases, and then lowered himself into a section of our new sofa. Hunched over the coffee table, hands locked together and folded in his lap, he looked like a football coach about to review a series of plays for the game of the week.

Same pattern as always. He was alert and alive in the late evening; I was exhausted, barely able to keep my eyes open. Still, I sat patiently and listened. I really didn't know what else to do.

"I'm leaving you this way because the law says I can," he said. I was struck by his words. The law says I can.

Curtis had been doing his homework. Curtis *always* did his homework. He was always prepared. "A no-fault divorce means no one is at fault. There is no penalty to me for leaving you in this way."

I didn't believe him, but I didn't say anything. Although I knew nothing about the changing divorce laws, I was sure he was wrong. He just couldn't walk out and set up housekeeping with another woman and suffer no consequences. Hadn't he heard of desertion? Adultery? Mental cruelty? Yes, he *had* to be wrong.

But I didn't challenge him. Didn't want to give away my thoughts. I'll find out the *real* story later, I thought, and then we'll really talk. You're going to pay for this, I thought. But for now I couldn't mobilize myself to do more than listen. He was very soothing and conciliatory as he talked about *my* feelings regarding the failure of our marriage and the extent to which *I* had contributed toward the marital breakdown.

*My* contribution to the marital breakdown? For a moment I started to respond. I could feel the words bubbling on my tongue. But I stopped. I didn't want him to see me cry.

My husband is leaving me for another woman and he's talking about it as if it were a discussion about who's going to do the shopping. My insides burned. How could he do this? So our marriage wasn't so great. Didn't people get counseling, try and work things out? Maybe we could get some help, maybe things could be different.

Did I want to beg him to stay? Should I? I felt a rush of emotions battering my skull. I was about to enter the ranks of being an unmarried woman. I didn't want to be one. I wanted to work things out, try again. One more chance, that's all I want, one more chance, I thought.

What should I say? What should I do? How could I stop him? Should I stop him? I was frantic inside, cool and removed outside. I remembered the advice of a boss from long ago. "When in doubt, do nothing," he had said. "Things have a way of working out."

So I did nothing but listen and seethe. I kept wondering if I was going to throw up. My stomach was churning ominously, and my head was killing me. Curtis sailed through his presentation as though he were chairing a well-organized business meeting.

"I know this is a great relief to you," he said with a paternal air. "We were just two people who grew in different directions. Now you can get on with your life and I can get on with mine."

He was almost acting as though he were doing me a favor.

"If you like, I'll be glad to help you find an attorney, Phyllis," he said graciously. "I don't think mine ought to represent both of us. Or maybe one of your female attorney friends could represent you."

"Thank you," I said almost in a whisper, "but I'll find my own attorney."

"I think you ought to see a therapist, too," he continued, "to help you work through your emotional problems."

Emotional problems? I thought to myself. What on earth was he talking about? I didn't have any "emotional problems." But I let that pass. I'd figure out what he was getting at later, when I could think straight. He looked up, waiting for my reaction then, proceeded to the next category.

"I'd like to lock up a separation agreement fairly soon," he said. "I'll have my attorney draft up something so that we can be divorced by the end of the year. I want to get this behind me."

Behind him? He wants to put this behind him? Eleven years of marriage wiped out in three months? I started to splutter, then caught myself again. No, I was not going to be a bitch, I was going to be professional, I thought. I was seesawing back and forth. What should I do? How should I react?

He handed me a yellow legal tablet and a freshly-sharpened pencil.

"Now, let's go over some of the details," he said.

Details? I hadn't even become accustomed to the general concept. A queasy feeling of dread began to descend over me. He was so *very* well prepared, almost too prepared. He knew all the answers and the prearranged outcome. He was totally in charge. I, on the other hand, was a simpleminded fool. Why hadn't I been able to see this coming?

I shoved myself into a corner of the couch and, as Curtis dictated numbers, I wrote them down.

"I will pay the following directly," he told me. "Mortgage, taxes, insurance, your car payment—mine is paid by my company—Nathaniel's school, camp, and sports activities, the gardener, and medical coverage. I will send you $100 a week for food, $20 a week for fuel, and $50 a week child support. That should enable you to live comfortably until we have a temporary settlement. Tomorrow we will go to the bank, divide whatever is left of our joint funds, and set up an account for you."

As he spoke I thought about our checkbooks, the safe-deposit box. He had probably been through everything. I wondered what was left, but in these early morning hours I had no choice but to wait until the bank opened at nine.

Still, the numbers and procedure *sounded* fair. I didn't question or comment, I just obediently wrote everything down, much the same way I had written down, every Sunday evening, Curtis's list of my weekly errands, activities, or obligations requiring attention. For the most part with Curtis it was always easier to acquiesce than to argue. Sometimes the items on the list were completed, sometimes not, but the format was always the same. He gave the orders; I tried to carry out all his instructions. Now and then I would rebel at an order or two. But rarely, very rarely. Some independent wife, I thought groggily. Obviously, I would have to change. But at two in the morning, I wasn't about to challenge or change this long-entrenched pattern.

The sound of my son's name brought me back to my husband's instructions.

"I want Nathaniel to spend part of the week with me," he was saying. "The bottom line for me is full joint physical custody. If you don't challenge me on Nathaniel, I'll be fair financially."

That was a silly statement, I thought, but still I said nothing. Nathaniel needed his father and was both familiar with and fond of the other woman. I had no idea what joint physical custody meant, but I had no intention of withholding our child from his father.

"I think you should write a note to Nathaniel's school informing them of the separation and specifying that his tuition payments won't be affected," Curtis continued. "You are the custodian of his educational fund and you can use the monies to cover his tuition in case of an emergency."

There was just one more thing: Jackie. "She feels just terrible about this whole thing," my husband said meekly. Would I write a note to her, telling her I had no hard feelings and that I hoped we would remain friends? Why he wanted this, I don't know. Why I agreed, I know not either, but I wrote my friend—I still thought of her as my friend—a note telling her I had no hard feelings.

I had no idea what my actions or acquiescence that night meant. By the time I saw an attorney five days later to find out what my rights were, I would learn that I had already given up many of them. I had forgotten that any legal matters should be approached with caution, not co-operation.

Before we retired for the night (at three A.M.!) we agreed to break the news to Nathaniel when he returned home after school the next day. It all seemed so civilized, I thought. We even shared the same bed, although we occupied territorially distinct areas.

When I woke up the next morning, I wondered if I had dreamt it all. Curtis's side of the bed was empty. I looked around the room to see if anything had been disturbed, my eyes searching the dresser tops for a clue to whether this was fact or fiction.

Curtis emerged from the shower, a towel wrapped around his torso.

"After you take Nathaniel to the school bus," he said

crisply, "there are a few minor things I want to go over with you."

This was no dream. I pulled on a sweater and a pair of jeans and continued my usual early morning routine as if I were locked into it.

After delivering a still sleepy Nathaniel to the school bus, I made Curtis breakfast. He looked serene. Over a second cup of coffee he discussed his plans for the day.

"I have to get out of here," he said, looking at his watch. "Our furniture is being delivered and I have to meet the truck."

My hands started to shake. I wrapped my palms around my mug to hide their tremor.

"How about if I take some towels, sheets, and pillowcases?" he asked nonchalantly. "You know that fifty percent of our things belong to me. Equitable distribution says I get half."

I gave him everything he asked for and then some. Utensils. Plates. Cups. He wandered through my kitchen poking into the drawers and shelves, looking at the contents.

"I need a vase," he said, as he stared at my Tiffany glass, a wedding gift from my closest friend.

"A vase? Why do you need a vase," I asked jokingly. "Do you plan on sending Jackie flowers this morning?"

"Well, yes," he answered sheepishly.

I swallowed hard. "Well, you can't have it," I said. I wasn't going to be that much of a lady.

He seemed mildly surprised.

By 8:30 I was alone. I washed the dishes, took a shower, and retreated to my home-based office, where I wrote for three hours, completing a stack of paperwork for my business venture and writing a portion of a book for which I had signed a contract less than two weeks earlier. It was good that I had things to do, I thought. Routine was important at times like these. When I took a break later that morning, I made a few telephone calls to friends and neighbors. To my surprise, no one was surprised.

"You're a strong woman," said the wife of one of Curtis's business associates. "I know you'll handle it really well."

"It's probably the best thing that ever happened to you," said a neighbor. "You'll be fine."

"I guess it had to happen sooner or later," said another neighbor. "You've been so busy with so many other things."

Well, maybe I hadn't been the best wife lately, I thought, but certainly Curtis should have understood. I guess he didn't, it occurred to me then.

"Why didn't *I* see it coming?" I asked myself. "How could I have been so blind? And why did everyone else see it?"

Months later I would find out that virtually every divorced woman I spoke with had been caught blind-sided too. Sure, we knew that our marriages had some flaws, but we considered those part of the normal ebb and flow of marriage. It was very different from a "relationship" that was winding down. In a marriage, you were much more willing to make excuses, willing to rationalize behavior and stick your head in the sand like an ostrich, believing that somehow it wasn't so bad, or that the problems would go away.

In my case, I had kept hoping things would change. And I looked to everything around me for possibilities that could help things change. The inn was just the latest in a long line of such artificial helpers. But nothing could help. The real problem was with Curtis—and with me. Our marriage was simply over.

Now I was finding out that not only was it over, but the people around me also thought I could pick myself up, dust myself off, and, after a brief interlude, breeze along as if nothing had happened.

"Give it a few months—you'll be back on your feet again," said a business friend. "Who knows? Maybe he'll get it out of his system and move back in."

I was taken aback. I wanted sympathy, sensitivity, support, a warm and comforting arm around my shoulders.

Instead they thought I could "handle" it, get "back on my feet" again.

But now I fell right in with their casual "business as usual" attitude. They were probably right, I thought. Why play the role of the bitter divorcee? These things happen all the time. The fact that it was happening to me shouldn't alter my calm, businesslike outlook. I was the consummate professional. I *could* handle it. Life goes on, I told myself philosophically, and felt as if I had achieved a great insight.

In retrospect, I was probably in shock.

# CHAPTER 2

# "WE'RE GETTING A DIVORCE"

The rest of "the day after" was another beautiful fall day, warm, with a casual breeze. I continued working on my book, ran errands, and tried to concentrate on not thinking about my impending divorce. The day seemed to take an eternity to pass. Like Limbo. That was all right with me. I wanted to think things over slowly, meet with an attorney and see where I stood.

Before that happened, Nathaniel had to be told about the breakup. I debated with myself over the wisdom of telling him so soon. I wanted to shield him from the confusion and pain I was certain would follow. Up-front honesty prevailed. Better to get it over with now than to prolong it. Not telling him would be a lie and I didn't want to do that to him.

Curtis had volunteered to pick Nat up at the bus stop and bring him home so we could break the news together. While he was waiting for the bus, I, unsure of what to say or how to explain the separation to a six-year-old, had called the pediatrician for advice.

"Make it simple," he said. "Don't go into long explanations. Let him ask the questions."

Around four P.M. I started pacing the floor, waiting for father and son to arrive. The enormity of what Curtis and I were about to tell him overwhelmed me. I rehearsed the doctor's suggested words over and over again.

"Sometimes people start loving each other and then they stop liking each other. Sometimes people start loving each other and then they stop liking each other." Liking each other. Loving each other . . . not any more, I guessed.

The two of them burst into the house, with Nathaniel talking nonstop about the activities of the day. Earlier that week his elderly first-grade teacher had suffered a massive heart attack in class. Two days ago Nathaniel had accidently been left behind by the school bus. And it was only the first month of his first year at a new school. Now he was about to get this.

"We're getting a new teacher!" he cried. "She's really pretty."

Maybe that would be a good diversion for the next few weeks. I poured him a glass of milk and pulled a few Oreos from a package lying open on the kitchen counter, then motioned for him to come and sit on the family room couch. Curtis was already seated. I positioned Nathaniel between us. He looked a little surprised.

"Sometimes people start loving each other," I said, following our pediatrician's advice, "and then they stop liking each other. Mommy and Daddy have been fighting a lot. We've decided to live separately so that we won't fight anymore."

Nathaniel listened quietly. I wondered if anything was sinking in. He munched the cookies and looked at both of us. We waited for questions. There was only one.

"Can I go outside and play now?" he asked.

Curtis didn't stick around after the announcement. He had to get back to his new apartment to await a furniture delivery. I stood alone by the kitchen window watching my son kick a soccer ball across the lawn. He appeared to be completely oblivious to what we had just told him.

Was this normal, I wondered? Should I have said more? I really needed to talk to someone, to bounce Nathaniel's reaction off a seasoned mother. Meredith. She should be back by now. Almost without thinking I picked up the phone and dialed. My friend Meredith possessed the required combination of qualities. She was also a psychologist. We had never discussed personal concerns. That would have been an intrusion upon our friendship and an abuse of her professional credentials, but now I was certain she wouldn't object to listening to me and perhaps offering a dose of objective feedback. That would be nice, I thought, a real help.

"Hello?" The lilting voice always answered the telephone with a question.

"Meredith, Curtis has left me for Jackie." To my surprise, I couldn't control the tremor in my voice.

For a moment there was only silence, deadly silence.

Then, "Bring Nathaniel and come over right now. We'll talk," she said.

Meredith had been my "other" next-door neighbor for years, our homes separated by the dense woods and almost invisible to each other. We lived parallel lives, rarely seeing each other socially because of our diverse work lives and family activities. While I was striving to prove myself in the business world, she was studying for her doctorate and teaching.

Meredith was waiting for us on her second-floor outdoor deck. Holding two wine glasses in one hand and a just-opened bottle of Bollini Chardonnay in the other, she watched us pick our way through the undergrowth of fallen limbs and branches. As we approached the house she called out and directed Nathaniel downstairs to her eight-year-old daughter's playroom. The children would busy themselves so that we could talk.

We dropped into opposing chairs in her living room.

I was amazed at how relieved I felt to be here. As she filled our glasses she told me that one of her favorite patients had just died after a long bout with cancer. I was touched that, despite her own distress, she was reaching out to me.

I started hesitantly to talk about Nathaniel, but Meredith didn't want to talk about him. She wanted to talk about me.

"Kids are resilient," she said. "He'll be okay. Really. You'll have to wait and see what happens, how he responds. He's too young to fully understand. He'll take his cues from you. You'll see."

I suspected that she was right. If Mommy got upset, Nathaniel would get upset. If Mommy didn't get upset, then maybe neither would he. Mommy was not going to get upset.

"What happened?" she asked. It was the same question I had heard that morning and would hear over and over again in the ensuing months. Meredith's tone was different, however. It said she cared, not like the cool, almost impersonal reactions I'd gotten earlier from people who, I realized now, just wanted to get off the phone.

"Do call if you need anything."

"Don't you worry. Things will work out just fine."

"Let's have lunch sometime. Call me."

I had thought they were friends. Meredith really was.

I gave her a halting rundown, trying to inject as much levity as I could into my account. After all, it must be pretty boring stuff for a psychologist. She stared at me.

"Phyllis, aren't you upset?" she asked. "Aren't you angry? How do you feel?"

I told her I felt no pain, no bitterness, no hostility. I didn't know how I was supposed to feel, how I was supposed to act. Though I did feel somewhat confused and off-balance. I kept telling Meredith that I intended to maintain my composure and control so that I could objectively plan for my future and present an image of strength that my son could depend on and draw from. I was, I realize now, even rather proud at how calm I was. I didn't understand why Meredith was looking so concerned and asking me so many questions.

"I think perhaps that rather than planning for your future," she counseled, "you should concentrate on the present. Think more about yourself. There's nothing wrong with that."

I *was* thinking about myself. I was thinking about how I was going to live, what was going to happen to me, how I would be able to take care of my child. Wasn't that a responsible way to act?

"Is there anyone who can help you through this?" she asked gently.

"What do you mean?" I asked.

"I mean do you have anyone you can talk to." Of course I knew what she meant. I had my parents, but they were 1500 miles away in Florida. I had friends, or people I considered real friends, but every one of them was geographically removed. I thought a while. No one had really helped me through anything before. I'd always been Supermom, Superwife, Superwoman. I was the wife in the Hollywood version of a successful role-model marriage. And proud of it. No wonder my local friends and neighbors thought I was so strong that I didn't need any help. As a result, I was embarrassed to have to acknowledge that for all my practical skills, my human connections were almost practically nonexistent. I had virtually no one around—except Meredith—whom I could call up and really talk to.

Meredith's gentle probing was interrupted by the children, who had decided that pizza sounded like a good idea for dinner. Okay by us. It meant we didn't have to fool with dishes and clean up.

The four of us trooped off to the neighborhood pizza palace, which was packed with customers. The tumult provided a welcome distraction for me and a hindrance to any more intense conversation. I'd had enough of being on the stand, witness to my own prosecution. The children entertained each other as Meredith and I talked in spurts above the din.

"You're not reacting properly, Phyllis," she told me. "Don't be surprised if you have a delayed reaction. It's like getting hit over the head and you forget for a minute about the pain. I think you're in shock. I don't think you've digested what has happened to you."

I disregarded her words. Just like a therapist, I thought, even a friend-therapist, always looking for the hidden emotional response.

"I'm a strong woman, Meredith," I told her. "I'll be just fine. I'm okay, really. Besides, this is going to be civilized. Curtis and I parted on good terms. I think he'll make an effort to do right and act in good faith."

She looked at me quizzically.

"He will, will he?" she asked.

"Of course. He doesn't want a fight and neither do I."

I didn't want to talk about this any more. I motioned for the check, but she beat me to it.

"This one's on me," she said. "Save your money.

"Just remember," she added as we walked out the door to her car, "this is like any other emotional tragedy. You don't necessarily react the moment it happens, or, if you do, you may not react with what most people consider an appropriate emotional response.

"You know, Phyllis," she concluded. "It's all right to show anger or hurt. Those emotions are natural and help heal the pain."

I nodded confidently. I could handle them, I thought; I *was* handling them.

As we were all driving back home in the early evening darkness, Nathaniel finally began to ask questions.

"Is Daddy coming home tonight?"

"No, honey. He has his own apartment now. He's staying there."

"Why did he go?"

"So he and I won't fight anymore."

"Who will take care of us, Mommy?"

"I will, honey."

I could feel Meredith stiffen with empathy over the questions. "Please," she said as we parted, "call me if you need to talk, even if it is in the middle of the night."

*I* didn't need to talk in the middle of the night, not then anyway, but it turned out that Nathaniel did. It was well after midnight when I heard his footsteps coming down the stairs and then felt his slight body as he climbed into my bed. Curling himself up fetuslike next to me, he whimpered that he couldn't sleep and that he was afraid and needed to cuddle. I pulled him closer to me and felt his frame relax.

"You can have my white blanket to sleep with until Dad comes back," Nathaniel whispered. "I'll bet he'll change his mind."

I knew there was no chance, but I ignored the question, resolving to answer in the morning. We slept, accompanied by the dog curled around us on the bed until she woke at 6:30 A.M. with a canine need to be let out.

My tears finally came that morning behind the privacy of a shower curtain. As I stood and let the hot water rush over my body, I suddenly burst into tears. I just stood there and cried and cried. Ten minutes. Twenty minutes. Thirty minutes, until the hot water turned frigid and I was forced to turn off the soothing flow.

As I stumbled from the shower, tears streaming down my cheeks, I heard the phone ringing. I wiped my face, threw a towel around my wet head, slipped on a robe, and reached for the receiver. It was my mother, calling from south Florida for one of her regularly scheduled early morning weekend check-in calls. I hadn't broken the news to them yet. I wasn't ready to handle their questions, and thought I would delay telling my parents of my separation for another week or two. Nathaniel wandered into the bedroom.

"Who are you talking to?" he asked.

"Grandma Kay," I answered.

"Can I talk to her?"

"Sure."

"Hi grandma. We're getting a divorce."

So much for delaying the news. He handed the receiver back to me.

"She wants to talk to you," he said.

Both my parents were sympathetic, supportive, and not surprised.

"We knew it would never work," said my mother. "We knew it was wrong years ago, but your father and I didn't want to be meddling parents. We saw things you didn't. What are you going to do if he wants to come back?"

I was surprised at how negative they were now, how critical of their former son-in-law.

"You're not letting him have Nat, are you?" my mother plunged right along. Of course not, I assured her, but the child did need his father. They would see each other frequently, but Nathaniel would live with me.

My father had more practical concerns.

"How much money do you have?" he asked.

I explained how we had divided the existing savings account, how Curtis had allocated temporary support, and that I expected the divorce to be settled quickly and amicably.

"You better start stashing away as much as you can," my dad said. "I wish I had some extra money to send you, but I just don't."

I knew that, living on a retiree's income and Social Security, they had little to spare. "I'm fine, Dad," I said, adding that I was in good spirits and able to weather a tough financial negotiation if necessary. I didn't think it would be necessary. I told them I would call them again in a few days. I wanted to get off the line, away from the questions. Something in me had begun to hurt very badly. I just didn't want to think about the divorce. But, before I turned off the divorce talk, I made one final call to my in-laws, with whom I had enjoyed a loving relationship. I cared very much for both of them and hoped we would continue as friends. I also wanted to make certain that they heard directly from me that Nathaniel would continue his relationship with both sets of grandparents. I imagined Curtis had already told them the news, but I wanted to tell them too.

Their response was one of surprised sadness, but they too had seen cracks and fissures in our marriage. (Had everybody seen things but me? I wondered to myself.) I rang off, after we all assured each other once again that we would keep in touch.

The remainder of the weekend was packed with previously arranged social activities—a friend's birthday party for Nathaniel, a community fund-raiser and political cocktail party for me. Neither Nathaniel nor I considered bowing out of anything. I delivered Nathaniel to his friend's party, held at a local roller-skating rink. Three of his friends and their mothers were gathered in the lobby.

"Hi everyone," my son called to the group. "My mom and dad are divorcing!"

Disbelief showed on their faces, but I was uncertain whether their reaction stemmed from the manner in which they learned the news or the news itself.

These parents of Nathaniel's school friends were wonderful, providing an unexpected source of support.

"I'll take Nathaniel to hockey practice next week," said one.

"He can stay with us overnight," said another. "It's tough being a single parent."

"Why don't the two of you come to dinner next Saturday," said another.

"Thank you," I said, feeling suddenly overwhelmed by their show of concern and kindness.

Curtis was to pick up his son from the birthday party and show him his new digs. Until now, neither of us had mentioned that he would be sharing his new quarters with Jackie. I hadn't had time to discuss this with Curtis, and did not want Nathaniel to be surprised at Jackie's presence, so I wrote a brief note telling Curtis that I felt it was his responsibility to break this news to his son. I left the note in a sealed envelope with the hostess. I don't know whether I was passing the buck or placing the responsibility where I felt it belonged, but I wanted the marriage-go-round to be explained by Curtis.

This wasn't, after all, just a separation. One day Curtis was living with me, the next day with someone else. I was not only concerned about any possible future effect on Nathaniel's view of relationships and the integrity of a family; I was also concerned about how he would respond to his two friends living with his father.

"Mom!" he shouted upon returning from dinner, "you should see Dad's apartment! It's great! He's got everything. I even have a bed there!"

Eleven years of marriage and I was still living in a mostly vacant house. It had never seemed all that important to me. Someday I'd get around to furnishing it, I always thought. Now it seemed like the world's biggest clue. After only two days of separation, Curtis was living in a completely furnished and decorated apartment.

"I have brothers now, Mom!" he continued. "You don't have to have any more babies! Scott and Corey are now my brothers!"

I didn't attempt to broach any sort of conversation about this revelation. Had Curtis told him that his two buddies were now his brothers? Or had Nathaniel drawn this conclusion himself? I put off even thinking about that one.

Instead, I picked up the baby-sitter, threw on some clothing, and took off for the community fund-raiser. I was certain that the neighborhood wags were already beginning to talk, and I wanted to spread the news myself. Firsthand, right from the horse's mouth, though I wasn't sure exactly what I was going to say, or how I was going to break the news.

What I did do was steel myself and work the room, talking to "old friends" and stating flatly that in case they heard any gossip, I wanted them to know it was true. Curtis and I had separated and he had taken a place with Jackie. What grist for the neighborhood gossips! Next-door neighbors! How long had it been going on? Did I have any idea? What was I going to do? *Tsk-tsk-tsk*. Not one person suggested that I call them if I needed help. Not one person suggested dinner. Not one person offered any show of support. I felt as if I'd been slapped. Obviously there had been more wrong with my life than just my marriage. I felt removed, isolated, and abandoned in the midst of people I had lived with for more than a decade.

But, I rationalized, these were "couple people," people I had seen only at social functions, at community and political functions, people with whom I had exchanged small talk and conversational niceties. I had never had any personal relationships with any of them because all my energies had been devoted to my home and to my career. In my new state of singleness, I was as foreign to their lives as they were to mine.

Much later I would find out that many other newly "unmarried women" had fallen victim to the same syndrome I experienced. I had, within forty-eight hours, become yet another living, breathing representative of the "surplus woman" syndrome, okay to talk to, but still only another woman and now a single one to boot. Hardly someone you wanted to associate with.

There *was* one positive aspect to the party, however. I received a referral to the man with whom I would ultimately develop one of the most intense relationships of my life—my attorney.

"Talk to Roger Spenser," a colleague's husband, a judge on the Superior Court, advised. "He's ethical, well-respected, and tough."

I telephoned him first thing Monday morning. Spenser had an appointment free the next afternoon. I took it. After I hung up, I drove Nathaniel to school, and gave him a note for the headmistress informing her of the separation. The school always wanted to be kept informed about any upheavals at home. Deaths of grandparents, dogs, goldfish. They pitched in on the school front to support the home front.

I had barely returned home when the headmistress phoned about my note. The school had been worried about my son, she said, because he had seemed so tense and anxious of late. This was fresh news to me. She recommended I speak with the school's therapist, whose major concern now was how to neutralize Nathaniel's potential reaction about his father living with another woman and her two sons, without any sort of interim time for him to get used to the separation itself.

That evening—it was only day four but it seemed like decade four—was capped by a spontaneous visit from Curtis. Nathaniel and I were seated at the kitchen table, talking over the events of the day as we usually did, when the front door opened and in swept Curtis. He had left some personal papers at the house and had come to collect them.

I took advantage of his unexpected arrival to ask him a few questions. (It was so hard to get ahold of him these days.) Did he want me to hold his mail or forward it? Had he spoken with the school psychologist? When was he planning to move his clothing from the house?

"Enough! Every time I walk into this house I am ambushed!" he exploded. "No more questions. If you want to talk to me call me at my office between ten and eleven A.M. That's when I'll talk to you."

I glanced at Nathaniel. My son said nothing during our exchange, but simply watched us with wide eyes. Curtis silently gathered his papers together, hoisted them under his left arm, retreated toward the door, and slammed it shut. Nathaniel set his fork down politely on his plate and looked at me. I waited for tears or questions. He offered one comment:

"I think we made the right decision, Mom."

Two days later, as I waited to meet "Spenser," as he was generally referred to by his staff and around the county,

I was *also* certain "we" had made the right decision. Sitting
in his waiting room furnished in basic attorney—leather
chairs, subdued colors, bookcases filled with legal volumes,
canned background music—I felt like a patient waiting to
see a prominent specialist. I fantasized that, like a top-
flight medical man, Spenser would quickly diagnose the
problem and prescribe the appropriate treatment, and my
discomfort would be cured.

Then he bounded out of his office. I don't know what
I expected—perhaps Jimmy Stewart or Gregory Peck—
but I was totally unprepared for the mass of kinetic energy
that greeted me. He was perhaps five feet eight, his body
firmly packed. He reminded me of a wrestler—strong,
agile, and wiry. His face was broad, surrounded by curly
salt-and-pepper hair. He appeared to be in his mid-fifties.
Later I would find out he was closer to the mid-sixties. His
blue eyes were warm, sympathetic. I liked him immediately. I wondered if he would take my case.

"Ms. Ellsworth? Roger Spenser. Come on in."

He guided me to his office. I had prepared a summary
and list of questions and, before I even sat down, I had
begun to reel them off. Years of preparing briefings and
background papers for employers had made me a com-
pulsive memo writer. I knew that the more fully I prepared
Spenser in advance, the less time would accrue to my bill.
I also wanted to organize my case on paper for both of us.

My four-page document detailed the background of
the breakup, my husband's initial financial offer, my goals,
the points on which I was willing to compromise, general
information about my husband-adversary, including his
occupation, income, and outlook, and a description of my
emotional state of mind. I'm holding my own, I wrote in
that memo. I anticipate some hard bargaining, but an amicable settlement. I'm on the case, in control. Always in
control, I thought.

"What I'd like to discuss with you are my legal rights,"
I went on briskly. "I want to know what I'm entitled to.
Can Curtis force the sale of the house? Does the fact that

he is living with someone mean anything? Do you know anything about joint physical custody?"

The questions kept pouring from my mouth.

Spenser, I noticed, had a bemused expression on his face.

"Hold on, hold on," he interrupted. He smiled warmly. "Let me get some background information on you first and then you can hit me with your questions."

For the next half-hour he conducted an intake interview. My name, husband's name, children, age, residence, place of marriage, occupation. Was there any chance of reconciliation?

"Ah . . ." I paused, then replied: "No." I guess not, I thought. The new apartment, all furnished, seemed awfully final.

Spenser looked up from his writing. Was this a case or not? I imagined him thinking.

Only after he had completed that and given me a rundown of his credentials and experience was I allowed to summarize the events of the past few days.

He listened to my story, taking occasional notes.

"By the way," he asked. "Out of curiosity. Did you notice any recent changes in your husband's behavior?"

At nearly forty, Curtis was a classic case of self-renewal. A type-A personality, successful businessman, he had recently taken up dieting, six A.M. jogs, tennis, and rock concerts. Spenser nodded briskly. That kind of behavior, he said, was standard for a departing husband. Curtis had not, however, gone so far as to have his hair restyled or taken to wearing jewelry. Spenser asked whether I had noticed any other pre-separation giveaways.

"There's been an awful lot of friction in the house lately," I said.

"That's not what I mean," he answered. "Have you noticed anything funny like him directing mail away from the house to another address or post office box? Has he changed insurance policies lately? Is he complaining that you are spending too much money or that he's broke?"

"I don't know," I answered hesitantly, then thought more about his question. "Well, yes, he has been complaining a lot about my spending habits."

"Most men, particularly those in business," Spenser said, "plan their divorces well in advance of the actual event. When a man walks into my office he has usually made the decision and is consulting an attorney to discuss strategy. A woman, on the other hand, comes in and wants to know her rights."

I certainly fit into that category, I thought, with a slight sinking feeling. "But there are laws to protect me," I said confidently.

Spenser smiled at me as if he knew something that I didn't and was debating whether or not to fill me in. He rose warily from behind his desk and began pulling documents from his files which he piled in front of me.

"Take these home and read them carefully," he said. "These will show you what the laws are. The main issues are property, money, and children, but under the current laws a woman is no longer assured alimony, property, or full custody of her children. The bottom line for you is that under the new laws things aren't so good."

I listened with an increasing sense of dismay as he outlined the basic provisions of the Connecticut divorce code—a code paralleling those of almost every state in the country.

"There are three parts to the present law," he said patiently. "No-fault, financial settlements, and custody."

I settled into my chair and he settled into a lawyerly lecture. Leaning forward, his hands folded on his desk, Spenser played teacher to my pupil.

"Under the no-fault system," Spenser began, "either party is permitted to sue for divorce without cause. It used to be that someone had to be at fault, a *cause* had to be cited—adultery, desertion, mental cruelty, things like that. But in an effort to eliminate marital mud-slinging and shorten the length of time needed to get a divorce, no-fault was enacted. Today the most common basis for divorce is irretrievable breakdown of the marriage. This means neither party is to blame, no one is at fault. No-fault."

I turned over Curtis's departing statement in my head. "Phyllis," he had said, "I'm leaving you this way because under the No Fault laws there is no fault. I lose nothing. There is no penalty to me."

"When your husband said he could leave you in the way he did," Spenser said, as if he were reading my thoughts, "he was absolutely correct."

Curtis had done his homework, I thought again. The game was already over and I hadn't even arrived on the court.

"In the old days," my lawyer told me, "if a couple wanted a divorce, an economic bargain would be struck. You support me and I'll give you your divorce. Call it blackmail, but it helped place a premium on the marital contract.

"Today," he continued, "the liberalized divorce codes have made the process easier, but in no way has it become any fairer."

His tone emphasized the words *in no way has it become any fairer*.

"The second part of the law involves property settlements," he continued, looking directly at me to see if I was paying attention. Everything, every word was being logged into my gray cells.

"In Connecticut we have the concept of equitable distribution," he went on. "Marriage is treated as an economic partnership. In principle, all the marital assets are put into a common pot and divided according to a set of ten factors—including length of the marriage, relative incomes, employability, earning power, age, health, standard of living, and economic circumstances of each party at the time of separation."

I reached for a notebook that I always carried with me. I wanted to put some of this in writing. Spenser stopped me.

"You don't have to write this down," he said. "Everything is included with the papers I'm giving you. I want you to listen."

I put away my pen and listened.

"Unfortunately, in practice the assets are divided on a lopsided basis. Men usually have a greater income to begin with and greater earning power. They are familiar with business deals and know how to put away funds far in advance of the actual separation. Many times I've seen situations where the wife is living in a big house, driving a big car, the works, and when it comes time to divide the marital assets, the house has been mortgaged to the hilt so there's no equity left, the bills haven't been paid, and the checking accounts are empty. Then it's the wife's problem to find out what happened to the money so she can get her rightful share."

"What exactly are marital assets?" I asked. I felt foolish asking the question.

"All assets of either party—acquired either before or during the marriage," he said. "House, stocks, savings and checking accounts, art, antiques, anything that you can place a value on. It doesn't matter whose name is down as owner. All assets of either party are subject to equitable distribution."

"I thought I was entitled to half," I said.

"You may be entitled to half," he told me. "You may be entitled to more than half. The word is 'equitable.' And equitable means fair share. You start with the proposition that everything is equal, then move up and down the ten factors which make up equitable distribution until each partner's share is fair. We just have to make sure that we have accounted for all the assets."

"It all sounds so arbitrary," I sighed.

"It is," he responded. "It is arbitrary and capricious. The final settlement is basically whatever you can negotiate, or, if it goes to court, what the court will award. Unfortunately, it's often he who holds the gold who makes the rules. The man with the deep pockets. And I say man because it usually is."

My head started to spin. What Spenser was telling me was that I was dependent upon my husband's goodwill to grant me a fair share of the assets *to which I was legally entitled.*

"This is why I want you to do your homework," he repeated, motioning to the papers before him. "I want you to fill these out so that we have a feel for what assets exist. Only then can we divide them up. Maybe fifty-fifty is fair in your case. Maybe there are things that he'll want to keep all of, or that you'll want all of. I want to see the whole pot before we start agreeing to ladle out portions."

I hesitated to ask him about alimony. He beat me to it.

"Now, on the subject of alimony," he said. "In this state there is no presumption of lifetime alimony. You have to prove that you need it. You're a professional woman with a track record. We'll have to see what we can negotiate."

I was shocked. Although I had been the "second" income in a dual-career family, had given up a well-paid job in the city to move to the country with my husband because of his career needs, and had altered my career direction to become a part-time free-lance writer for the good of the family unit, in all likelihood I would now be penalized for these efforts. My husband's salary currently averaged over $100,000; I earned about $12,000 a year from my various part-time efforts. Yet, since I was a woman who had worked and who could work, I would therefore probably not be awarded alimony.

The knockout blow came when he told me about custody.

"Curtis insists upon joint custody," I said. "I don't even know what it means, but I intend that Nathaniel live with me and have open free access to his father."

"I don't think you'll have a choice here," he said. "Joint custody is pretty much the rule of thumb today. It was initially intended to rectify past abuses where fathers were denied access to their children and mothers dictated when, where, and under what conditions the children would be seen. Today, unless a father is incarcerated, an alcoholic, a drug addict, or certifiably mentally unstable, some form of joint custody is the norm."

I pressed him again.

"But what does that mean?" I asked.

"Depends. There's a lot of custody terminology swirling around that means very different things today," he said noncommittally. "Joint physical custody means one thing; joint legal, still another. It's all negotiable. For some men," Spenser continued, "the custody issue is a bargaining chip. Some dads use the threat of taking the child away from Mom to get her to agree to any sort of financial settlement to keep her children."

Bargaining chips, I thought. Use my child as a bargaining chip? I was dismayed. Negotiate, bargain, barter. It occurred to me then that we were basically talking about a business deal. My divorce was going to be based upon whatever we could negotiate. And Curtis was very, very good at negotiation.

"You have any money to live on?" he asked.

I told him we had divided what existed in our joint bank accounts and that I expected a few thousand dollars shortly as partial payment for a book contract. The total was perhaps $9,000.

"Okay," he said crisply. "I think we should do nothing for a while. Sometimes a husband will try and cut off a wife, starve her out so that she'll settle for anything. You have a little money behind you, let's see what he does next."

Nine thousand dollars would not take me very far, I thought. The mortgage payment on the house alone was $700 a month. Though Curtis had said he would pay the mortgage on the house, I wondered if he would and for how long.

"Don't tell your husband what you want," he cautioned. "Don't bob your head up and down. Don't agree or disagree. You be a good listener. Maybe we can get him to put his cards on the table because he has only one way to go—up! I want you to get him talking and keep him talking so that we can flush out his strategy."

He asked me if I participated in any community activities. I told him I was on the board of directors of the League of Women Voters and the local historic society.

"Good," he said. "Get more active. Stay visible and be a lady at all times. You are the injured party. I want you to be seen as a pillar of the community. This is a small town. People talk."

I realized that Spenser already was treating my divorce as a business deal to be backed by a carefully orchestrated campaign of image-polishing through public diplomacy. I felt glad I had worn a tailored suit for my first appointment.

He handed me the stack of papers, pulling one sheet from the file.

"By the way, you must be very careful about accepting any dates," he said, "because if your husband is able to prove adultery prior to the date when you actually began living apart, he may not have to provide support for you according to the law."

"What?" I cried. "You can't be serious!"

He shrugged his shoulders and nodded his head in affirmation. If we were going to request spousal support or alimony—I could not go out with a man except in a group and I had to say good night at the door. My husband could move out of the house and move in with another woman, but I couldn't even date until settlement papers were signed, no matter how long that might be.

"Don't blame me," Spenser said lightheartedly. "I'm just warning you. You wanted to know your rights."

I certainly had.

"This is your homework," he said, motioning toward the papers in my hand. "Take your time, answer all the questions as fully as possible. Your answers will help me prepare your case."

I thought my four-page backgrounder memo had provided an adequate briefing, but Spenser wanted even more details. I glanced over sheets labeled "Checklist—Property Settlement Agreements," "Client Specifics," "Standard of

Living and Location of Marital Assets," and "Important Leads for Trial Evidence." There were twenty-seven pages in all.

"Do you really need all *this*?" I asked.

Yes, Spenser insisted. He wanted to learn as much as possible about me and my marriage. By making me put my answers on paper he was hoping to separate fact from fiction and get me thinking about my priorities.

I flipped through the papers. "Client Specifics" asked for personal information. Education; work experience ("If you are not presently employed, state why"); children; religious, professional, and social organizations; emotional and physical health. A résumé for divorce. It also asked me to list my priorities in decreasing importance, what I was willing to settle for, and the reasons for the breakdown of the marriage. I would have to think about that one. Later.

I moved on to the "Standard of Living and Location of Marital Assets" checklist, which was described as "useful in opening up avenues of discussion." The answers to these questions, I read, "can also be beneficial to your accountant and to this office" and "can also help us formulate questions in examination of your spouse at the time of the trial."

Really, this was going overboard. I didn't have an accountant (my husband's business accountant always did our joint tax returns), nor did I think I needed one. Neither did I expect a simple case like mine to go to court.

"Don't you think this is a little much?" I asked him. "I have no intention of going to court."

"I don't either," Spenser assured me, "but you seem like a smart woman, more level-headed than the type I usually get. Most of my cases come in so emotional that they sabotage their own case. It's to your advantage to be fully informed. I like a client who participates in her own defense."

*Defense*, I thought? I was the innocent party. Why should I have to defend myself?

"Besides," my lawyer continued, "we can't win anyway.

It's a terrible environment for women, a backlash against the days when the wife got everything. If we go to court, you take a chance. We'll come out best with a negotiated settlement. I just want to rattle the sabers a while, let them think we're willing to go down the line if necessary."

If I hadn't caught a twinkle in Spenser's eye I would have thought he was setting me up for a courtroom battle rather than trying to settle the issues over a conference table. He was having fun! He was playing a *game*. The divorce game. A flash of instinct told me I would learn a lot from this man. I felt like I had just taken a seat on a roller coaster that was about to begin its uphill climb. Okay, Spenser, I'm with you, I thought. I strapped myself in, mentally turned myself over to his care, and returned to the lists in my lap.

"Standard of Living": babysitters, clothing, tailored clothing, charge accounts, entertainment—at home and away. The house (were photos available?). Automobiles, gardener, furniture, vacations, schools and camps. The list was endless. He wanted to know everything. Answering the twenty-seven pages of questions might take me weeks.

I thought of Curtis and the sense of urgency he had conveyed about our settlement. He wanted things done with, completed by the end of the year. That was less than three months away and, according to Spenser, the waiting time from the date of filing the divorce complaint papers until a no-fault divorce could be granted was ninety days. We'd never make it.

"We're not going to rush into anything," said Spenser. "That's what he wants you to do."

I protested that I had promised Curtis I would be co-operative.

"You *will* be," my lawyer assured me, "but not at the expense of giving away what is rightfully yours. You don't have to settle everything overnight."

I cringed a little inside and realized I was afraid Curtis would be angry and accuse me of not dealing in good faith, then took a deep breath and pushed these concerns aside. I'd deal with that problem when it happened, I told myself firmly.

Finally, I turned to the last questionnaire: "Important Leads for Trial Evidence." Even if we had no intention of going to court, Spenser's insistence upon answers made me aware that I would have to fill this one out too. This would be the toughie.

This questionnaire wanted a list of all of our marital assets, financial dealings, and loans (banks, credit unions, insurance companies, savings and loans). Also, insurance and brokerage records, check stubs and employers, credit card receipts, telephone bills (was one number called frequently and whose was it?)—every financial transaction we had ever had.

Curtis had been pretty good about keeping me informed about financial matters, but I did not have an on-going personal list of all the transactions made during the course of the marriage. I wasn't even certain where the records might be, but I expected that a good rummage through shelves, drawers, and filing cabinets would yield the answers.

"I will need your past three years of income tax returns," Spenser was saying. "Make sure they include any schedules. These show sources of income other than salary. If you can't find them, we'll write IRS and request them. You *have* signed them each year, haven't you?"

I assured him that we had filed joint returns and that our assets were held in joint names. At least those I was aware of.

"How about financial statements for any bank loans?" he continued. "Do you have any of those?"

"Why?" I asked. "Aren't the tax records enough?"

"No," he told me. "Tax returns only reflect the income upon which taxes are figured. A financial statement lists everything. It always reflects you most positively. See if you can get a copy of any of these."

Spenser had one other area he wanted to cover during this first session. I noticed his eyes check the clock and the time elapsed. Almost two hours had passed.

"I want you to get a post office box so that any mail I send you will be opened solely by you," he said, "and I want you *never* to keep your divorce records in your house. Keep them at a trusted friend's home or locked in a safe-deposit box. You must begin thinking defensively. I'm not saying that your husband will go through your records, I'm just telling you to take precautions because I've had other husbands carrying around *my* case in their briefcases. I don't want to give away our position.

"Any questions?" he asked.

"No." I had just had a fast course in family law, the principles of negotiation, and the psychology of the departed spouse.

"Don't you think you should ask me my fees?"

"Of course," I replied sheepishly. "What is this going to cost me?"

"I require a $2,000 retainer up front. My hourly rate is $90 billable against your initial payment. I'll send you a contract and complete explanation of our billing system. When I receive a signed contract and a check, your case begins."

He had one more question for me.

"Do you know who your husband has retained for his counsel?"

"Someone by the name of Michael Rawson," I said. "Do you know him?"

Spenser leaned back in his chair and tossed his pencil onto his desk. He looked me straight in the eyes.

"He's the very best," he told me.

I felt my stomach hit the floor.

Spenser smiled. "Of course the word is that I'm also the best. We're in for a good fight."

A fight? I felt completely unhinged. This was an amicable divorce?

I shakily gathered my papers together and got up to

leave. Spenser rose with me, absently fingering the loose papers littering his desk. He looked up at me, waited a moment as if he were collecting his thoughts, then spoke.

"Look, from what you've told me, this guy's got everything worked out," he said. "Well, we have to do some checking, ask some questions. Maybe he's being up-front and maybe he's not, but please, don't be in a rush to settle."

Curtis's sense of urgency had been transmitted to me. I had thought we had to wrap things up quickly. Now my lawyer kept telling me to take my time. Obviously this was going to take longer than Curtis expected. Lots longer.

I was not unpleased at the thought. Although I feared Curtis's anger if he sensed that I was dragging my heels on a settlement, the thought that not everything would be going his way as fast as he wanted was reassuring.

"Generally, it's two years out of the chute until you start living again," Spenser continued. "You have to plan now for the economics of life after divorce. This is more than just ending a marriage. Don't rush the process. It's your future."

*Two years?* It was a sobering thought. I was beginning to gain a sense of a massive undertaking.

He walked me to my car and opened the door for me.

"Don't sign the joint tax return. Never feel secure and *never* let your guard down. We'll talk again in a few days. Now go home and do your homework."

I drove off with the realization that this was not going to be as simple and as easy as I had thought, or rather as Curtis had told me. But I wasn't worried. I trusted my lawyer. I had been with him for only two hours and I trusted him in a way that I had never trusted my husband.

Funny, I thought, reflecting on my trust of Spenser. I was suddenly admitting to myself that I had never trusted my husband. Maybe my marriage wasn't all I had thought it was cracked up to be.

But Spenser . . . I felt very good about Spenser. We were really partners. He was on *my* side.

# CHAPTER 3

# JUST BEFORE THE BATTLE: GAMBITS, SORTIES, AND SALVOS

Five days after the split Curtis arrived unannounced at the house. He was edgy, obviously unsure of his reception. "I have to pick up some personal items. Don't try and stop me. You have no right to prevent me from removing anything," he said as he came in the front door.

"Take what you want," I snapped in response to his testiness.

I glanced past him and saw the shadowy outlines of two forms sitting in his car. Were they business associates or witnesses? Why would he bring witnesses? What did he think I was going to do? Prevent him from entering the house and taking his clothes? And why was he so angry?

"I thought this was supposed to be an amicable separation," he said as he brushed past me and swept on toward the downstairs bedroom. "Who gave you Spenser's name? I hear he's a son of a bitch."

Curtis himself had suggested that I hire my own attorney, that we not use the same person. Now that I had done it, he was angry. I felt, somewhat obscurely, as if I were guilty of something. Bad faith, maybe?

Still, I decided to write off Curtis's negativism as being part of the "your lawyer is no good" script most husbands delivered. Spenser had cautioned me about the dialogue. It was designed to undermine my confidence, make me doubt my lawyer and give in to my husband's demands. I was prepared for Curtis's words but not his attitude. Still, I was *not* going to get into an argument.

Let him blow off steam, I thought. The storm would blow over. It always did. All I had to do was be my usual calm self.

I followed Curtis into the bedroom, lowered myself into our Bentwood rocker, and watched as he swiftly but carefully arranged underwear, shirts, ties, cufflinks, and odds and ends into a suitcase.

What's all the rush? I wondered. It was midmorning, he had already missed half a day of work. Where did he have to be? Why was he sweeping through his drawers in such a big hurry? I wanted to justify myself to him, deflect his charge that I was not acting in good faith. He seemed to want to get away from me as quickly as possible, as though I had some contagious disease.

Curtis appeared to be ransacking the drawers. What was he looking for? I wondered. *Was* he looking for anything? Or was I beginning to be paranoid? Neither of us had anything of value like jewelry or collectibles that he might have left behind or that might have been stashed in these drawers. Any papers or records were stored in the office upstairs.

"I need to get some things from the office," he said abruptly, turned and bolted from the room with a few giant steps. He took the stairs two at a time. I resisted a strong impulse to follow him. I was already being accused of bad faith and I didn't want to add still another charge to the growing litany of offenses. I listened hard as he opened closets and banged desk drawers, trying to pinpoint where he was and what documents he could have been searching for. Within moments he was back downstairs—empty-handed. Had he found what he was searching for? I couldn't tell.

As he re-entered the bedroom, I remembered that I had had the locks changed the day before.

"By the way, I had the locks changed," I told him, my voice sounding smugly triumphant.

His simmering anger exploded into a full boil.

"You cannot do that!" he shouted. "You cannot change the locks on the house and lock me out. I own half this house and you cannot breach my marital rights."

I *had* acted on my own, but it *did* seem logical that if he had left and I was living here I had the right to change the locks. Besides, if he had left me, I rationalized, why should he have the right to come back into the house? Spenser hadn't said anything to me about the locks and entry into the house, and I hadn't thought to ask. The minute Curtis slammed the door behind him still fuming and threatening, I raced for the phone and called Spenser's office.

"Your husband is right," said his assistant, repeating Curtis's explanation. "The house is in both of your names. Therefore, he has full access to it at any time. You must provide him with a key. Otherwise you jeopardize your case."

I felt like a child being reprimanded for bratty behavior. Now I had to apologize though I didn't really feel like it. I picked up the phone and called Curtis at his office. The receptionist asked who was calling.

"Mrs. Ellsworth," I said without thinking.

I could hear the silence on the other end of the phone. Mrs. Ellsworth? I was certain she was saying with a sly inflection. How would she ring me through? "She *says* it's Mrs. Ellsworth." "It's your wife." "Do you want to talk with someone named Mrs. Ellsworth?"

I was relieved to hear the familiar voice of Curtis's secretary.

"Hello, Donna, it's Phyllis. Is Curtis around?"

"He's in a meeting." Her voice was strained, distant. "I'll see if he wants to talk." It occurred to me that she was *on his side*. For an "amicable" no-fault divorce, this seemed to have gotten adversarial pretty fast.

Curtis's voice was brusque. "Yes, Phyllis, what is it?"

"I owe you an apology about the keys. I was wrong. I have copies for you. I'll bring them over this afternoon."

"You must have talked with your lawyer," he said. "Good. Now you'll see that I know what I'm talking about. I always do my homework. You still haven't faced that fact. You always do things without thinking, without realizing their *effect*. This is just another example."

My silence slowly penetrated the telephone lines. Curtis began to talk. His tone was conciliatory, but firm.

"The enormity of the situation is beginning to catch up with you, Phyllis. You are realizing that you are alone, but you're a big girl, and you've got a lot going for you. Relax, kid, you're not going to go homeless, penniless, and jobless. Now, that's a bit of a pep talk, but that's the way it goes."

This was more like it. The Curtis I used to know. He really did mean well after all. How I wanted to believe in him. Feelings began to flood in on me. Maybe he would reconsider. I would change. I'd be a better wife. I'd be what he wanted me to be. If only we could talk. Really talk.

Maybe this was only a mid-life crisis. Lots of men had them. Maybe if he got it out of his system he'd come back to me. Then we could be happy.

Give me a chance, I thought, give me some time . . . If only . . . If only.

Why not give it another shot?

"I've been feeling a tremendous amount of pressure, Curtis," I said tentatively. "It's so emotional. With Nathaniel, with the attorney, with you . . ."

"Look, as long as you and I cooperate," he interrupted, "we will both come out with dignity, money, and peace."

There was no mention of a marriage. Still I persisted.

"I feel like you are treating me like a union negotiator," I responded. "I'm your wife—Phyllis—remember? There was no need to show up at the house with witnesses—or whatever they were."

No reason at all. In fact, he had hurt my feelings.

"After all, we've lived together almost eleven years," I said haltingly. "It's as if you don't trust me. I haven't done anything to make you act like this."

"I didn't know what to expect." He seemed slightly abashed. "I was only taking precautions. Look, I'm more than willing to go down the line with you—unless I feel that you are not playing ethically, morally, and above-board."

I opened my mouth to assure him how ethical, moral, and above-board I intended to be, but he cut me off.

"Phyllis," he continued, "our marriage is over."

He paused, as if waiting for his words to sink in, then continued slowly.

"I know it's difficult to accept this, especially when you think about the good times we had—and we *did* have a lot of good times. But it's all over and it's time for both of us to move on."

My head was spinning. My throat was closing up. I wasn't sure I could talk without bursting into tears. He didn't even want to listen. How could I make him see that we should try to save what we had—*whatever* that was?

He continued in the same paternal tone.

"You are resentful of my relationship with Jackie," he said. "You are angry that I am happy and you will try and take your anger out on me by getting even."

He paused to let this sink in.

"You were my mate for ten and a half years," he went on. Five were pretty good, two were okay. The last three stank. I've been thinking about leaving you for three years, Phyllis. I can't even talk with you except on the telephone."

I almost dropped the receiver. I could not comprehend what he was telling me. *Three years?*

He continued in this same level voice. I didn't say a thing, couldn't say a thing. It was as if he were speaking in a foreign language and his words were incomprehensible. I was speechless with shock.

"I didn't accept our marriage and the way we lived," he said slowly. "I still don't and I never will."

He paused, then continued again. "All the years we were married I supported you with money, Phyllis. I never supported you emotionally. I know that and I'm sorry about it. But you need someone different from me. I just wasn't in control of my life then. Now I am."

He had one more thing to add.

"I would have gone last week with or without Jackie," he said. "I'm not blaming you. I just wanted out."

I recoiled from his words, stunned at what he had just told me. His delivery was flat, devoid of emotion, robotlike. There was no feeling, no empathy for how I might respond to his revelations. I was writhing away from the rejection. He didn't care about me *at all*.

He had just wanted out. I *hated* him!

I hung up abruptly and slumped down into the corner of our new couch. I wanted to disappear into the cushions. I was seething with rage. How could he treat me like this? He didn't want to try and save our marriage. He didn't want a reconciliation. Nothing. He had walked out five days earlier and closed the door behind him forever. For Curtis, the past had ceased to exist.

How stupid I had been! Trying to negotiate a reconciliation, thinking that if somehow I could change, we could patch up our differences, piece our marriage back together and make it work . . .

I still didn't want to believe his words. He had just wanted out. I kept murmuring over and over to myself that things hadn't been so bad. We should try and compromise, meet each other half way. Denial. Pure denial. I couldn't face the fact that I was about to become a statistic. One in two marriages ended in divorce. Ours was about to.

How could I have been so blind? I repeated. How could I have *not* seen it? The past six months had been so convulsive. I must have been sleepwalking. Then the details of his confession suddenly struck me.

*Three years?* He had wanted to leave *three years ago?* He had to be joking. Nobody could think about leaving for three years—or could they? Where were we? What were we doing? I thought and thought. Everything was a run-on blur. No particular event stuck in my mind. Then I remembered my desk calendars. They might provide a clue! I went running to my upstairs office, pulled open my file drawers, and retrieved my old calendars. I kept them for years. Curtis had insisted on that. I always recorded everything on these calendars—appointments, meetings, telephone calls, expenses. Mostly they served as year-end tax records. Now I was really glad I had kept them. My calendars provided a history of our marriage. Three years back. I pulled out 1979. What were we doing then?

The first date to catch my eye was January 30, two P.M. I had had an appointment with a prominent Boston neurologist, arranged by my internist for a consultation on murky symptoms. Intense headaches, fatigue, discharge from my breasts. Breast cancer, pituitary tumors, brain tumors, all fell within the possibilities. He took a thorough history and physical exam, then asked me to dress and meet him in his office.

"Is everything all right at home, Mrs. Ellsworth?" was his first question, which I remembered as vividly now as I had then.

I had bristled at the question, the implication that somehow everything was not all right at home, that my symptoms were stress-induced. "Yes, of course," I had said firmly. Curtis and I were the *model* dual-career couple.

I had a lot invested in this view of our marriage. But were we? At the time I had just left a demanding full-time job to pursue a free-lance writing career, working out of my home so I could spend more time with my son, who was just entering the toddler stage, and with Curtis, who seemed to be placing more and more demands upon me as a corporate wife. Company dinners, social events, travel—with family or alone with spouse, the obligations seemed never-ending. Six, eight, sometimes ten a month.

I continued flipping through the calendar. The dates were marked almost exclusively with child- and family-related responsibilities. Mother-toddler gym, playgroup, toddler art class, preschool interviews, dog to the vet, wifely business dinners, social engagements, conventions and Curtis's business travel, household responsibilities.

There were also appointments for interviews for the free-lance articles I was beginning to have accepted by a variety of women's magazines. The year also saw the publication of my first book, *The New Pregnancy*, which explored the rights and responsibilities of the pregnant working woman. How ironic, I mused, to have written a book about the ease with which work and mothering could be combined. One chapter even counseled how to get a spouse to be more supportive. Some authority I was, I thought ruefully.

As I passed through the months, another set of notations caught my eye. Whose handwriting was it? Mine? Curtis's? I couldn't tell. Every few pages contained an almost invisible pencil-etched number with a circle around it. Thirty-five, thirty-six, forty. I searched through the calendar. The notations appeared to match the days when I was at work and when my son had been left in the care of his nurse. Did I make them? And why?

What did they mean? When—and more importantly, why—had they been made? Was this Curtis doodling in my calendars? Or was it my own handwriting on behalf of some long-forgotten tabulation? I didn't know. I *did* know I was feeling rather paranoid at this point.

My thoughts returned to the present as I realized it was time to meet the school bus. I threw the calendars into a pile next to my desk, composed myself so that my son would see a pulled-together Mom, and resolved to continue my calendar review later.

The next day Curtis called again. His tone was short; though he didn't mention it, I suspected he was angry that I had concluded our last telephone conversation by hanging up on him. Maybe he was afraid I would do it again. Maybe I would, I thought.

"Have you seen a therapist yet?" he asked.

"A therapist? What for?"

"You have been extremely hostile to me," he said.

"I don't think so. I thought I was being pretty cooperative under the circumstances. How many wives do you know who would give a husband fresh sheets for their new living arrangements?"

"You weren't cooperative," he continued. "You were hostile."

"Why, because I wouldn't give you a vase for your girlfriend's flowers? Because I picked my own attorney? How am I supposed to act?" I challenged him.

"Listen, Phyllis, I'm just trying to help," he said. "As long as you are still covered under my company's medical plan, go get some help. Get it all out. It won't hurt to have someone to talk to. There is so much shit we have to deal with anyway."

I felt my spirits drooping. Perhaps he was right. Maybe he *was* looking out for me, in his own manner.

"I do feel insecure," I confessed meekly.

"It shows," he said. "You're digging your heels in."

"This isn't the most secure-making situation," I said quietly.

"Look, Phyllis," he said. "I'm not going to make life so difficult for you that you can't breathe. And you're not going to make life so difficult for me that all I can afford is a hotel room or a one-room shack. The law doesn't allow for that. What you need to do is give up this idea of the inn project, finish your book, and get back to writing."

I had barely thought about the inn over the past few days. My opening was less than two weeks away and Curtis was my partner. Now he was telling me to give up a project I had dreamed about and prepared for two years, and suggesting that I go back to a career that he had never approved of in the first place.

I didn't know what I wanted. What I did know was that somehow Curtis had thought out *my* life without letting me in on the decisions. It was all so confusing. I didn't want to make a decision now about my future. I didn't want to think about anything. Curtis seemed to have his life in order, and expected mine to fall into place as well. It wasn't so easy. I tried to get through to him.

"Being a writer is very insecure, Curtis. You know that. You also know that I've put all my energies into the inn for the past two years. That was to be my business. If I give up the inn, I'm starting over again. I've been away from corporate work for years. Things have changed."

"Forget the inn," he said emphatically. "You're not married to it. You've managed to squeak through with at least $12,000 free-lancing the past few years. You have a track record. You'll be able to start over again."

Twelve thousand dollars. How could I live on that? The yearly mortgage on the house alone was $8,400. Curtis *was* paying that. But what if he stopped? My paranoia was increasing moment by moment. Where would I go? And with a small child?

Point, counterpoint. I felt I was making a last-ditch effort to convince Curtis that I could succeed at the inn. I had put so much of myself into the project, it was so close to being a reality. I couldn't bear the thought of giving it up.

"I gave up two years of my life to develop the inn," I pleaded. "I gave up my nine-to-five job for us to have a better family lifestyle."

"Good. I gave up the last three years of my life as a human. It's not easy when a home breaks up, but you don't stay together for bricks and sticks or money." He paused, then continued. "We grew separately, Phyllis. We both knew it. You knew it. It was a great sense of relief for you when I left. I'm positive of that. The last few years were the pits. In fact, I think the pits would have been the high point. Don't you see it that way?"

"Well, we did have some ups and downs," I said lamely.

I didn't want to talk to him anymore. I felt pressured, under fire. And enormously depressed. Curtis was trying to tell me what my feelings and my future should be when I was uncertain about the direction of either. I did think of hanging up again, but I decided not to.

"I'm not going to screw you out of anything," he said, "but you're on your own. I haven't been able to communicate with you for years now. You don't want a partner in your life. You're the Lone Ranger."

The Lone Ranger? How could he say that? I thought I was one half of a modern dual-career couple. It struck me how little we really knew each other after more than a decade of marriage. The Lone Ranger! I'd have to think about that one.

"I know you're feeling resentful over the fact that I am having a good time," he concluded, bringing me back to the conversation, "but I just couldn't live with you anymore because of my feelings for Jackie."

Aha! Finally!

The presence of another woman in our separation had hovered in the background, but somehow my friendship with her gave her relationship with my husband a surrealistic flavor. I still liked her. To me she was not "the other woman." She was a nice, kind person. I couldn't finger her as a participant in my defunct marriage.

I don't know whether Curtis had intended to bring up his feelings for Jackie, but now it was out in the open. I didn't respond. There was nothing I wanted to say. My husband had left me for another woman. He had even wanted to take my Tiffany vase to hold a bouquet of red roses for her. What does a wife say? How nice? What lovely flowers? I hope you'll be very happy? I didn't want to hear it any more. Tears were threatening to well up in my eyes, and I had to swallow very hard.

"You should read up on divorce law," Curtis went on. He even recommended a book.

I was convinced he had flipped, suggesting that I read a book on divorce. (Still, I bought a copy the next day in the fruitless hope that I could read between the lines and decipher something about his strategy.)

"Now I want you to contact Spenser and ask if he'll let us handle some of the preliminary arrangements ourselves," Curtis continued. "The more you and I can do, the fewer legal bills we will have. We need a temporary settlement, we need to split up certain pieces of property. You need a new car, or at least one to get you through the winter, and I need to have you sign a joint income tax agreement. If you refuse to get moving on these issues, it shows me that you are unwilling to bargain in good faith."

Spenser's words came back to me.

"Never sign anything, don't agree to anything . . ."

I wavered. But Spenser had been very firm.

"I don't think I can do that, Curtis," I said finally.

"When I tell you to believe me when I say I can't afford certain things, I want you to believe me," Curtis was saying, with an edge to his voice. I had barely been listening as my mind flip-flopped over his request to talk. "I need to get a few of these things taken care of. I don't need to pay a lawyer to handle them."

"I'll have to get back to you, Curtis," I said. "Let me think about this."

I hung up and called Spenser.

"Go," Spenser said.

"Go?"

"Sure, but don't agree to anything," he said. "I want you to keep the lines of communication open. The more he talks the more we learn about what he wants, and what he's willing to give up. Don't sign anything. Don't agree to anything, but go. Be pleasant. Be a good listener and let me hear from you after your meeting."

I called Curtis back and agreed to meet with him as soon as he returned from a week-long business trip to California, where he was going the next day with Jackie.

While he was gone, I spent much of the time looking through my calendars and brooding. I remained baffled over just when everything had started going downhill with Curtis and me, and why I just hadn't seen it.

And how could he say that I was resentful of Jackie? That was one point I was sure of (then, anyway). She didn't break up our marriage. She was just there to pick up the pieces.

What *had* gone wrong between Curtis and me? And why had it become so irrevocably beyond repair? I tried to piece together the disintegration. Curtis had said the first five years were pretty good. Agreed. It was the late 1960s, the years prior to the surge of the women's movement. While I had always worked, I never considered making the choice of job over husband. When he was transferred to St. Louis I went with him.

We did discuss my finding "something" to do in St. Louis, but he assured me from the beginning that I didn't have to work. His salary was sufficient for both of us. I spent most of our first year of marriage cooking my way through Julia Child, baking bread, taking pottery lessons, riding my bike, traveling with him on business, entertaining his customers, and generally being a wife. I was not unhappy.

Finally I grew restless toward the end of that year and began to interview for jobs. Just as I was offered a position he was transferred back East. His office was in New Haven, but he had tired of urban life and wanted to live in the country. We rented an eleven-room house in questionable living condition. I painted, spackled, battled bats, snakes, and insects, and shooed away our neighbor's cows. It was not unpleasant, but, stuck in the countryside day in day out, I began to long for a different life.

Finally I went back to work, landing a full-time job only a forty-five-minute commute away. Those *were* good years. We traveled, entertained. He took care of finances; I took care of the house. We were young marrieds, happy and in love.

Our son was born. At that time women were forced to

leave their jobs as soon as they began to "show," and it was widely assumed that any pregnant woman would retire from the work force to assume her proper position as a full-time mother. I never did. I had other ideas. I loved my job. I loved my baby. I wanted both the security of a home life and the stimulation of a career. Was this where we had begun to "go wrong" for each other? Did I love my baby in a way and with an intensity I had never loved Curtis?

A blur of infant and toddler incidents passed through my mind.

Nathaniel and I planting peas in the garden. He was three.

"When do we put the butter in?" he asked.

"What butter?"

"The butter, so that the peas will taste better when we pick them."

Nathaniel, age four: "Mom, if you eat the seeds from an apple will an apple tree grow out of your head?"

Nathaniel, age five, keeping me company while I recuperated from temporary loss of sight after stopping a tennis ball with my right eye.

"I'll draw pictures for you," he said. "It won't make your eye feel better, but it will make your feelings feel better."

The jubilant memories of those first years clouded as I remembered other parts.

"You can't do both," my husband told me repeatedly. "You can't be a responsible mother *and* a businesswoman." While I thought he was probably right, somehow I couldn't help wanting to prove that I could. Around the time Nathaniel was born I was offered a new job. It was a part-time, flexible-hours position with a New York—based firm. I would have to commute two hours in each direction. I would be dependent upon child care. But I would be combining work and mothering. Here was my opportunity to show Curtis he was wrong, that I could combine two very important parts of my life. I never thought at the time that maybe Curtis would begin to feel neglected. To my (then) way of thinking, we were simply a two-career family, and we had to pull together to make it all work. The only problem was that I was pushing and Curtis wound up pulling.

After two weary years I had to admit that Curtis was right. As usual. My single-minded stubbornness had prevented me from seeing the practical drawbacks to the long-distance job. The job itself was fabulous: wonderful associates, a challenge, decent pay. What wasn't so fabulous was the day-to-day jockeying over getting to work and then worrying about the welfare of my child. For despite the not-to-be-excelled retired maternity nurse I had hired as Nathaniel's caretaker, I worried about him constantly. Did he have his bath? Had he eaten enough? Was he watching too much television? I worried about everything and nothing. Somewhere in all this I stopped worrying and thinking about Curtis. He was an adult, he could take care of himself; Nathaniel was a baby. It was obvious, at least to me, who came first in my worrying and fussing energies.

"You are unthinking," Curtis complained. "You think only of yourself and your needs. What about *our* needs? I'm not going to come home from work after a long day and then have to put in another two hours baby-sitting for you until you show up at eight o'clock."

That's when the headaches started. Whether their source was my stress-induced schedule, the lack of practical spousal support, or simply a desire to spend more time with my son who was growing into a toddler without any help from me, I gave up. I retreated from the traditional work world to spend more time as a country-bound wife and mother.

Maybe Curtis did have a legitimate complaint, I thought, riding the bumpy train home on my last day of work. With Curtis feeling shut out from my baby and my job, and with me no longer available to be the corporate partner he seemed to want, maybe things hadn't been so great. Maybe I *was* being unfair.

"Is everything all right at home, Mrs. Ellsworth?"

The words of the neurologist came back to me. In discussing my symptoms the physician and I had concluded that I was overextended and that my decision to pursue a free-lance career was best for me and my family. I accepted the diagnosis, explanation, and resolution of the problem.

I continued flipping the pages of the calendars. 1980. 1981. Lots of magazine work, mothering, and family activities. My fingers stopped when I came to a week marked "Florida trip."

Another turning point. A family vacation to see my parents, who had just moved to Florida, and to visit my brother and his wife, who had recently established a joint medical practice in Palm Beach. Leaving Nathaniel with his grandparents, Curtis and I took a few days away together at Palmaire, the luxurious health spa located nearby.

It was a wonderful getaway. We played tennis, made love, had time off together, the first time we had allowed ourselves the luxury of doing so since Nathaniel was born. I felt good about us. *But by then, he had already made the decision to leave.* Or so he said. I couldn't believe it.

During that leisurely vacation I rationalized that maybe I *was* overextended, maybe it would be better to settle into something closer to home. I would be available for Nathaniel, available for Curtis. We could spend more time together as a couple, as a family. I felt restless, true, but I couldn't see any way of fulfilling my yearnings for a full-time career without damaging (or destroying) the fragile and precious happiness we finally seemed to have achieved. I loved my baby and my husband and was loved in return. It wasn't such a tough price to pay for that.

Then the whole business of the inn had come into our lives.

A message awaited me on my telephone answering machine upon our return. Curtis and I had been silent partners in a nonworking inn for many years, renting the kitchen space to a local chef who served dinners only. The message was from the chef's sister, who told me that he was ill, his recovery uncertain.

During his long, slow convalescence, the chef approached me with a novel proposition. Since I was already an accomplished home cook, why not become more involved in the business? I could do lunch; he could do dinners.

I could easily pick Nathaniel up from the school bus after we closed down the lunch service. I would be close to home, accessible. I could have a business, something of my own, plus be available for my family.

It sounded perfect. Curtis, however, was not only unsupportive of the venture, he wanted to sell the building. He must have been horribly shocked, probably even felt betrayed, by my proposed new venture—just when I'd given him what he wanted.

He said his company was having a bad year, they were cutting back, there would be no salary increases or bonuses. It was the first time I had heard about the cutbacks. Since I was no longer working full-time, I had no way of contributing financially to the inn.

But finally, Curtis did go along with the project. He really didn't have much of a choice actually. Four of us owned equal shares of the building, a federally registered historic site. Three of us were wildly enthusiastic about the prospect of turning a passive real estate investment into an active bed-and-breakfast tourist establishment. Curtis was outvoted. So, at a time when his own company was in transition, he was more or less pressured into helping bankroll a speculative venture. I was ecstatic. I would make it up to him. He'd see.

To prepare myself, I enrolled in a series of restaurant school courses, learning basic professional skills and techniques. I contracted with a local produce store to bake breads. Word of mouth spread the news. I soon was baking desserts and catering small parties. Nathaniel helped me prepare and deliver my orders. The three of us ate my practice meals and Curtis grumbled a little because it wasn't all that necessary for me to work. I reassured him that the inn was going to be a smashing success and that things were going to be terrific for us as a family.

The closer I came to opening, the more satisfied I became—and the more testy and critical Curtis became. Mostly we argued about money and his contention that I lacked an understanding of what it really took to run a business. He knew. After all, he had run a business for years.

Later I realized our arguments weren't about money and taxes and business skills. They were about control and dependency. We both wanted some measure of control over our lives.

My birthday arrived, and, in an effort to dissipate the tension, I suggested we go out. He agreed, albeit a trifle peevishly. Pick any place you would like to go, he told me. I made the reservation at a chic French restaurant in the suburbs. Maybe we could have a nice dinner with a good bottle of wine and talk about our differences.

He was almost two hours late in getting home. We were an hour late for our reservation. I could feel a headache begin to brew. The pain began to intensify in the back of my skull and neck. I was nauseated and woozy.

We were finishing our first course when he told me about my birthday gift. He'd always bought me a gift.

"I haven't bought you a gift this year," he said nonchalantly. "I don't intend to. It doesn't mean anything."

He never stopped eating, never even looked at me as he spoke. I thought he might be getting back at me for my carping at him.

Still, the food turned to sawdust in my mouth. I felt my stomach begin to churn. I excused myself from the table and raced for the ladies' room.

I barely made it into a stall when the first wave of vomiting hit me. I was wearing a lavender silk dress and I hiked the skirt around my waist to avoid splattering myself. I heaved again and again, toppling over my dress shoes as I leaned toward the bowl.

He said nothing when I returned to the table. His attention was directed solely toward the rack of lamb which he was deftly carving into mouth-size bites.

"It's not the gift, Curtis," I said as I seated myself shakily and fumbled for words to tell him how crushed I was. "It's the meaning. I don't need anything. It's just that . . ."

I waited for him to say something. Anything. An apology. Nothing. His statement went through me like a razor. He wasn't sorry. He *meant* what he said. The pain was so intense, so incisive. I pushed my veal, wild rice, and carrots around my plate for the rest of the meal. I wanted to leave, couldn't wait to leave, but he wanted to finish eating. So I sat there and waited, and thought of what I could say without it actually erupting into a scene.

Curtis even ordered dessert—a nut tart topped with freshly whipped cream and espresso coffee with a lemon twist. I accepted a dollop of fresh raspberries from the hostess, but with the first taste, my stomach started up again and I pushed the plate away.

By the time we returned home my headache had gotten so bad that I could not remain in a vertical position any longer. I went searching for something, anything, to relieve the pain. Emperin codeine, prescribed for menstrual cramps, was the first medication I saw. I took one and lay down. An hour later I was still awake, with no relief from the pounding in my head. I took another pill. Another hour, still no respite. Maybe a Valium. Curtis always had Valium. I took one. I had no sooner swallowed than the nausea, lightheadedness, and hot and cold sweats began again. I returned to the bathroom and proceeded to throw up for the better part of the early morning hours. The dry heaves continued well into the next day.

I stayed in bed, exhausted and too ill to move. Nathaniel went swimming with a neighbor. Curtis paced the house and finally came into our bedroom.

"I want every pill you have," he screamed at me. "You are not going to pull that trick again. Next time you will succeed in killing yourself and I don't want you to do that."

What on earth was he talking about? Then I remembered my friend Alice. She was a former college roommate who had suffered a complete breakdown not too long ago, sparked by her intensely competitive work life and her inability to manage three small children, a husband, a home, and a fast-tracked career. Curtis had often told me we were so much alike. Alice had taken an overdose of pills.

Now I had taken all of three pills and he was afraid I was suicidal.

I couldn't believe what I was hearing. "Curt, I'm not Alice," I muttered weakly. He didn't look like he believed me.

A few days later I received a telephone call from a medical examiner sent to interview me by our insurance company. She needed to conduct a physical exam for my new life insurance policy. When would I be available?

Since I hadn't purchased any life insurance, I called Curtis at his office. Curtis already had a substantial policy on my life.

"I just got a call from the insurance company," I said. "They're sending a medical examiner to do a physical on me. What's this about? You already hold $75,000 on me."

"You're not going to kill yourself and leave me penniless," he said. He sounded frightened and angry. "You're unstable and I have a son to take care of. I need you."

The whole scenario was so out of scale that I thought it laughable. Well, if this would make him happy, okay, I'd take the exam and sign the policy. I did both.

Even with my compliance, there was still tension on both sides. He thought I was doing myself in. I thought I was getting no support.

I was nearing the date I had set to begin serving lunch at the inn. Remembering the last family vacation in Florida, I suggested we spend a few days away. We would go together, the three of us. He agreed, and we drove to a small town on Cape Cod. We sunned on the beach, ate lobster, explored the area. He was tense, I was trying not to be.

We made love for the last time after Nathaniel had gone to sleep the evening prior to our departure. It was awful. There was no feeling, no passion, no warmth. I lay there afterward, empty and confused. Something was very wrong, I thought, as a kind of dread began to lap at the edges of my consciousness. In the light of day, I pushed these thoughts away.

But for the next three weeks the tension never let up; and for three weeks my head ached. Curtis was argumentative, snappish. At one point we discussed separating, then dropped the subject.

Somehow we had to resolve the friction. I sat for hours on our back porch in the warm autumn air and asked myself what I could do differently to alleviate the situation.

I was certain that once my restaurant was open, the friction would dissolve. If only Curtis would understand. The inn would bring us closer. It would be something we could be involved in as a family. I began to feel better. Yes, the inn *was* the answer.

As the day for my opening drew closer, I felt more and more optimistic. Things were getting better between us. Curtis seemed more cheerful, more at ease, happy. Maybe he was finally beginning to accept my venture and our new life. He no longer sullenly avoided my gaze.

"Curtis, it's time we should talk," I ventured that morning as he prepared to go off to his office.

He paused. "I guess we should," he said, putting on his jacket and walking out the door.

Good, I thought to myself. We've made a breakthrough. We were going to make it after all. I thought I'd found the perfect solution to combining a career, motherhood, and marriage, but then that evening Curtis came home with his own solution.

"Phyllis, I'm leaving you."

# CHAPTER 4

# PUSH COMES TO $HOVE

Three months had passed. Curtis and I hadn't even come close to civil discussions about formalizing the separation, let alone achieving his year-end deadline for divorce. About the only thing that had changed was that Nathaniel was seeing a psychiatrist and I was worrying more about how we would live after the final divorce decree was handed down. It seemed a long way off. Still, I worried a lot.

There wasn't much else to do legally. Most of the legal process entailed waiting. My case went into Spenser's pipeline; Curtis's into his attorney's. Ours weren't their only cases, after all.

Our lawyers had exchanged correspondence citing our respective demands. Curtis said I was asking too much. I said he was offering too little. We had a four-way lawyer-client negotiating session to get some of the issues on the table, but we were no closer to any sort of financial or custody agreement than we had been the day Curtis left. He repeatedly accused me of dragging my feet to avoid finalizing a settlement. I repeatedly told him it wasn't my fault that both of our attorneys had other cases and other court appearances for other clients.

Spenser kept reminding me not to rush into any final decisions. I felt like a tennis ball in the midst of a fast-moving volley. I didn't want to make a quick decision because I might be locked into financial terms I would later regret. I needed time to sort out what I wanted to do. The trouble was, I didn't know what I wanted to do. Should I keep the inn or give it up? Agree to split the house with Curtis, sell, and move into an apartment? Go back to commuting? How would I *ever* know what *was* best for me?

"Phyllis, you *must* make a decision," Curtis told me repeatedly.

But I couldn't. *He* was frustrated over the lack of momentum in ending our life together. I was frustrated and confused over how to start a new life. And Nathaniel was torn between his past as a member of a two-parent family, his present status as a child in limbo, and his future place in two homes.

As Nathaniel's anxieties over the changes in his new life increased, he became more and more the focus of my attention. Curtis and I remained locked in a legal impasse as my role as Nathaniel's mother intercepted Curtis's demands for a speedy settlement.

Curtis had insisted from the very first upon a joint physical custody arrangement. I asked Spenser what that meant at our very first session and he had tossed the ball back to me.

"It usually means a fifty-fifty split of time with the child," he said.

"Fifty-fifty?" I gulped. "But Curtis travels. He isn't around fifty percent of the time. He never has been!"

"Some form of joint custody is the thing these days, Phyllis," Spenser continued, "but there are no absolutes. It's basically whatever the parties agree upon."

"He's not getting *my* child," I said adamantly.

I had assumed—mistakenly—that joint custody would

mean that Nathaniel would live with me and have open and free access to his father. I also assumed we would be flexible and cooperative in sharing time with our son until a formal custody agreement could be reached. I couldn't see any other logical way of assuring that, in the interim, Nathaniel would have ongoing contact with both of us.

Then I found out that there were many variations on the custody theme. Joint physical. Shared legal. Split. Sole. All of them with different meanings and all subject to different interpretation.

Not that the different meanings and interpretations came to the fore all at once.

In the days and weeks immediately following our split, Curtis had been so immersed in the enchantment of an all-consuming love affair, the practical realignment of his living conditions, and the urgencies of his day-to-day business responsibilities, that Nathaniel received low priority. It wasn't that Curtis was deliberately avoiding or abandoning his child. There was simply little time left for fathering, quality or otherwise.

I reasoned that, until the pink cloud of romance evaporated, it was better for Nathaniel to have a strong base in a familiar setting and be able to see his father frequently, virtually on demand, but know that his "place" remained the home in which he had grown up.

Curtis did not initially object. Sometimes he and Nathaniel were together for a few hours on a weekend. Sometimes for a midweek dinner. Occasionally overnight for an entire weekend. To me, it seemed like hit-and-miss visitation, but Nathaniel wanted—and needed—to be with his father.

He missed him desperately and was angry that his two friends—Jackie's sons—were living under a roof that Nathaniel saw as being his familial turf. I was reluctant to hold back on any time the two of them could be together, no matter how broadly inclusive the arrangement.

"You're letting Nathaniel stay overnight? With them?

How could you?" It was my mother on the phone, asking the same question she asked every time she called and found Nathaniel not around.

"I could very well, Mom," I said. "Nat needs his father too."

As the weeks passed, the unstructured visits and household shifts grew increasingly confusing and upsetting to my six-year-old. He looked forward to the time spent with his dad, but was left alternately angry and withdrawn after each visit. I was torn between letting him go whenever his father asked and wanting to protect him from the emotional upsets the roller-coaster spontaneity engendered.

*I* knew he was anxious and upset, but I wasn't aware just how obvious it was to others until I received a call from the headmistress at Nathaniel's school.

"We've been keeping an eye on Nathaniel," she said, then told me about an incident earlier in the week. A teacher on afternoon bus duty found him crying hysterically as he waited for the school bus.

"I don't want to go to my dad's house," he said. "Please don't make me go."

It didn't make sense. He wanted to go, but he didn't want to go.

She referred me to the school psychologist, who diagnosed him as showing a sense of loss and deprivation.

"He's anxious, depressed, and needs outside help," she said, and referred me to a child psychiatrist who handled private cases outside the school setting.

My initial reaction was embarrassment. I thought Nathaniel and I had been making great strides on the home front, trying to come to terms with the separation, divided loyalties, "sibling conflict," and the two-household setup. But soon the embarrassment turned to anger and resentment that my son was not coping as well as he should have been—or as I thought he should. The residential flip-flops, the other children, his father's new life, were all, I was certain, to blame.

I wanted to put a stop to Nat's insecurities, protect him

from his anxieties. My first step was to call our pediatrician for a second round of advice.

"Go," he said, after I explained that the school had recommended outside help. "It can't hurt."

"Nathaniel's reaction isn't unusual," the pediatrician continued. "Divorce isn't just one dramatic event. Boom! Then it's over. Most children experience a complex chain of reactions as they readjust to new lives and new relationships. Just don't rush him. Let him come to terms with the upheaval on his time schedule."

As I hung up I thought about how best to break this news to Curtis. I didn't know how he would react to his son seeing a psychiatrist. The doctor had explained that there were fairly predictable behavior patterns to expect in a child, including anxiety, fear, anger, guilt, sadness, loneliness, and conflicted loyalties between parents. He also told me to expect Nathaniel to harbor the classic fantasy of a reconciliation between us.

But he also said—and here is where I feared most getting into an argument with Curtis—that Nathaniel needed a sense of structure built around Curtis's spending concentrated time alone with his son.

"These spontaneous visits are harmful," he said, repeating what the school psychologist had said earlier. "The separation and divorce is confusing enough. Joint custody and flexible scheduling may work, but at this early stage, it's important for Nathaniel to know ahead of time when he will be seeing his father and then spend that time alone with him in order to establish a secure one-on-one relationship between the two of them."

I broached the subject with Curtis as tactfully as I could, first bringing up the issue of visitation and scheduling. We now communicated only by phone.

"Nathaniel needs to spend some time alone with you," I said, parroting the words of our pediatrician. "He misses you and needs to be with you alone, away from the other children and away from Jackie."

"You are preventing me from seeing him," he responded. "You're raising a lot of roadblocks. I want Nathaniel to be able to come over in the middle of the week, play with the boys, have dinner, and go home. He has to be able to do that. You cannot dictate schedules. He's going to be with me and be part of my life. My home has lots of love, affection, and caring."

"Curtis, you're not listening to what I'm saying," I said testily. "All I'm suggesting is that you spend some time alone with Nathaniel."

"You can't tell me that he misses me and then tell me I can't see him," Curtis insisted. "You are denying me access. You don't get to dictate my arrangements with Nathaniel. If I don't like the schedule, I'll be in court the next day."

"On what grounds?" I asked, dumbfounded.

"Preventing access and visitation rights."

"I am Nathaniel's mother," I stated ponderously. "My concern is for the welfare of my child. Sometimes mothers have an instinct about their children. What I have been trying to tell you is that sometimes I know him better than you do. Give me some credit for trying to work with you and get him through this period. It has been very disorienting."

"You will not get veto power over this child," he replied softly. I hadn't thought I *was* going to get it. "I want a full fifty-percent joint physical custody agreement—nothing less."

"What do you mean? Are you threatening me?" I asked, my voice beginning to rise in tone another octave. I could feel my emotional juices begin to flow, an irrational sense of the unreal began to settle over me.

"I'm not going to allow any bargaining when it comes to Nathaniel," he replied.

A hazy picture was beginning to emerge from the rhetoric. Spenser! I remember him telling me how many men force their wives to trade money for the children. The husband often threatens to go for custody, until the mother gives up her financial demands. He keeps the cash; she keeps the kids. Was this Curtis's plan? Could *he* seriously think I would bargain for money over my child? I thought he was overreacting and decided to try and deflect the argument.

"Sometimes you have to trust me, Curtis," I said.

"I *do* trust you, Phyllis," he said. "I haven't pressed you on seeing him, have I?"

One minute he was saying he didn't see him enough. The next minute he was saying he wasn't pushing me to see him.

"I thought you were too busy," I said coolly.

"That's not it. It's because it doesn't work for me to see a lot of him now. He needs his mother and his own environment, his room, his toys. But he needs to see his father when he wants to. He's going to be living primarily with you. I know that. I don't want him just on weekends. I want him during the week, some weekends, and some holidays. And I want a joint custody agreement to make sure I get it."

I reluctantly agreed to a loosely defined but structured schedule. Nathaniel would spend every other weekend with Curtis and have dinner with him once a week, and we would split holidays and vacation times.

Then I told him about the child psychiatrist. To my surprise, Curtis agreed to go along with the child therapy sessions for a trial period. We differed on approach. He favored the more pragmatic "Let's find a solution to the problem" technique practiced by many psychologists, as opposed to the "Let's delve into the mind and see what the dynamics of the conflict are" psychiatric method.

Nathaniel and I were still officially covered under Curtis's corporate medical plan. I called the recommended professional, a female Harvard-trained child psychiatrist specializing in divorce-related problems, and made an appointment. She suggested I introduce her as someone who would be Nathaniel's special friend with whom he could talk about his feelings. We set up a session for the following week.

Since Nathaniel was now scheduled for his first week-end-long visit, I dropped him off at Curtis's apartment on Friday after school. Nathaniel was excited to be spending the weekend on a "sleep-over" at his father's.

Beginning at eight P.M. that evening I received four telephone calls over a period of two hours.

"Mommy," my son was crying hysterically. "Please come and get me. I don't want to stay. I want to come home."

What on earth was this about, I wondered. When I asked to speak to Curtis, Nathaniel sobbed that his father and Jackie had gone out for the evening and had hired a sitter to stay with him. The other two boys were spending the weekend with *their* father.

"Please, Mommy, come and get me. Can't I come home?" he pleaded.

He knew and liked the sitter, a mature young girl whom I had also used on occasion, but my six-year-old was terrified at being left alone in a strange bed at his father's new and unfamiliar apartment. I was incensed. How could Curtis do this? Still, I had no legal right to go get Nathaniel.

The fifth call came from the sitter. Nathaniel was asleep in her arms on the couch, she would let him stay there until Curtis returned, and not to worry. I lay in bed thinking about my inaction all night.

"I want to come home," Nathaniel began to say on the phone the next morning at eight A.M., until Curtis interrupted the call.

"This child is manipulating you," Curtis said. "He's having a great time."

"Why did you tell him you would be spending the weekend with him if you had no plans to be around?" I asked angrily.

"Your son can go home," I was told curtly. "You are sabotaging the father-son relationship. I'll bring him back in an hour."

As precise as ever, Curtis arrived with Nathaniel one hour later. I watched from an upstairs window as Nathaniel opened the front door on the passenger side, jumped from the car, and ran toward the house. Curtis waited until Nathaniel had opened the front door, then drove off.

Nathaniel flew into my arms the moment he entered the house.

"I love you, Mommy," he said, hugging me tightly. "I love you more than anything in the whole wide world."

I hugged him until I thought he would burst. I was so afraid that somehow he would be taken from me.

Obviously Curtis and I were coming at custody from two different directions. Curtis's idea of it was radically different from mine, and, with no guidelines and no ground rules to follow, we had nothing to go on but good faith.

Good faith. More like the Solomonic question of how do you divide a child in half. Who thought up this one? In principle, the idea of both parents continuing their involvement with their children after divorce appeared to be an improvement over the previous nobody-wins arrangement where mothers were awarded sole custody and fathers were visitors in their children's lives. But joint custody simply didn't play out in practice. In practical terms, the real custody question for me remained unanswered: Who was in charge of the child on a day-in day-out basis?

Both the school psychologist and our pediatrician had emphasized that a crucial factor in the successful post-divorce adjustment of the child was a predictable, stable environment. Six- to eight-year-olds just taking their first steps toward independence were especially liable to upsets. Sleep disturbances, fears, and physical ailments—real and psychosomatic—could all be expected in early school-age children of divorce.

Curtis, in his demands for "joint physical custody," ignored all this carefully solicited advice. He had a new ready-made family and wanted Nathaniel to take his place in it, immediately.

What was mystifying to me, however, was Curtis's persistent demands for joint physical custody while his actions indicated otherwise.

"Why do I have to go to Dad's house if he's not there?" asked my son.

I assumed he *was* there, since Curtis had assured me when we worked out the scheduling arrangements that he would pick Nathaniel up after school, they would spend time together, and he would return him to my place after dinner. Inevitably, Nathaniel would be picked up by Jackie and stay with her and the boys at the apartment, then Curtis would arrive for a quick dinner, after which Nathaniel would be returned to me.

Sometimes pickup responsibilities even devolved to Jackie's mother, a nice woman, but still another person for Nathaniel to contend with. Occasionally, Nathaniel would be dropped off at a neighbor's home to wait until Jackie or Curtis returned from work. All these crazy pickups and deliveries—when I was at home, less than two miles away, and fully available for cooperation. I was co-parenting with a chain of third parties. All to pay homage to the principle of joint physical custody.

I wondered fearfully if Nathaniel would think I was abandoning him or that I didn't want him when he was placed in the care of these third parties, knowing that I was at home. When I mentioned my concerns to others, I was told that a multiplicity of child-care arrangements was common practice in joint custody households. Rock-bottom instinct told me this may have been a common practice, but that didn't make it right. *Someone* had to be in charge. Someone was always in charge in a family that remained intact. In divorce, I was certain it was even more important for a child to have a strong sense of attachment to a parent. With an erratic blend of flip-flopping child-care arrangements, how, I asked myself, could this be possible? What would it do to the child's mental health?

Sure, co-parenting sounded fine on the surface. We lived in an age of dual-career couples and role reversals. But—and here is where I differed from those who compromised away their day-to-day parenting obligations in favor of a nod to the theoretical principles of sharing a child after divorce—the question for me remained a big one. Why should I hand over my day-to-day role as the child's on-site, involved, and available mother to a series of others simply to participate in the ideal of dual child rearing? This wasn't dual child rearing at all. This was multi-party child rearing.

After a series of these pickup-and-delivery circuses I telephoned Curtis to discuss my concerns.

"Why do you tell me you're going to be taking care of Nathaniel when you're not?" I asked him.

"You hire baby-sitters when you aren't home," he said.

"Your son is disappointed when you tell him you'll be there and then you send someone else," I said.

Curtis's response was predictable: "You are denying me access."

It became the catch-all response for everything having to do with the child. "How," I asked, "am I denying you access when you are not there?"

If I expressed concern over Nathaniel's bedtime, if I accepted an invitation for him to attend a birthday party on "their" time, if I objected to child-care arrangements, or to the language he brought home, I was accused of interference. I probably shouldn't have accepted commitments for Nathaniel when he was with his father, but I saw no reason not to express concern over my son's rearing and welfare.

"You can't control what I do with Nathaniel when he's with me," Curtis repeated again and again.

Why couldn't I? I was the child's mother and wanted to know where he would be, what he would be doing, and who would be taking care of him. Was that so wrong?

"Are you taking time off during vacation?" I asked when he said he wanted Nathaniel during spring break. "Will you be taking care of him or will someone else be? Where will he be?"

"It's none of your business."

I began to get angry.

"I did not agree to Nathaniel spending time with anyone but you. You are his father."

I was very much on the defensive. I wanted to give Curtis every benefit of the doubt, but I was beginning to fray at the edges. Nathaniel would be seeing the child psychiatrist soon. Maybe then I would get some answers about what to do, what was right and what was wrong, and how much maternal control I could rightfully exert.

Something had to be resolved—and pretty soon. Nathaniel's nights had become a battle zone. He would wake screaming from nightmares, or not be able to sleep at all. Bedtime, always trying, became a go-for-broke tug-of-war as he tried to avoid sleep and the terrifying dreams that haunted him each night.

"Mommy, Mommy, there's a man coming through the window who's trying to saw me in half," he cried one night. I didn't need an in-depth psychiatric explanation of that one.

We had always set aside two times of the day for special talks. Dinner had been a family event. We sat and ate together, rehashing the events of the day and reaffirming our existence as a family. Bedtime had always been reserved for one-on-one conversation. Sometimes Curtis had handled bedtime responsibilities, but more often it was I who had tucked Nathaniel between his covers and talked with him about any special thoughts or problems he had.

Nathaniel referred to it as "private time," and with the concept in place, I created a game called the "Divorce Reporter" where we talked into a tape recorder about the separation and his feelings. I wasn't looking for any great insights. I just wanted him to talk about how he felt, to get his fears and feelings out in the open. I thought he would respond better to making it a game with the help of a tape recorder.

"Can we talk about anything?" he asked.

"Sure," I said. I wanted him to begin talking about the

divorce, but I knew it was a painful subject. Talking about our family's disintegration was hard for me, virtually impossible for him, but I thought if maybe he could get his feelings out, I could help settle his anxieties.

"Mommy, this is hard to talk about."

"That's okay—just talk about anything and I'll try and answer the best I can."

"Well, it's about watches. How do you make watches?"

"That's pretty hard to explain."

"Could we open up one and see what's inside?"

"Maybe. Why do you want to know about that?"

"I want to know about the eastern time, the central time, and the mountain time. How do they split it up?"

This was not what I had expected.

"That's a pretty hard question. How come you're asking me all these hard questions?"

"Because it got dark early today. Why does it get dark early?"

"Why don't you ask your science teacher?" I paused, trying to gather the nerve to direct him toward the subject of divorce.

"Don't you have some questions about the divorce to ask me?" I said quietly.

"I have some other questions."

"Okay—shoot."

"After you chew your food, how does it get down inside you?"

"Oh good, that's a question I can answer. You swallow it. It goes down your throat to the esophagus and then into your stomach where it's digested."

"Where does it stop? Is it like a hose?"

"Sort of. It leads to your stomach, then it gets digested in your stomach."

"I think I know what happens when it all piles up. The food all bangs together. Boom, boom, boom, then you get a stomachache, right?

"Right."

"Mom, I have another question."

Maybe this was something about the divorce.

"Who invented the world?"

"God made the world from a chunk of matter that was split up into Earth and lots of other planets."

I was trying hard not to get impatient.

"Mom, is there such a thing as Martians?"

"There may be other forms of life on other planets that we don't know about. In fact, there may be a little Martian whose mother is trying to get him to go to bed right now and he's asking his mother if there is such a thing as Earthlings. He's probably sitting up in bed right now asking his mother for a glass of water and trying to convince her to let him stay up for just five more minutes so he can see a special program on television."

"You're kidding me, Mom. There's no such thing as Martians."

"Look at *E.T.*"

"That's pretend. Mommy, there's no such thing as Martians. I think I'll go to bed now."

I kissed him good night, tucked his covers tightly around him, and vowed to try again. He was giggling when I left his room.

The bedtime nonsense continued for several weeks. Rather than discouraging his silly questions, I answered them as objectively as possible. I wanted him to feel he could talk about any subject freely and openly.

Once he became fully comfortable with this bedtime routine, I planned to introduce more delicate divorce-related issues. The first breakthrough had unexpectedly frightening results.

"Will you keep me company until I fall asleep?"

"You have all your stuffed animals. In fact, you have so many that there is barely enough room for you in your bed."

"I need a human."

"Go to bed."

"Are we separated yet?"

"No, it takes a long time."

"What do we have to do to get separated?"

"Well, we have to split up everything, then the lawyers meet and draw up some papers that say we have agreed to divorce and then we sign some papers and that's it."

"I'm not giving up any of my stuff."

"You don't have to."

"Mom, I love you and Dad the same. Are you both one-hundred-percent in love with me?"

"Of course darling."

I kissed him, hugged him tightly, and turned off the light.

"Good night Mommy," I heard him say. "I love you."

Less than an hour later I heard him screaming.

I ran to his room.

"Mommy, mommy," he cried, "I can't see!"

I snapped on the light and stopped cold. His eyes had swollen, the lids so puffed he looked like a bullfrog.

"Wait right there, don't move," I instructed him, trying to remain calm. He was off-the-wall hysterical. My fingers shakily dialed the pediatrician whose answering service reached him within minutes.

"Sounds like an allergic reaction to something," he said, prescribing cold compresses and an antihistamine. "Wait forty-eight hours and see if the swelling subsides."

Nathaniel clung to me for an hour, finally falling asleep, exhausted.

Over the course of the next few months we would have five more incidents of the mysterious frog eyes. Dozens of allergy and other tests yielded nothing. There was no obvious pattern and no physical basis for the symptoms. His eyes would pop. He would refuse to go to school.

"I look like a monster. The kids will make fun of me," he cried.

I let him stay home. The swelling would subside and all would return to normal.

Just when I thought some progress was being made, the nightmares would start again. He was up half the night, I was up half the night, and I was tired and angry. When would it end? The eyes, the arguments, the divorce? I wanted my life to be like it was in the movies—like in *An Unmarried Woman*—all problems speedily sailed through, the abandoned heroine finally left holding all the cards. But in a real-life divorce things just drag on and on . . .

Nathaniel's anxiety transferred to the school setting. He always had been a happy, well-adjusted child. Suddenly he was rebelling against even attending school.

"I don't want to go back to school," Nathaniel said during one of our bedtime talk sessions. "We played keepaway and the kids wouldn't let me have the ball. And I liked the bun on the cheesesteak, but not the cheese, and I feel like I'm getting a cold and I can't swallow and I don't want you and Dad to get a divorce."

He disintegrated into tears.

"I want my dad to come back. It's all my fault."

"Nathaniel, it is not your fault," I told him, gently smoothing his hair. He lay across my chest, sobbing, cuddled in my arms.

"Did you argue about *me*, Mommy?"

"Never, honey," I said. "We argued about a lot of things, but we never—*ever*—argued about you."

Nathaniel responded instantly to his psychiatrist. She played chess and checkers with him and he liked that. What she was really doing was engaging him in play therapy to see how he viewed the family breakup.

She also let him draw pictures and play with blocks and cartoons.

His artwork was instructive. His family pictures, all drawn with smiling faces, indicated that he had positive feelings toward both Curtis and me. When she asked him to draw a picture of his mother, he drew a woman with a smiling face standing in front of an orange house (ours was redwood) surrounded by a rainbow. The woman, however, had brown hair on one side of her head, blond on the other. I was a brunette, Jackie a blonde.

Nathaniel and I continued our bedtime talks. The doctor felt these bedtime sessions were helpful because they encouraged Nathaniel to talk about his feelings. The more he talked, the more comfortable and accepting he would be of the separation.

"Do I have to go to the doctor's?" he asked one night before a therapy session. "I never do anything there except play. Sometimes we talk a little, but I don't want to talk with her, I want to talk with you."

Sometimes, when she began to draw him out, he resisted going the next time. In most successful therapy, the closer the dicussions get to the problem and the pain, the more the patient resists. Nathaniel was resisting.

I told him that I had gone to talk with her too.

"You did?" he asked in amazement. "What did you talk about?"

"The divorce and how I felt." Maybe if he saw that I had feelings too, he would feel it was okay to talk about his. "I was scared and I didn't know what was going to happen."

"Sometimes I feel that way too," he told me, "but I know what's going to happen."

"You do?" Maybe Nathaniel had some inside information about the case.

"Of course," he said. "You're going to get a divorce!"

Bingo! A breakthrough. It was the first time that Nathaniel had verbally indicated an awareness that his parents were split and separated. Psychologically, it was a giant step for a small child. It was a beginning. I knew I could nurture him back to being an emotionally strong child, but it was going to take time, lots of time, and Curtis and his demands and his timetable would just have to wait. My child came first.

The months whirled by. Thanksgiving. Christmas. New Year's. Whenever I talked with Curtis he urged me to settle, to sell the house, split it up, find an apartment, and get on with my life. I still was rushing to complete my book project, and hadn't thought about what I could do or where I could live after that. I had been cautioned by both Nathaniel's psychiatrist and our pediatrician not to dislodge any more of his anchors—school, friends, living conditions—until our son came to terms with our separation and stabilized emotionally. Spenser, when I spoke with him, continued to urge me to take my time and not be pushed into any decisions I would later regret.

I needed time to sort things out, I kept reminding myself. Perhaps I *was* dragging my feet, but I couldn't think straight. Later, *much* later, I would learn that my inability to get myself together was part and parcel of the emotional fallout of the post-separation phase of the divorce process. Many husbands capitalize on this disequilibrium to get their wives to settle up and "get things over with." Thanks to my lawyer, I wasn't about to do that. Still, this was hardly a pretty phase in which to find myself. At this point I wasn't making decisions because I couldn't. I literally couldn't.

Curtis's and my attorneys were also caught up with other cases, sometimes to the point that they were unable to meet with either of us for weeks on end. So we waited, both of us becoming more frustrated and farther removed from a quick settlement than either of us had anticipated.

"Phyllis, you have got to make some decisions," Curtis tried once more during one of our "making arrangements for Nathaniel" telephone conversations. "I want to get on with my life."

"I want to get on with my life too," I retorted, though at that point I really couldn't say I had much of a life.

For the moment we seemed to be at an impasse.

February 11, 1983. There was not a trace of snow when we awoke, but the school bus driver called at six A.M. to say there would be no transportation because of the impending storm. Having grown up in the Great Lakes snowbelt, where no one stopped until the accumulation reached two feet, I dismissed the warning as another day of typical

East Coast pre-snow hysteria where everything ground to a stop as soon as the first flurries appeared.

We had been receiving false snow warnings all week. School was still open, but I decided to keep Nathaniel home this time. It was the beginning of a three-day holiday weekend and school was scheduled to let out at noon. My car, a touch-and-go source of transportation, had been in the shop for repairs three times over the past month, and the chance of a snowbound breakdown dampened my enthusiasm for the long commute.

The flurries started around nine A.M. at the same time Nathaniel remembered that today was his school's Valentine's celebration. The thought of his carefully selected and addressed cards for his classmates, party decorations, games, and his own nonattendance brought frantic tears and outsized disappointment.

I remembered my own childhood disappointment whenever I had missed a special school party or celebration. I looked at the flurries with a practiced eye and decided that they might just not materialize into the promised snow.

We packed ourselves into the car and drove off to school. The party was supposed to begin around 11:15. We could easily make it. I walked Nathaniel into his class at 9:30 to explain our tardy arrival. He was greeted by his classmates with cries of:

"You missed the party! Where were you? We just had the party!"

The scene was straight out of the "Peanuts" gang, with my child playing the role of Charlie Brown. All those carefully addressed Valentine's Day cards, dreams of sugary candy hearts, and the excitement of the ritual opening of the cards vanished. He was crestfallen.

His teacher stepped in to remedy the situation. Now I had firsthand evidence of why he had fallen in love with her. She quickly consulted with me as we fabricated a trumped-up story allowing him to save face before his classmates.

"Nathaniel's bus didn't come this morning," she said.

"Now that he's here, how about if we celebrate Valentine's Day again?"

Any excuse for a party is a good one for a class of six-year-olds. None of them were going to turn down a second celebration only moments after the first.

As one friend ran to the cooler to bring him an ice cream cone, another ferreted out a slightly squished left-over cupcake with candy hearts and red and pink sprinkles. The rest of the children circled his desk as he slowly picked his way through the stack of cards.

"Oh, isn't that cute?"

"Look at the bear on the motorcycle!"

"Here's one with a frog!"

His classmates commented appreciatively on each card he opened. He had no sooner finished the stack when an announcement was made over the loudspeaker that school was closing early due to the storm. The snow had picked up considerably and was now swirling dervish-fashion outside the windows.

We packed his cards and goodies together and returned to my car, which had become encrusted with heavy, wet snow in less than half an hour. The roads were uncleared, icy, and drift-swept, the wind and the speed of the snowfall impeding the efforts of the snow removal trucks. The wipers, set on high, could barely keep the snow off the windshield. My car, even with its front-wheel drive, and at a tortoiselike pace, was skidding unmercifully. The winds rocked us each time we stopped.

"Did you ever miss a school party when you were a kid, Mom?" Nathaniel was perched in the back seat. He leaned forward as he asked the question and I felt his fingers lightly play with the fur of my curly lamb coat.

I told him the same thing had happened to me once, except it had been a Halloween party. We talked about feelings and disappointments. I tried to keep the conversation going to distract both of us from the weather conditions, which were worsening by the minute.

We talked about the years I spent growing up in the

Midwest, how it snowed much more than on the East Coast, and what my brother and I did as children when schools were shut and we were home snowbound.

"Mom, when are we going to be home? Are you scared? You never get scared. When do you get scared?"

"What are you scared about?" I asked him. "I'm the one who's driving. You're only sitting there. Remember the play we saw a few weeks ago? What did the little boy do when he was afraid?"

Nathaniel thought a while, trying to remember the play and the scene.

"I remember. The little boy was about my age and he whistled a happy tune."

Thank you, Rodgers and Hammerstein, Yul Brynner, and the cast and crew of *The King and I*. Nathaniel sang and whistled for the next two hours—the time it took us to arrive at the base of our driveway. I decided it would be foolhardy to try to get the car up the hill in this storm. I wedged the car into eight inches of snow just barely off the street to allow room for the snowplow I hoped would come soon. As I lifted my foot from the clutch I felt it spring loose. Damn! I would have to have the car towed to the dealer. We would probably be snowbound for a few days anyway, so I decided to put off thinking about it until the end of the weekend.

Nathaniel and I crawled up the steep hill—falling repeatedly as we struggled to gain any sort of footing against the base of ice. The sleet and icy snow whipped around us, stinging our faces and covering our snow clothes. Nathaniel took a belly flop and fell flat on his face, bloodying his nose. The bag of valentines never left his hand.

"I'm trying to be brave, Mom," he gasped.

I was never so happy to be inside my house. I lit a fire in the wood-burning stove, put up a pot of hot chocolate, and sat before the television watching the emergency weather reports.

Less than an hour later the telephone rang. The caller introduced himself as the credit manager of my oil supplier. He was sorry to be calling me on a day like this, but they were canceling my credit and would be stopping my oil deliveries.

"There must be a mistake," I told him lightheartedly. "We've been customers for years. Why don't you check your records. It's probably a computer error. Horrible day, isn't it?"

He said nothing for a minute. I thought he was checking the records.

"There's no mistake," he said kindly and sympathetically. They had received a letter from my husband stating that he was no longer responsible for the house bills and requesting his credit deposit be returned. Since Curtis was not living in the house any more and since both the credit records and billings were in his name, they were required to return the deposit.

Because I had no deposit nor a credit record established with the firm, he said, the only way they would deliver oil was COD. According to his estimates, the delivery would run about $375. Since I was due for a delivery and most probably had enough fuel for only the next few days, he wanted to let me know in advance so that I could make a decision. After payment was made, he would set up a monthly budget account to spread out my total oil bills over a year's time period, but until then, no payment, no oil.

"I'm sorry Mrs. Ellsworth, but you're not alone," he said. "We get letters like this all the time. I assume you and your husband have separated. Maybe you should talk to your lawyer."

This couldn't be. On a day like this? How could this be happening?

I barely heard his final words as he assured me that he would try and schedule an emergency delivery. Three or four days of fuel remained, and I was stuck at the top of an impassable hill. An inoperative car blocked the driveway. And the snowstorm was shaping up to be the area's worst blizzard in twenty years.

Within minutes the phone was ringing again. This time it was a representative of the electric company. Same story. No deposit, no credit, no electricity. By the time I heard from the insurance company providing coverage for my car, the words were committed to memory. The car was no longer drivable, but because the title was in joint names, I couldn't sell it, nor could I obtain new insurance because mine was not the name on the title.

Curtis hadn't sent his voluntary support check this week either.

I was dumbfounded. Curtis and I did have our differences over how the divorce settlement was proceeding, but he had repeatedly assured me that he would provide for us and the household expenses until we reached an agreement. And he had been doing so—until now, when everything stopped. I thought about our vows of good faith to each other. What was going on here?

I reached for the phone to dial my attorney. He was on vacation for two weeks. I was referred to a young woman named Elizabeth Weber, who told me she had read the correspondence between Spenser and myself and that she would probably be handling the custody end of the case.

Hold everything here! My deal was with Spenser, not with an associate. I knew nothing about her, and certainly did not want a recent law-school graduate handling my son's destiny. But Elizabeth Weber, working late on that Friday afternoon with fifteen inches of snow on the ground and another ten to go before the storm ended, was the only game in town.

She sensed my dissatisfaction and coolly deflected my challenging, confrontational attitude as we discussed the financial sanctions and what they meant.

"This is a very common tactic," Weber said. "I'm only surprised it didn't happen earlier."

Weber explained that when negotiations were at a standstill, husbands often tried "wife-busting" tactics in an attempt to break the logjam.

"You're damned if you do and damned if you don't,"

she said. "If you cave in, you're in a weak bargaining position. If you pick up the pieces and show an ability to support yourself, your financial settlement is usually lessened. Do you have any money to cover these bills until we can get you a court date?"

"A few thousand maybe," I said, thinking of my dwindling bank account, "but no income either."

"You can either file a motion for temporary support—called pendente lite motions—and force the issue through the courts, or accept the intimidation and give in," Weber explained. "The decision is up to you."

Courts? Judges? This was supposed to be a civilized, negotiated settlement. I had a few days to think things over, because the courthouse was closed until Tuesday when we could file our request for support. Basically I had two options—give in or go to battle.

Snowbound at the top of my hill, I tried to rationally assess my status. I was really trapped. I had a book contract, but would not receive final payment until I delivered the manuscript. I couldn't take time from the book for a competing assignment because my contractual commitments contained a "time is of the essence" clause. If I failed to deliver the book on time, I would forfeit the advance paid to me. I lived in a rural community where professional jobs were scarce. With my car on the fritz and no money to repair it, I had no reliable transportation to take me to the closest job market, approximately forty-five minutes away. Most important, I had a young child who needed his mother. Nor could I move. I had been cautioned by Spenser and Weber not to unilaterally move Nathaniel away from Curtis because it might be a factor—a negative one—in my custody case. No way was I going to jeopardize my position there.

As I mulled over my options, or rather the lack of them, I was alternately enraged and wounded. I had been operating in what I thought had been good faith since the separation. All the threats I had turned aside as bluff had now become reality. All along I had assumed Curtis and I would reach a compromise settlement. Now it was becoming apparent that any compromising was to be done by me. For the first time since October 1, reality set in. I was in the middle of a divorce, my previous life was over, and my estranged husband wanted no part of me. For months I had been trying to go on with my life in exactly the same fashion as before, but without Curtis. Now I knew I couldn't. I had to change my attitude and tactics, and, to do this, I had to change myself.

I was so confused and so angry I couldn't even pick up the phone to call Curtis. He was coming to pick up Nathaniel the next day, and I wanted to confront him face-to-face. I couldn't understand his actions. This was his son's home. How could he cancel our basic utilities in midwinter? Was *this* the way he considered his son's welfare? Why should I even cooperate when the subject of his time with Nathaniel came up if this was the way he was going to treat us?

Weber had warned me that I could not—and should not—withhold Curtis's visits with his son, not even under these circumstances.

"He's just playing hardball with you," she said. "The sanctions have nothing to do with you personally or how he feels about Nathaniel. Try and stay objective and keep your emotions out of the conflict. He's just treating the divorce as a business deal, trying to force your hand."

A *business* deal, I thought. He's treating us like a business deal? Leaving us to shiver in an unheated house in the worst snowstorm in decades?

I cried through the night, my tears turning to intense anger when Curtis arrived to pick up Nathaniel the following afternoon. I could feel my blood start to simmer at the sound of his knock on the front door. He had just slogged his way up the driveway, which was now packed with twenty-five inches of fresh snow, and was standing in two feet of snow on my front doorstep. I pushed open the front door to let Nathaniel, who was already dressed and waiting in his snowsuit and boots, out, at the same time barring Curtis from coming in with my left arm.

I started to speak, but he beat me to it.

"I should have made you bring him down," he snapped, as he shuddered in the frigid winter air.

My face turned purple and Ms. "Got-It-Together Business-As-Usual" threw a fit, totally forgetting Weber's warning about keeping her emotions out of the conflict. A complete, full-fledged volcanic fit. I lost any semblance of a rational being.

"What is the meaning of these financial sanctions?" I screamed. "We're supposed to be civilized adults. We're supposed to be negotiating. Are you a child who packs up his toys and goes home if he doesn't get his own way? What is this business with the utilities, cutting off everything in the middle of winter? This is your son's home. Are you crazy? Why are you doing this to us?"

He looked at me with a bemused expression as if I were a naughty, unreasonable little girl.

"I want to bring you to the bargaining table, Phyllis," he said, quietly and without emotion. "I want to go on with my life. I am not going to continue to support you. I have another life and other obligations. The well has run dry. As for this being my son's house, he has two homes. He doesn't live with you—he lives with both of us."

My mind swirled with thoughts of his recent vacation to Saint Thomas, his purchase of a car for Jackie, their expensive evenings out, and their weekends away. I knew he had purchased gifts and clothing for the other boys and furnishings for their home. And now he was trying to undermine my position as Nathaniel's mother.

"Get out," I screamed.

Nathaniel was standing a little way off outside the door, bundled in his snow clothes, playing with the icicles which hung from the evergreens. He looked up in amazement and shock over the tone and level of my voice. My knees were weak, my voice strained. I was crying, shaking, and screaming at the same time. There was no stopping me.

"Get out, you bastard! I will not be intimidated or coerced or brought to the bargaining table under this kind of pressure! Any kind of pressure! You have been dealing with a crooked deck! And you know what? It's not going to get you *anywhere!*"

I paused, gasping for breath, then continued slowly and deliberately.

"If you think . . . I am going to give up my child, my home, and my way of life so that your girlfriend can maintain her tennis habit, you've got another thing coming. Now you're in for a *real* fight!"

He slowly backed away from me, keeping his eyes on me at all times. His expression had changed from amusement to amazement, tinged with some apprehension. I think he thought I was ready to jump on him. I was. I had never been so enraged, so completely out of control—*ever!* Curtis had never seen me like this before because I had never *been* like this before. My brain was alternately red hot, then blue-white with anger. I was a human volcano that had lain dormant for years, and that now was suddenly exploding, spewing forth layers of ignited emotions and feelings as if they were bands of molten lava and ash.

I stepped back inside the house with new resolve and, with one grand dramatic gesture, swung the door wide open and then slammed it in his *face.* I was amazed at myself and at my portrayal of the wounded wife. Still shaking, I marched down the hallway, up the stairs, and into my office. I'd show him! I sat down at my desk, pulled out my checkbook, and began to calculate how long I could hold out against Curtis's financial siege.

The figures were not encouraging.

# CHAPTER 5

# DIVORCE DIPLOMACY

I went to bed that night and tried to sleep. I thought of money, of how I didn't have it and how desperately I needed it. I thought about what I should do, where I should go and whom I could turn to. No answers came from anywhere. I struggled to hold on to myself, to try and think clearly and calmly, but I was battered by an onslaught of emotions and feelings whose intensity I had never experienced. Extreme rage. Terror. Hurt. Anguish. And over and over my child's words played in my head, "Who will take care of us, Mommy?"

I fell into a turbulent sleep and woke around midnight, my head pounding. It was the first headache I had had since Curtis left. I had grown used to being free from pain during the past five months and now the dull pounding pressure which pushed inward against my skull seemed unbearable.

Nausea, chills, swollen eyes, disorientation. I knew I had a classic migraine. And I also knew there was nothing I could do except ride it out. I was to remember very little of that holiday weekend.

With Nathaniel at Curtis's and me snowbound and in excruciating pain, I stayed in bed, arising only to use the bathroom and walk twenty steps into the kitchen to pour myself a glass of juice or soda. My head throbbed with each step I took and it seemed an eternity until I was able to return to the security of my bed and rest my head lightly on the pillow. Every time I thought of Curtis, the knots in my neck tightened. Every time I thought of Nathaniel, his innocence and anxieties, the dull drumming in my eyes, temples, and forehead seemed to get worse.

When the migraine finally passed, it was Tuesday morning. I had spent forty-eight hours in another world, fogged in, disoriented, blinded by pain. When I woke, I felt as if I had emerged from a torturous jungle after hacking my way through the world's densest undergrowth. And suddenly a clearing was in sight. As the pain lifted I felt a new resolve, a new determination to take care of my child.

Later that morning, when Spenser returned from his vacation and called to check in, I barely let him say hello before I started to blurt out my version of the weekend's events. As I did so, I began to shake again. "I can't believe how angry I was," I said to Spenser, hoping he didn't detect any sign of weakness in my voice. I'm still angry, I thought to myself in surprise—and afraid too. Very afraid. Curtis had used financial power against me and I had found out just how vulnerable I was. However, my tone with Spenser betrayed none of this.

"I have very little money to live on," I said as if we were discussing the weather. I'd always prided myself on being a cool customer. Why change now? "That's what it comes down to."

"I've filed a short calendar motion for temporary alimony and child support," said Spenser, getting right to the business at hand. "We should receive a hearing date in about a month or two."

"That long?" I cried, my mask slipping a bit. "I don't know whether I'll be able to hold out until then."

Spenser said something meant to be bright and funny and maybe even comforting about the wheels of justice grinding slowly, then assured me, "We're moving ahead as fast as we can."

It seemed that a long backlog in domestic court calendars prevented any hearings from being immediately scheduled. I would have to wait my turn. If I was lucky, I would wait a month. If not, two months or more.

My "job" during this wait was to get all my financial records in order. I gulped. I hadn't exactly been getting myself together these past five months. Days passed without my doing anything. I don't know what I *did* do. I was so confused by the shifts in our case—back and forth between cooperation to confrontation and back and forth again—plus my indecisiveness about what to do, where to go, and how to earn enough money to do anything, that all I could do was burrow into my home on the side of my hill and stay there.

I tried to ignore the hurts, tried to push aside my fears, tried to concentrate on keeping a strong face for Nathaniel and against the outer world. I knew I had to come to terms with my new circumstances, but I didn't know how. I was simply overwhelmed by my own indecisiveness, my depression and anxiety, Nathaniel's problems, and the interminable legal process. Now I had a task: I needed to organize my facts and figures for this upcoming support conference.

Get it together, Phyllis, I told myself, and wanly wondered if I'd be able to.

"This is the very first step on what may be a long ladder," Spenser continued. "A request for temporary support is just that. We make our case for a weekly stipend to carry you over until a final settlement can be negotiated."

A hearing officer would evaluate my financial needs by comparing Curtis's figures against mine. That all seemed rather black and white, but the hearing's outcome was usually decided on a more subjective basis—by the family relations officer. If either of us objected, it would go before a judge. All this—just for *temporary* alimony and child support.

"It's all a question of which set of numbers—the husband's or the wife's—are more believable," Spenser told me. "We have to establish a moderately successful but not extravagant standard of living. You work on your numbers, I've got some other papers to file, and we'll regroup a week or so before the hearing date."

"One other thing," Spenser said. "I'm going to try and set up a four-way meeting between you and me, Rawson and your husband. We know their opening position; they have a sense of ours. Let's see if we can get some of the issues on the table and keep this case out of court."

Spenser's conciliatory attitude toward Curtis and his attorney was just show. We both knew we were miles apart on everything and one two-hour session would not even begin to settle our differences.

I felt I knew how it would go: like a series of summit meetings. The two opposing sides agree to meet. We would express our good faith and our intent to cooperate. We would each put our position on the table, neither of us would budge, and we would leave the meeting empty-handed, while expressing goodwill and high hopes that our efforts would lead to another session.

Divorce diplomacy, with the winner decided by an exceptional show of cunning, strategy, precision, and skill. You also needed an iron stomach and steely nerves. I wasn't sure I could summon up either.

"Have you thought about what you really want?" asked Spenser. His voice was less lawyerly now, more fatherly. He was referring to what I expected from the settlement negotiations. It was the same question Curtis had asked repeatedly since his departure.

"I don't know," I replied in a flat voice. "It depends upon what Curtis will do, what he will give up."

I couldn't tell Spenser or Curtis what I wanted, because I didn't know myself. Whatever he'll give me, was what I was thinking. I kept rationalizing that I couldn't make a decision about what I wanted to do until I knew how much money I would have to do it with. It was a circle. I didn't want to make a decision until we had reached a financial agreement and we couldn't reach a financial agreement until I decided what I wanted to do. But whenever I thought about trying to figure out what I wanted to do, I began to get very depressed. So I avoided the issue and did nothing. Not very productive, but it was the best I could do just now.

Curtis and I had been separated for several months now, but I still couldn't think straight. I felt that everyone was trying to pressure me into making decisions that would affect the rest of my life when I really wasn't in any condition to do so. Even Spenser. On the one hand he was telling me to take my time. On the other hand he was asking me if I had decided what I was going to do. Only a little while ago I had been planning to open a restaurant and turn an historic inn into a country bed-and-breakfast lodging. I still had hopes of running the restaurant, but would Curtis give up his financial stake in the building? And even if he would, could I make it work? With barely any funds of my own, no cash flow, no investors, and the panic which set in whenever I thought of how much money I needed to care for my child, maintain the house, and keep my head above water in the day-to-day struggle to survive . . .

The best I could offer Spenser was a series of "if . . . then" scenarios. Each alternative was based on Curtis's action and generosity. I had never felt so out of control of my life.

"If he's willing to turn over his share of the inn to me," I said, "I'll give up half the house, put it on the market for a quick sale, and move with Nathaniel to an apartment at the inn."

At least I had figured *this* much out. There were three large apartments in the building and a tenant would be leaving soon. I could live above the restaurant. We would be in the center of a small town, Nat would have friends to play with, I would have a source of income with which to begin a new life.

"If he's not willing to do that, I'll have to rethink my future. I can't depend upon free-lance writing as a steady source of income. That's unrealistic. I may have to move to find a job that pays a decent living, but I don't know where to go, or what kind of job I can find."

I *did* know that I didn't want to be forced into a decision just for the sake of satisfying the other side. Curtis had his future completely planned out. Mine was up for grabs. I was full of resentment that his new life had fallen into place so easily while mine lingered interminably on hold.

More than a month passed before Spenser was able to schedule a four-way meeting between Curtis, his attorney, himself, and me. The session was held in Spenser's office on a damp Saturday morning. I had arranged to arrive an hour early for a final briefing before the others arrived.

I had wanted to skip the meeting. I doubted it would accomplish anything, and, worse, I had a real dread of confronting Curtis in this way; but Spenser insisted. He needed to meet Curtis face-to-face to get not only a sense of how much or how little Curtis was willing to give up, but, more importantly, to get a feel for how Curt might respond in the presence of a court official.

I signaled my reluctance to Spenser by showing up twenty minutes late and very casually dressed: Levis, boots, an old turtleneck, and a tweed jacket.

"Aren't you ever on time?" asked Spenser a bit brusquely as he directed me into his conference room. Over the years I had grown accustomed to never wearing a watch because I never seemed to have to be anywhere at any precise time of day. My tardy habits remained now. Aside from our very first meeting, I had never arrived at Spenser's office on time. Since he scheduled and billed clients on the hour, I knew this was aggravating, but, try as I might, something always prevented me from being there precisely when I was supposed to. Today, however, I had deliberately taken my time in driving to his office. That'll show him, I thought.

"They'll be here in half an hour and I want to review our status."

"This is a waste of my time," I told him sullenly. Not that I had much else to do.

He chose to ignore my attitude.

"What property are we talking about?" my attorney asked without looking up from the papers held in his hands. He was curt and ultraprofessional. I knew his manner masked his annoyance with my behavior.

I grumpily produced my financial papers. We had been over this at least three times before. Spenser started firing questions at me.

"Property?"

"The house, the inn, and some stock," I replied resentfully.

"Alimony. How much do you think you are entitled to and for how long?"

"As much as you can get me," I spat out. Spenser discreetly said nothing, didn't even bother to look up. His face was pure attorney. I couldn't read a thing.

"Pension and profit sharing?"

"There are monies in both funds," I said. "I don't know how much."

"Stock?"

"Privately owned," I said. "Curtis's company is a family business. I've told you that. The family owns the stock. It's not traded publicly. Unless it goes public it's not worth anything but grief."

"It *is* worth something."

I sat and sulked. I wondered if Spenser still liked me, if he still thought of me as the type of client he liked to represent. One who participated in her own defense. I sure wasn't doing much participating now.

"What about the car?" he asked.

"I don't need a car," I replied.

"I thought that was a big issue with you," he said. "Even your husband admitted that yours was in its final days."

I wanted to say that if I waited for all of them to get around to making a decision about the car I would have worn out the soles of a dozen pairs of sneakers by now from walking. But I bit my tongue.

"I bought a used Subaru from a neighbor who sells cars and my banker gave me a car loan," I said meekly.

The title was in my name, the payments were a workable $103 a month, and my transportation was now reliable.

"I'm letting our jointly owned, unusable car sit in the driveway," I said, summoning up my new-found courage. "To sell the car Curtis needs my signature. I can't sell it and he can't sell it. Let him wait."

"Now you're showing some initiative," said Spenser admiringly. He finally looked up.

"About time, don't you think?" I asked with a grin.

He responded to my retort with a grin of his own. We were back in business. Partners on the same team again. Why was I being so contrary? I really shouldn't take my anger out on this man, I thought. It wasn't *his* fault I was getting a divorce.

The four-way meeting went off as scheduled. I was hostile and confrontational because of the Valentine's Day harrassment I'd just endured. Curtis was equally unfriendly. Spenser had added fuel to the fire by filing documents earlier that week with the court stating that I denied that the marriage was "irretrievably broken" in addition to our request for alimony, court costs, equitable distribution of property, temporary alimony, and attorney's fees.

Then Curtis announced that he wanted the house sold and the proceeds split equally. He wanted me out and resettled within months.

I smiled sweetly, trying to give Curtis the impression that I might be willing to consider a reconciliation.

"And I want a no-fault divorce within ninety days,"

Curtis stated, firmly looking at me. "Our marriage is over. I want you to be very clear about that." He also asked for a relocation limitation, preventing me from leaving the area.

I balked. I didn't know where I wanted to live, nor whether I could find a suitable apartment to house me, my child, and my dog. I was also concerned that Nathaniel might find a major move extremely upsetting now.

"That's nonsense," said Curtis.

Curtis wanted a full joint physical custody agreement, with Nathaniel spending 50 percent of his time with them, 50 percent with me.

"That's impossible," I said. Nathaniel was showing increasing signs of insecurity over the two-household flip-flops. "Nathaniel's only six—he needs a base of security."

"He doesn't need a base," Curtis said. "He needs love."

Love? I thought.

Alimony. Curtis said $150 weekly was sufficient, two years long enough. I said I needed a bridge to help me through the transition to financial stability. What he proposed wouldn't even cover the mortgage for the house.

"But we're going to sell the house," he said smoothly. "Your share of the proceeds will pay the rent on a decent apartment. You don't need a house."

He also wanted to sell our share of the inn to our partners. The building was suddenly a cash drain rather than a tax-sheltered investment.

The meeting lasted two hours. The only thing we agreed upon was a schedule for split, alternating holidays for Nat.

"See you in court," we challenged each other grimly as the session concluded.

Spenser was his usual noncommittal self, politely thanking everyone for coming. "That was most enlightening," he said to me when we were alone. I waited for him to continue, but instead he started to give me instructions about preparing for the support hearing.

"Let's see if we can get you some money to live on while we fight for a settlement. I want to buy us some time so we can negotiate without staring down the barrel of a loaded gun."

I still had a few thousand dollars in reserve, but my monies were running out fast. And nothing at all was coming in. Maybe I could last another two months. At most. Spenser, I thought, get me some money *soon!* Please!

It was two weeks before our motions for temporary support would be heard. Spenser telephoned on a Sunday morning at eleven A.M. to see if I was ready for our presentation before the court official the next day.

"We will only have a short time to meet with a family relations officer," he said. "We will present our income and expense statements and hope for the best." He wanted to go over my financial records again—now, on the telephone.

I was ready. My income was limited to one $6,000 payment from a book contract. Curtis had stopped all his voluntary payments. The mortgage was due soon. I didn't know whether he would pay that or not, since he kept insisting that he wanted the house sold. My expense statement listed the mortgage, home maintenance, electricity, gas, oil, telephone, and taxes. Total weekly average: $333.68. There were also listings for insurance, automobile payments, medical, education, and child-care costs. Total weekly costs here: $234.81. A second sheet listed payments for trash collection, children's clothing, yard upkeep, pet care, shoe repair, and other personal expenses: $88.28. Total estimated weekly household expense, *not including food or clothing:* $656.77.

Proof of any unusual expenses was also required. I had none. I was concerned with the cost of daily living.

Another form listed property owned (the house, the inn, a small portion of a real estate partnership) and outstanding loans. I listed my $103.33 monthly car payments. Since Curtis had canceled my credit cards, I had no other outside credit balances.

A third form showed my assets and other non–real

estate forms of property owned (including checking, savings, retirement accounts, and insurance).

I also had copies of three years of income tax returns, including all the schedules.

Satisfied that my financial records were in order, Spenser switched the subject.

"What are you going to wear?" he asked.

I was certain he was recalling my sloppy country attire at our last meeting.

"Probably a suit. Why?"

"Don't you have a tailored dress?" he asked. "I want you to look like the well-kept wife of a successful executive, not a businesswoman."

"Why?"

"We're in the middle of a backlash," he explained. "Years ago everything went to the wife. Today things are erratic. There is no guarantee for anything. On the surface *you* appear to be the one who is faultless, but we can never tell how the other side will present its case. I don't want you coming off as a financially extravagant, successful professional woman. The way you present yourself may affect our case."

"This is ridiculous," I sputtered. Any fool could see the vast difference in earnings and income on paper. But I knew he was right. The "bitch wife," guilty without trial, automatically at fault for any marital dissolution and needing to be punished: that was my assigned role, whether I liked it or not. I had read articles about the inequities of divorce, but I never thought it would happen to me. Most women never do.

"You are the injured wife of a successful executive," he said calmly, "but you also have a track record as a professional woman capable of earning a living. You are without money now, there is a substantial income differential between you and your husband, and I want to provide for your future. You cannot appear to be too capable or too successful because, if you do, our arguments for financial need will not be taken seriously. Now, look through your wardrobe and see what you can come up with."

I said good-bye and obediently started to rummage through my closets.

Spenser was on the line again at 8:30 the next morning.

"I just got a call from Rawson," he said drily. "They want a postponement. How do you feel about that?"

A postponement? I was due at Spenser's office in an hour.

"Your husband says we didn't give him enough time to prepare his case," Spenser said. "It's your decision. We may need the same courtesy from them some day."

I considered granting the request for less than a moment.

"No," I snapped. "I'm the one without the funds. Let him be angry. He's had enough time to prepare."

"Good girl," said my attorney. "That was the answer I expected."

Spenser smiled approvingly as he greeted me at the door to his office. I was dressed in a classic blue crepe model trimmed in taupe. I wore a string of pearls, navy stockings, and black pumps. Rather than carry a briefcase that might mark me as a businesswoman, I carried a blue leather clutch. My papers were neatly categorized in a legal folder.

"C'mon," he said, taking me by the elbow and directing me out the front door, "we don't have much time. We'll talk on the way over."

As Spenser and I walked the two blocks from his office to the courthouse, I nervously pressed him for possible outcomes of the hearing.

"We could win, we could lose," he repeated again. "The two sets of figures are presented. The decision rests with whose set of figures and presentation is more believable."

Spenser didn't want to build up any expectations.

"Let me do the talking," he instructed me. "Don't volunteer any information, and answer any questions you are asked with simple answers, preferably yes and no.

"I want you to come across as a gracious, but wounded, wife."

At the courthouse Spenser checked in with the clerk of the courts. We would be meeting with a young female family relations officer.

Curtis and his attorney had arrived a few minutes earlier. Curtis was surly, angry that I had not agreed to a postponement. He had been away for the weekend and muttered to Spenser and his attorney that I was pulling a fast one by not giving him enough time to prepare his case. We had only been on the courthouse docket for weeks.

Rawson drew Spenser aside and tried to press for a postponement. They looked like a couple of bookies discussing the odds on the Kentucky Derby. Rawson was tall and elegant, clad in a perfectly coordinated dress suit, shirt with his monogrammed initials on the vest pocket, and a complementary tie. He had hair graying at the temples and cool blue eyes, he bent slightly, his head cocked, and spoke softly but firmly, trying to convince Spenser of his case.

Spenser, short, stocky, dressed in a gray pinstriped business suit, gesturing rapidly, looked up at Rawson. Suddenly, they parted. Apparently all bets were off. Curtis and I had been forced to wait together in the corridor outside the conference room while our attorneys met in another corner of the hall. Neither of us said a word to the other, each of us strained to hear what our attorneys were saying.

Spenser motioned for me to follow him, and directed me down a hallway toward our hearing room.

Spenser knew all the court officials, having appeared before all of them at one time or another. No bones would be thrown to us by any of them, he cautioned. Each case was heard on its own merits, and whether we drew a man or a woman, no favored treatment could be expected. Still, Spenser's personal familiarity with the people who staffed the Family Relations Office made me feel more secure.

We were ushered into a windowless room dominated

by a rectangular table which almost filled the eight-foot
by-ten-foot space and introduced to our hearing officer, a
woman in her late twenties or early thirties. Seated at the
head of the table, conservatively attired, hair pulled back,
she betrayed no emotion, showed no partiality. Spenser
and I sat next to each other on one side of the table. Rawson
and Curtis sat facing us on the other.

Since we were the petitioners, Spenser had the floor.
He stated the facts simply and succinctly. From the date
of separation, Curtis had been voluntarily paying $170 a
week in support in addition to the mortgage, taxes, and
insurance on the house. The two attorneys had met or
spoken on several occasions and a four-way client-attorney
meeting had been held in an attempt to arrive at a temporary support agreement.

Spenser then stated that, while my husband had assured me that he would voluntarily take care of household
and child-support bills until a settlement could be agreed
upon, he had stopped doing so: that oil and electric bills
were no longer being paid, that school and medical bills,
and automobile payments, insurance, and repairs were being
refused. Therefore, as a last resort, we were being forced
to petition the court for an interim source of financial aid
until full settlement could be agreed upon. "We have made
overtures, we are trying, we are showing our good faith,
our willingness to bargain," Spenser emphasized. "Our efforts have not been met with cooperation and we have had
to resort to the last means available to us—the judicial
system." I found myself very moved by his presentation.
But then, I reminded myself, this was *my* life, *my* predic-
ament. I scanned the face of the family relations officer
anxiously, but it was closed, impassive. As it should be, I
thought, but still . . .

Curtis's attorney took the floor. He looked like a successful trial attorney about to face the jury. Spencer Tracy,
Paul Newman came to mind. He was filled with flair and
confidence. A shiver of fear ran down my spine. His presence, cool, controlled, and condescending, disturbed me.

I had complete confidence in Spenser, but Rawson's demeanor made me feel like *I* was completely at fault.

"My client had no choice," he said, staring directly at me. "Phyllis's extravagance forced him to cut back on his voluntary payments."

I was shocked and angry. But thanks to Spenser, I was also ready. I didn't respond or show any facial movement, just as Spenser had counseled me.

Rawson continued, claiming that during the years of our marriage I had spent outrageous sums on clothing, on the house, that Curtis was now still paying off my bills, that I had refused to negotiate out of vindictiveness toward Curtis and his relationship with Jackie, and that I flat-out refused to get a job.

"She's more capable than most people of finding work," he said. "We don't feel she's entitled to any alimony. She's a professional woman, able to earn a living."

I *was* capable of making a living, I thought with a sinking feeling. They'd never award me any alimony now.

"No one is contesting that," Spenser replied calmly. "My client is just completing a book and will be looking for work as soon as her contractual obligations have been fulfilled."

Rawson smiled and turned toward me. At this point I could have cheerfully strangled him, and it was all I could do to maintain the calm demeanor Spenser had requested of me. How dare they cast me as some financial wanton for purchasing clothing and household items during our marriage? Apparently what were perfectly acceptable and reasonable expenditures then became, with the magic wand of divorce, suddenly unacceptable overnight. And their accusations about my unwillingness to get a job! If Curtis had been out of the work force for five years, would he be able to find an acceptable job within weeks? I was seething.

"Do you have a résumé?" Rawson asked me casually.

"Of course," I said irritably.

"Do you have one with you?" The question was asked

in a conciliatory manner, soft, interested rather than con-frontational. "I really would like to see what you've done."

I softened my attitude, giving in to his manner, which had become soft, stroking.

"I don't carry a résumé around with me," I said.

"Could you send me one?" he asked. "I really *would* like to see what you've written."

Spenser nudged me. I suddenly realized what Rawson was doing. I sat back and shut my mouth.

Had Rawson been able to actually show the conference officer my résumé, with all my professional credentials, my work history would have been on the record. While I hadn't earned any substantial monies in years, the résumé would have shown me on paper as *capable* of earning a decent sum and might have come into play in the awarding of temporary support and the final settlement. Rawson was clever, very, very clever.

After this little byplay, Curtis volunteered that he had proof of my unusual expenses that he had had to pay on my behalf. From his stacks of documents came papers item-izing payments for the inn. For years a real estate invest-ment and tax shelter, owned in partnership with another couple, the inn had suddenly become an "unusual ex-pense."

"I've paid all her contributions to the partnership," he said earnestly. "This is *her* business that I've been bank-rolling."

"The inn was always a real estate investment," I said, barely containing my rage, remembering the checkbook scenario at the bank months earlier. "You saw it as *your* tax shelter."

He just looked at me, innocently shrugging off my countercharge. I was furious at how easily he could change his stories in midstream to reflect a new stance. And he was so believable! Curtis would have made a fine attorney himself.

I could see Spenser wanted us off the subject: he swiftly

directed the questioning to Curtis's job, income, and expenses. His forms showed an "adult roommate and two children" to be sharing his apartment.

"Where does your 'roommate' work?" Spenser asked.

"She helps me at my office," Curtis replied.

One point for our side. Spenser had established that Curtis was supporting Jackie and her children rather than his own family.

Spenser continued to probe, asking questions about income, car payments, bonuses, pension and profit sharing, and other sources of income. Curtis answered each query with his usual technical precision, matter-of-factly citing exact amounts and providing backup documents to justify his figures.

"What kind of work do you do, exactly?" my attorney asked, shifting onto other ground.

"I'm in the contracting business," Curtis told him.

"That's interesting," said Spenser chattily. "Do you do a lot of travel for that?"

I couldn't figure out what Spenser was doing. Why was he having a pleasant conversation about Curtis's business?

"Yes, we go all over, coast-to-coast."

"Do *you* travel for your job?"

"No, not too much, occasional business trips."

"What were you doing in Saint Thomas last month?"

Bingo! Spenser had zapped him. Curtis had taken Jackie to Saint Thomas for ten days. He had even sent Nathaniel a postcard which I had slipped into my files as proof of their vacation and which my attorney now produced as evidence of the availability of "discretionary" funds.

"That was a business trip," Curtis cried. "My company paid for everything."

"I thought you said you rarely traveled on business," my attorney replied, a droll smile blanketing his face.

The conference officer, still expressionless, interjected with a suggestion that we move along. Our hour was almost up.

"Mr. Spenser, we have to wrap this up," she said. "What do you feel would be a reasonable amount of support for your client?"

Spenser said nothing for a moment or two. We had just received an indication that there *would* be an award for support. I knew he was trying to determine how much we should go for.

"How much would *you* advise?" Spenser asked.

"I think we should leave the actual amount up to the court to decide," Rawson interjected hastily.

"Your client indicated he would be willing to pay $450 a week during our four-way meeting two weeks ago," said Spenser, not wanting to leave the room without some number being tossed out for consideration.

"You had to get that in," Rawson spat.

"That was *his* figure, Mike, not mine," Spenser protested with feigned innocence.

"Enough," Rawson replied. "We'll leave the figure up to the court. And then if we are not satisfied, we will appeal."

After the conference, I felt as though I had been sitting in the airless room for a decade. However, there would be no decision that day. Normally, we would have made our case before a judge that same day, but the court calendar was so filled, that we would have to return for a second go-round a few weeks down the road. To speed things along, the judge asked the family relations officer for a recommendation of how much temporary support would be appropriate.

I felt as if every ounce of energy had oozed from my body. Why, why, I kept asking myself, did we have to go through something like this? And this was only a hearing for *temporary* alimony and child support, a financial net to cover basic living expenses so I could look for a job in the meantime. There was something wrong with the divorce codes, no doubt about it.

I managed to keep a pleasant look on my face as Spenser thanked the family relations officer for her time, returned his copies of my financial documents to his case, and steered me toward the door. We threw a polite good-bye to Curtis and Rawson, who were still seated at table, talking about where to go for lunch. As we walked from the conference room, our backs to our opponents, Spenser's face finally assumed an emotion. He was visibly distressed.

"Your husband is a skilled negotiator," he said. "He's good. Very good. All that union-negotiating experience has made him a tough rival. Why didn't you tell me about the inn?" he asked. "He made a good case for bearing unusual expenses on your behalf."

Those were not the words I wanted to hear.

"Spenser, goddamn it!" I exploded. "That inn was never, ever intended to make money. We bought it eight years ago specifically as a real estate investment, as a way of sheltering our dual-career incomes. That was before we owned a house. We needed deductible expenses."

I wasn't any financial expert, but I knew basic IRS provisions. You either invested your money and paid taxes later or saved your money and paid taxes now. I hadn't lived with Curtis all those years and not picked up some of his financial savvy. It was only in the last year that *I* had begun to look at the inn differently, in terms of its ability to bring me a business.

Curtis, however, still looked at it as a way of sheltering income. Which was why it never even occurred to me to include the expenses of the inn on my financial record sheets. Even if it had occurred to me, I wouldn't have been able to. I didn't even know how much money *had* been spent there. Curtis kept all the records for the partnership. Now Curtis was using this knowledge to his benefit.

"You still should have told me," Spenser said. "When I said I wanted to know everything about any marital property, I meant *everything*! Is there anything else you haven't told me?"

"No," I said meekly.

"Good," said Spenser.

I looked at him anxiously.

"Well, what do you think? How did we do?" I asked.

"You never know until the decision is handed down," was all he would say.

One thing I had learned about attorneys. They were always noncommittal. Never build up a client's expectations. Always take a conservative view. That way, if you lose, you don't incur a client's wrath. And if you win—well . . .

As we walked back to his office, Spenser tried to temper my impatience with a review of the current legal environment toward no-fault wives. I had heard it all before, and I certainly didn't want to hear it again. Alimony wasn't a given. I was capable of earning a living. I had a track record. We had lived well, but many court officials took great offense at excessive support payments. Today's environment assured the husband of a decent financial share—even if he was supporting two households and sharing one of them with an "adult roommate."

At the same time that Spenser was, almost automatically, mouthing these words, I could see he was deep in thought. When we reached his office, he noted that his next client wasn't due for another quarter hour, and invited me in to continue our talk.

"Your husband is a tough nut," he said. "But this session was very instructive. It showed me how he negotiates in business deals, what his strengths and weaknesses are, and how we'll have to plan our course of action."

Spenser paused and looked at me as if debating whether to continue, apparently decided I could handle it, then went on: "This guy's no different from almost any other husband. He wants everything his way. He thinks that by trying to break you, he'll force you to give in and settle. Some guys have good intentions, but most want to get away with giving as little as possible. They've made a decision to leave, it's usually been well planned and long thought out, and now they want to wrap up the loose ends and get on with their lives. What happens is that the man puts together a package, presents it to the wife, and, in most instances, after some token negotiation, she accepts it.

"I don't want you to be in a hurry to settle," he continued. "You're not an exceptionally wealthy couple, but there *are* assets and you are entitled to a fair share under the equitable distribution provisions of the Connecticut Divorce Code. You've held up so far. A lot of women wouldn't have. I don't want you to give in now. Be patient. Hold out for what is rightfully yours."

He was talking to me like a Dutch uncle rather than an attorney.

"Most women don't realize, or don't want to face the unpleasant fact that, in most divorce cases, the husband has done all the planning well before the actual separation itself."

The light bulbs began to switch on in my brain. Could this have been what Curtis meant when he said he had wanted to leave me three years ago? Or was my divorce paranoia feeding my imagination? Spenser made it sound like a three-year strategic plan for business development. Only this was divorce development. Men were so different from women, able to plan their private lives, so able to compartmentalize, I thought. I couldn't compartmentalize at all. For me—as for most women, I realized—it was all or nothing, and right now it looked as though it were nothing.

I turned back to Spenser.

"Any husband who starts a divorce proceeding without a green light to go through with it is a fool," he was saying. "When a husband says, 'I want out' without his wife's acceptance, he is asking for a long, hard fight."

"Why?" I asked. "What if both parties know it's a bad marriage?"

"Because that's rarely the case," he answered. "Usually it's the man who wants out, and if a husband hasn't done the groundwork, the wife's usual reaction is a firm no or 'I'm going to punish the son-of-a-bitch' or 'He's a crazy mixed-up kid, I'll wait it out and he'll come home to Momma' or 'Damned if some other woman is going to get my husband.'

"That's why many lawyers tell their male clients to 'gaslight' the wife, to use the Chinese water drop treatment, to plant the seed that it's a bad marriage, that it would be better for both parties to separate. I'm not saying your husband has done this, though it's obvious he's done *some* planning. Ideally the husband wants the wife to make the decision because it places him in a more favorable strategic position—legally and economically."

I was stunned, dazed. Had *I* requested the divorce, Curtis would have been perceived as the injured party, and *he* would have had the upper hand in both the financial and custody negotiations. I thought of the headaches, the tension, the guilt I felt over believing I could have been a better wife.

"Could this possibly be what happened to me?" I was incredulous.

"I really don't know," Spenser said compassionately. "I'm telling you this to underscore my reasons for not rushing to settle. It's always the woman who suffers most in a divorce case. Society still blames the woman for failing to keep her husband happy. And it punishes her both economically and socially—even today. The husband can go freely about his business, date, spend money, and no one thinks anything about it. Divorced women, especially if they are over the age of thirty-five, are looked upon as discounted goods, flea-market specials. A man's income often goes up after a divorce, often as much as 40 percent; a woman's goes down 70 percent.

"He can skip out on child support," my attorney went on, "and it's very tough to get him to pay up—despite all the new federal laws to the contrary. A man usually marries again within three years. A woman may never marry again. Add to that the very real disparities in earning capabilities—women still only earn about 60 cents to every male dollar—and the woman's responsibility toward her children. It's usually the woman who winds up supporting the children. No matter what the law or society says about equal pay, equitable distribution, and the dual-career couple, it's still a lopsided bargain when a marriage sours."

I was subdued by his lecture. He stood up to usher me out and let his next client in.

"I want *all* his financial facts," he said, "a *full* financial disclosure. If he has been planning to leave for a long time, then he has surely taken care to protect himself financially. It's my job to help protect you."

We received the recommendation for temporary alimony and child support three weeks later on a warm May day. The languid air felt soothing against my skin, almost lulling me out of my daily emotional turmoil. I kept feeling I had to find something to do, but I was still too depressed to do much of anything.

"Do you want me to give you the news now or do you want to come in to the office and go over the figures?" I recognized Spenser's voice on the phone immediately.

"Is it good news or bad?" I asked.

"Depends upon your position. Be here at two. We'll talk it over."

He hung up. I was left hanging. The butterflies in my stomach were flapping so hard I thought my body's interior would explode. I had three hours to kill. I spent most of it wandering around the house and getting dressed. After trying on half a dozen outfits, I settled on a linen blouse and skirt, appropriate attire for a visit to my attorney.

I left my house half an hour early. The drive took ten minutes. I had decided if I had to wait for bad news, I would rather wait in my attorney's reception area, enjoying the dubious comfort of being surrounded by other clients in varying stages of marital disarray.

But Spenser's outer office was empty when I arrived. His assistant announced my presence. He poked his head around the corner of his office almost immediately and handed me a pile of papers.

"I have to take a telephone call," he said. "Read these. Page two, bottom line is the recommendation. I want an answer on the other document too. Your husband has filed a Cross Complaint against you."

His words about a Cross Complaint barely registered. I stood in the hallway, leaning against the wall outside his office, reading. The only number I saw was $450 a week for the support of wife and one child. We had won the first round! I wanted to giggle, wrap my arms around someone, share this wonderful news. We had won!

I pulled myself together and continued on down the page. The recommendation was not without qualifiers, of course. I was to pay *all* the household expenses, including the mortgage, taxes, and insurance. Those three payments alone ran $1,000 a month. Other household expenses, including electricity, oil, telephone, snow removal, and yard work totaled another $350. My car payments and insurance ran $150 a month. That was $1,500 in basic shelter expenses, not including food, clothing, shoes, haircuts, or any other personal items. Obviously, there was no cushion for any emergency. However, Curtis was also required to continue medical coverage for both Nathaniel and me. My initial elation subsided. What it really came down to was that I had been awarded borderline maintenance, based upon the expenses incurred on a monthly basis—the same expenses which existed before Curtis had left and which had not changed over the course of the past eight months.

Then I came to the qualifier which was set apart in capital letters: "NOTE: There is a major dispute re: custody and visitation which is pending. This recommendation is based on major *physical* custody of son with the mother (and therefore the burden of financial support) and liberal visitation with father . . ."

Spenser came to fetch me as I was turning to the second instrument, the Cross Complaint. Since Curtis and I were supposed to be filing for divorce under the no-fault provisions I was stunned to see a list of "indignities" charging me with being at fault for the disintegration of the marriage.

Again, a switch in tactics, a major shift in midstream. First Curtis had demanded a quickly settled no-fault divorce. Now, he was charging me with a list of indignities and switching to a fault divorce.

I could feel my temper begin to build. What did he want? I thought. What did all this switching really mean? He was using every trick in the book to undermine my confidence, to break me. First the money and the financial intimidation. Then the change in stories about the inn, and his support of *my* business undertaking. Then the zigzagging about Nat and my taking care of him. Now a document packed with half-truths and intimations.

Spenser grabbed my elbow and directed me into his office. I groped for a chair, my eyes still glued to the Cross Complaint.

"What do you think of the recommendation?" he asked gloatingly. "Pretty good, huh? Of course they object. We still have to go before the judge. Put June third down on your calendar. That's when we have our court hearing. I want to talk about that too, but before we do anything I want some truth from you."

I stopped scanning the Cross Complaint and looked up. Was my attorney all of a sudden questioning my honesty? First he was chirping away happily about our temporary support award and then in the same sentence and same breath questioning whether I had been leveling with him all along.

Men! I thought. What did any of them want? No wonder I was so emotionally disoriented. I couldn't figure out *any* of them! All right, Spenser, I thought. You want to play this game, I'll play your game.

He was referring to the Cross Complaint. "I want to go down the list right now," he said. "One by one, and I want a full explanation of what it means or what you think it means."

I turned to the list of "indignities" I had allegedly committed over the course of the marriage.

"Okay, let's take a look at the atrocities I perpetrated," I said grimly, but Spenser didn't seem to notice my mood.

The list went on for six pages and consisted of twenty-seven points. I was accused of being extravagant, a drug abuser, unfit mother, and unsupportive wife.

"During the years 1981 and 1982, defendant refused to invite plaintiff's parents to visit with them . . ."

Sloppy accusation, sloppy legal work. It wasn't like Curtis. He was always so careful. How had this document been prepared? Curtis's parents had visited on many occasions: six weeks after our separation they spent the Thanksgiving holiday with Nathaniel and me, staying at my home and sharing the holiday feast with eight other people—my potential witnesses.

There were conflicting sets of charges. One set accused me of doing no household chores, causing our home to be "dirty, strewn with clothing and leftover food," while another set stated that I had hired too many cleaning women and gardeners. If I had had that much help, how could the house have been in such disarray?

I was accused of leaving our son with nannies so that I could go to work.

I was accused of marital misconduct. I *had* spent blocks of time away from home in unidentified absences; that had been when I enrolled in a tennis clinic with a dozen other local wives, learning to be a better tennis player and making the effort to be more of the kind of wife Curtis wanted. Jackie had been on the courts with me much of the time. I had wanted to surprise Curtis with my new athletic skills and new friends. Every time he asked me where I had been I had deferred giving him a straight answer.

"Around . . ." I told him.

As he complimented me on an improved game, I attributed it to a new racket. Maybe I should have told him what I had been doing all those months.

The document also charged me with stating that I had my own "network and expected plaintiff to find his."

Anyone up to date on workplace terms knew that a "network" was a chain of contacts within one's own business world—and this was the context in which I had made a suggestion to Curtis. I remembered it vividly: my saying he needed to develop a wider "network" of business contacts to expand his business development efforts for his company and throughout his industry.

The kicker was point 19.

"During the latter part of the time that the parties lived together, there were continually loud arguments started by defendant," the document charged. "Most of the arguments were over money matters. Defendant often used vulgarity and raised her voice against plaintiff. Defendant seemed jealous of plaintiff's job and continually asserted her equality with him."

I started to laugh. *That* was wrongdoing? Asserting my equality? I was astonished that an attorney practicing law in the 1980s would file such a document with a court.

Spenser watched me as I moved down the list. As I checked off each point I went from anger to laughter and back again. I kept asking myself what did Curtis really want? To embarrass and humiliate me? Why? Why had he done this? The list of alleged "indignities" was so outrageous, so ludicrous, I burst out, that I couldn't believe my attorney wanted a response to these charges.

"I just wanted to hear what *you* had to say," he said. "If your case ever goes to court we may have to defend you against these charges. I needed to know your version of truth versus fiction."

Spenser was grinning at me mischievously. I let out a sigh of relief. My attorney believed me!

"I also need you to give me a list of the atrocities *he* committed against you," he said, laughing. His eyes were lit up with enjoyment at my discomfort. "We're not going to counterfile, but I'd like to have the information on hand."

"But *I* want to file," I said grimly. Pure revenge. Just for the personal satisfaction of getting back at Curtis. I was already formulating answers in my head. Spenser wouldn't hear of it.

"You're the *lady*," he said, toning me down. By counterfiling I would be asserting a confrontational attitude. That would be a mistake.

"I keep telling you, you're the *lady*. I don't want you to be perceived as the aggressor. I want to give this guy a long string, let him fight, struggle, get tangled up in his own actions. Then we reel him in, dead tired and exhausted, and that's when we scoop up the marbles. You just have to keep playing it cool."

I was sick of these instructions. The charges were ludicrous, but we still had to defend ourselves against them. It was a game, but a dangerous one. I still wanted to hit back, to counterfile, but I wouldn't. Spenser was right.

Spenser put aside the Cross Complaint and moved to another topic. "Did you get more involved in community activities like I told you to?"

"I sure did." I was the Voter's Service chair of the League of Women Voters, a member of the board of the historic society, and had been appointed by our congressman to a countywide task force on job development. I wasn't particularly active in these groups. I just went to meetings, but their presence in my schedule gave me something to do, something to fill in the long, lonely gaps of time in my new life.

"Not bad for starters," he said appreciatively, nodding his head up and down.

Spenser's tactic from the beginning had been to position me as the "gracious but wounded wife." He knew that if we ever went to court and had to defend ourselves in a fault divorce where a Cross Complaint listed wrongdoings, that judges frowned on the "He did this to me," "No, she did this to me" approach. Our strategy was to call into question the validity of the charges themselves.

"Anything else?" he asked.

"Well, the League of Women Voters is going to produce a local cable television show," I said, "and I'm going to be the hostess."

"How did that happen?" He was impressed.

"I wrote the proposal," I confessed.

As chair of the Voters Service Committee, my job was to expand citizen education efforts throughout the county. The local cable/public access station had a mandate from the community to provide programming on local issues. I discovered this while working at a voter registration booth at the local supermarket.

The league was exploring new ways of expanding their public service programs and the idea had just come along. I hadn't gone looking for it, but once the opportunity presented itself, it seemed like something worthwhile—for me and the community.

The local cable station was receptive to our suggestions that the local League of Women Voters sponsor a monthly series on community-based issues and agreed to train volunteers to staff the show. I selected a producer from the ranks of the league's volunteer members and gave the series a name—"At Issue." Then I wrote myself in as hostess.

Spenser was bouncing up and down in his chair.

"Fantastic! Wonderful!"

Now that I thought about it, I had to admit it was ingenious. Maybe all those weeks sitting in meetings were about to pay off after all. Several of the local judges were slated to be guests on the show. The community benefitted, as the series aired shows on toxic-waste disposal, domestic violence, and children and the law, sponsored political debates, and trained unskilled volunteer women in the use of the electronic media equipment.

"How's your money holding up?" Spenser asked after regaining his composure.

"So-so." So-so was a wild overstatement. I was counting pennies by the day. The $5 I might have spent on lunch with a friend was now calculated as five days of lunch money for Nathaniel. The tube of lipstick was a week's worth of gas for my car. The money for pizza after Nat's soccer game was used to replace his worn-out sneakers.

My book manuscript had been completed and submitted to my publisher and I had received my final payment, but that was it. I had a few thousand dollars in the bank. Nothing more. I needed to get out and get a job, but the thought of entering an unfamiliar workplace terrified me.

In the five years since I had held down a full-time job in corporate America, a complete revolution had occurred. I didn't know how to use the new electronic equipment; whole industries I had once been familiar with had changed, disappeared, or undergone massive cutbacks. My "real world" job skills were outdated.

I had no idea what I was now qualified for, where I could work, or what I could do. I hadn't kept up with any of the fields in which I had previously worked because they had been so unappealing when I had worked in them that I had never conceived that I would ever *want* to return to them.

Oh, I *had* gone on a few interviews, mostly at the behest of friends who had set up appointments for me. One, a fund-raising position with a local university, paid $16,000. I didn't get the job because I had no fund-raising experience, I was told. The other, paying $18,000, was a press relations job. I had been a member of the press years earlier, but I had no experience with press relations now. That too went to someone else.

In both instances, the men interviewing me kindly suggested that something part-time might be more suitable at present, something to brush up my work skills.

"Can you get some free-lance writing?" Spenser asked. "Something to tide you over?"

"I've already spoken with my agent," I told him. "I have a few proposals out, but even if they are accepted, writing them takes several weeks, the articles may not be published for several months, and payment is never made until publication."

We considered alternate jobs. I lived in a small tourist

town. Perhaps I could work in a shop or get a part-time clerical job. Or I could begin to look for a full-time position in a nearby city, but the closest towns were thirty minutes away.

Nathaniel's summer vacation started in three weeks. I had enrolled him in a day camp for six weeks, but it ended at 3:30 each afternoon and I had to be around to pick him up.

Moving was out of the question since a custody conference was pending. If I moved prior to a resolution of the custody issue, I might be cited for wrongful removal of my child from the area. I couldn't even move out of the house for fear of giving up my property rights.

"Face it," I said glumly, "I'm really stuck."

The exuberance of our early mutual back-patting over the temporary support award dissipated as both Spenser and I came back to earth. Seven months had passed since the cool September night that marked the beginning of my separate life. No monies would be forthcoming until after the court hearing was held five weeks from now, and only if the judge agreed with the recommendation of the family relations officer.

"We'll go before a judge next," Spenser said quietly, "and we'll need to be fully prepared. I want no surprises this time. I'll talk to you about it in a few days. In the meantime, try and find yourself a job, *any* job."

# CHAPTER 6

# THE JOB AND THE JUDGE

"Get a job, any job." Spenser's words haunted me nonstop. I had already been rejected from four job openings: "Thanks but no thanks." "The position has been filled internally." "We're keeping you in our active file."

My imagination started to peak again. An active file. What was that? I envisioned hundreds of manila folders wiggling and leaping like Mexican jumping beans in one metal cabinet drawer. The active file. Which folder would thrust itself forward for selection? Not mine. That was certain. At this point, I didn't think I had the strength, stamina, or initiative to pursue a full-fledged job search. I wasn't burned out. I couldn't even get ignited.

Sure I could participate in volunteer activities, but they weren't "real" jobs for me in terms of either my commitment to them or any monetary reward to me.

I *had* to get some kind of a "real" job. I bought a copy of the local newspaper and thumbed through the want ads to get a sense of what kind of jobs were available. I didn't really think I'd find anything. I knew the good professional jobs were never advertised. It was all networking. Who had heard about you, what you had done. "There's something opening at Acme Corp. Why don't you follow it up? Tell him I told you to call." That sort of thing. Only problem was I had let my corporate contacts lie fallow during my years as the country wife. I was out of touch. And to get a headhunter to call me—well, I hadn't done anything for years. How would a recruiter even know I existed?

I made myself a cup of coffee. Instant. I wasn't brewing the real thing lately. Me, who used to order gourmet beans from a coffee importer and then grind them to order, cup by cup. I pulled apart the paper, turned to the help wanted pages and spread them out on my kitchen table.

I ran my index finger down the first column.

Accountant. Nope. No financial credentials. Administrative assistant/Secretary. Fast growing national firm seeks mature (yes), personal (yes), well organized (sort of) self-starter (not any more) to work for top executives. Must have excel typing skills & exper with word proc & computers. That left me out.

I read on.

Appliance service technician. Artists. Auto body specialists. That's it, I laughed. My track record with cars certainly made me an automobile specialist—about bodies I wasn't so sure. That was it for the A's.

Banking. Barber. Bartender. Bindery. Bookkeeper. Cabinetmaker. Carpet installer. Chefs. Cooks. Lots of cooking positions. . . . I went on. Data entry. Delivery person. Drivers/school bus. With all the driving and chauffeuring I had done over the past few years I was certain I could qualify for that.

Gymnastic instructor. Hairstylist. Investigator. I always wanted to be a detective. I wondered what the qualifications were. Real estate. Every divorced woman I knew was in real estate. I eliminated that category on principle. Secretaries. Toolmakers. Waitresses.

Lots of waitresses and waiters. I had bused tables in college and that hadn't been so bad. I had also served hundreds of guests at the dinner parties I hosted for Curtis's business associates. The only thing I had ever dropped was a turkey and that had been behind the closed kitchen doors.

Maybe waitressing wouldn't be a bad idea. I could work flexible hours. Since I had a small child, flexible hours were really the key for me—and I knew good waitresses made decent money. I read the ads:

"Waiter/waitress. Floor service and food runners. Exper. required for fine dining establishment." *Fine dining* were the key words. Good tips here. I marked that one.

"Waiter M/F days. Mon. Thur. Sat. Apply in person. No calls." Forget that one. I didn't want to work days. Unless the place was located in a high-traffic commercial district the likelihood of steady lunchtime customers plying me with decent tips was nil. I knew that from restaurant management school.

"Waiter/waitress. Full time. Dinner shift. Some exp. nec." *Full time* drew the gong on that one.

"Waiter/waitress needed. Pt. time. Experience not as important as personality and basic knowledge of foods." Aha! I circled that one and reached for the phone, then stopped. Should I really call? I thought. I've been out of the job market for so long. They'd probably turn me down right away.

"Hi!" said a voice as the front door opened. It was Stan, my next-door neighbor, the "other spouse." We had developed a neutral next-door relationship since the departure of our respective spouses. We were neighbors first, friends next. I walked his dogs, he walked mine.

"Do you have any extra dog food?" he was asking, looking through my cupboards. "I can't handle a run to the store during homemaker rush hour." I looked at my watch. Almost four P.M. and time for the school-bus pickup. He was right. Every school mother in the community seemed to shop at the local grocery store between the hours of four and five each day. Both of us avoided shopping then. I preferred to shop when the supermarket opened and was nearly empty at eight A.M. or when it closed at nine.

That way I didn't bump into anyone who might ask questions about what was happening. The gossip vultures. I had been attacked with a "What happened?" vengeance in aisle 1, Produce, once, and vowed "Never again." Everyone I met seemed to be assessing my status by what my shopping cart contained. Fourteen cans of dog food and toilet paper. Some life.

I returned to Stan's rummaging.

"Bottom shelf under the sink," I replied, not rising from my seat at the table.

"What are you doing?" he asked as he located the dog food.

"I'm looking for a job," I told him. "I've decided to become a waitress."

"A waitress?" He was aghast. "Better a cook than a waitress. At least you have some experience there."

I thought about it. Somehow I had never thought of that alternative, but a job as a cook *did* make sense.

"Arturo's needs some kitchen help," he said, pulling out a chair and leaning over to look at the ads. "Why don't you see whether you can get a job as a relief cook?"

"Arturo's?" I recoiled from the thought. Arturo's was a local singles bar! "I'm not going to work in a singles bar."

Arturo's was one of the town's hot spots. It also drew the tourist trade. It was *always* busy.

"Why not?" he asked. "It's honest work and the food's pretty good. Besides I know the owners and they're a pretty nice crew."

I had never worked in a real restaurant kitchen before, although I had come close to opening my own place. Still, I *had* trained professionally.

"Here's the number," he said, scribbling a set of figures onto a corner of the newspaper. "Call them."

I folded the newspaper sections, put them aside, and walked out with Stan to the driveway where I got into my car and drove off to pick up my son at the school bus. Half an hour after we got back I received a telephone call from Arturo's owner.

"I hear you're looking for a job," he said. "We're looking for a cook on the night shift. Are you interested?"

"Well . . . yes," I hesitated. I really *did* want the job, but didn't know whether I could cut it. Arturo's was a real restaurant. Maybe they would start me out making salads and assisting.

"Good," he said, "why don't you come down in about an hour and we'll talk."

I had a job interview! They were interested in hiring me! I couldn't have been more ecstatic had I been under consideration for a $100,000 managerial post.

My thoughts turned to what to wear. I had always worn tailored clothes to my previous job interviews. But what did you wear for a job interview as a cook in a singles bar? I opted for an Oriental-style big shirt and black pants. A little trendy, but not so much that I might be perceived as being a flaky lady. I wanted the owner to think of me as a good, dependable employee. I couldn't believe I was actually thinking about how I was going to present myself as a potential employee to the owner of the town's niftiest hangout.

I arrived at Arturo's shortly before the evening dinner service began and met with the owner in the dimly lit bar area. He showed me the menu, asked about my past experience.

"I haven't had any real restaurant experience," I told him. I wanted to be up-front, honest, "but I am very, very dependable. You will be able to count on me. I'll show up."

"Experience isn't all that necessary," he replied.

"How about if I begin on salads and cold things?" I suggested.

"No, that won't do," he replied.

My heart sank. I'm not going to get the job, I thought.

"The only position we have available is line chef," he continued. "You'll work Mondays and Tuesdays to start. The hours are six to two. Don't worry. Your assistants know the ropes. They'll help you out. You'll do fine. I'll start you at $5.25 an hour. Can you be here next Monday?"

"Yes. Yes, of course," I stuttered.

"Okay," he stood up and reached to shake my hand. "See you then."

He turned and pushed open the swinging door to the kitchen. I looked around me. The bar crowd was stacked three deep. I had a job! I was going to be a cook working the night shift at Arturo's!

I tried to calculate mentally how much an eight-hour shift would bring me. My brain wouldn't function. Somewhere around $40 was the closest I could come to determining the amount. I didn't even negotiate; I didn't think I could. Most of all, I didn't want to, for fear that I would be turned down or that I would seem too greedy.

For now, I had a job!

I hung around the house most of Monday waiting to go to work. Nathaniel was with his father for a few days, so I didn't have to confront the problem of getting a sitter that night. What I had to do was get dressed and go to work.

I spent an hour deciding what to wear. Something cool and casual, I thought nervously, as I selected a pink polo shirt and white cotton trousers. A little makeup wouldn't hurt, either. After all, this was a singles bar, and, while I had never considered the bar scene as a social vehicle, here I would be staff. You could never tell. Things might be looking up all over.

I arrived for my first evening of work a few minutes before six, appropriately entering through the kitchen door. Four male faces looked up as I came in. They wore T-shirts and soiled kitchen whites. Two of them were obviously about to go off the day shift and were sitting on a counter smoking cigarettes. Their faces were scruffy; the aroma of their bodies signaled that they had been working hard. I thought dismally of my clean white pants and pressed shirt.

"Who are you?" one asked.

"I'm the new night chef," I replied.

"She's the 'chef,' " one repeated, and they all guffawed.

These were my new associates. I just stood there, looking from one to the next. They all looked so young. Maybe in their early twenties. The dishwasher hunched over the sink scrubbing pots was the first to move.

"Welcome to Arturo's," he said, extending his soapy hand. "Can you cook?"

A young man barely out of his teens came up to me, pulled an apron from the linen pile, threw it toward me, and moved toward the ovens.

"I'm Scott," he said. "I'll be assisting you. Come on, we have to get to work."

Fortunately, Scott was a seasoned employee of six months. He knew where the sauces and supplies were located. It was up to me to figure out how to produce the featured specialties. Restaurant school had certainly not prepared me for this.

Not that I was cooking brain-surgery comestibles. What I was putting out was high-quality, basic, fast bar food. The key word was fast. The more customers you serve, the more money you make. At Arturo's, turnover was the name of the game.

Within minutes I was drenched with sweat. I needn't have bothered about my clothing or appearance. Outside, the mid-summer temperature hovered in the upper nineties. Inside the non-air-conditioned kitchen the heat was unbearable. The two commercial ovens were set permanently at 500 degrees. I couldn't move away from them because I had to repeatedly check the items cooking rapidly inside or monitor the multitude of sauté pans frenetically sizzling on the burner tops.

Thank heaven for Scott. He set up the dishes and sauced down the foods and I slammed them into the oven. My main job consisted of making a judgment of whether or not the food was cooked. Most of the time I decided it was.

We pulled the ironstone cooking platters from the oven with our kitchen tongs, garnished up the plates with parsley and fruit slices, and sent it out. Some talent this took.

I wiped the sweat from my forehead then I wrapped

an iced-down tea towel around my head to keep the moisture from pouring into my eyes and onto the food. It also prevented my hair from singeing each time I bent to extract a dinner from the open oven door. I wrapped another iced-down towel around my neck to give my body some relief from the intense heat. By now my face was streaked with makeup and grime, my apron caked with food remnants. My clothing clung to my body. And how I stank! The fragrance was a mixture of grease, marinara sauce, and sweat.

I had never been so intensely physical in my entire life. Every pore was open and running, every sense alert. If I moved backward, my legs might graze the oven doors and I would be burned. If I moved sideways the fat from the deep fryer would splatter over my arms. Keeping up with the orders was a feat in itself. Sometimes I felt as though I were on a factory production line with a supervisor increasing the speed of the conveyor belt to see how fast I could go, how much food I could produce. I never knew my fingers could work so fast. Manual dexterity, I thought. I could add that to my list of job skills.

In the ensuing weeks, I lost myself in my work at Arturo's and quickly graduated to working several more shifts. It was variable, the shifts rotated: sometimes I'd work two nights, then three days, sometimes four nights in a row.

I tried to keep as busy as possible; I felt better that way. On slow nights I helped the prep staff prepare the food for the next day's menus.

"Tonight you learn how to prep chicken breasts," the prep chef told me one evening early on in my kitchen tenure, as she lugged a 100-pound plastic baggie filled with squishy chicken breasts from the walk-in. She heaved the sack over her shoulder as if it were a pillowcase filled with dirty laundry. It landed with a thud on the butcher block counter. A dozen previously deboned breasts spilled out of the bag, flooding the area with pinkish juices.

"Once you get the hang of it the job goes rather quickly," she continued, as she sharpened a knife against a whetstone. "See, you want to separate the membrane from the flesh. The more carefully you carve, the greater the yield. We should be able to get two full portions and one half portion from each breast."

I tried to follow her instructions. Good thing chicken was cheap, I thought, as I produced more waste than yield on my first few attempts at poultry picking.

"Nice work, Phyllis," said my chicken-breast instructor as she passed by me on her way to the vegetable bins, scooping up my wasted meat and popping it into the stock pot with one motion. *She* had opted for the broccoli-carrot-green-pepper patrol. The faint bit of praise stroked my badly bruised ego. In the months to come I would turn into Arturo's consummate chicken-breast prepper.

It was a great relief to be working at Arturo's, both financially and (quite unexpectedly) emotionally. I found a great sense of accomplishment in little tasks—chopping parsley or onions, sautéing chicken breasts—and great pleasure in producing hundreds of meals each week. I may not have used my brain as I might have in a white-collar job, but the athleticism of my kitchen work was more cathartic than *any* high-level corporate job could have been. I laughed to myself as I tried to imagine how some of my tonier acquaintances would have fared had they had to spend several hours deboning chicken breasts or lugging forty-gallon pots of marinara sauce into a frigid storage room.

I didn't mind the work itself. Nor did I mind telling people what I was doing. What was humiliating was the reaction of friends and acquaintances who crossed my path while I was working my shift at the restaurant. The way they looked at me made me feel naked and unclean, almost as if I were on welfare. A subtle class barrier had sprung up between me and my former peers. I was suddenly hired help—and one didn't socialize with the help.

One evening I left the kitchen to check an order with a waitress and passed by a table of neighbors. Since I hadn't seen them for months I stopped to say hello.

"Phyllis, is that you?" said one of the wives. "I can't believe it."

Another looked up from the menu. Her face froze in an awkward smile. I was covered with grease, my face was sweaty, my apron splattered with kitchen matter. They didn't know whether to laugh or die from embarrassment.

I broke the ice.

"I made it into the restaurant business after all," I said glibly. It was easier to make jokes and laugh at myself and my situation to ease their discomfort. They had decided not to "get involved" with me after my separation.

"I'm sure you understand, Phyllis," one of the wives explained patronizingly. "We like you both. We don't want to take sides." She paused, looking rather pleased with this decision, then continued, "Now, what's good? What are you cooking tonight? What would you suggest?"

I hoped she couldn't see my face reddening behind the sweat, grease, and grime. I told her everything was wonderful and she should order whatever appealed to her. Then I excused myself and turned toward my kitchen sanctuary where no customers were permitted. As I pressed through the bar crowd, I felt the hands of an all-too-regular Happy Hour patron sliding around me. I shoved him wordlessly aside and stormed into the kitchen. I was so angry I was ready to burst into tears.

I suddenly noticed that no one was at their stations. Instead they were all congregated at the triple sink at the far end of the room, clustered around Jesse, who was standing silent, head bowed, with his arms around two of the other dishwashers.

"What's going on?" I asked.

"Jesse's dog died," one of them said. "He was run over by a car."

I offered my sympathy with the others. We finished

the evening more subdued than at any other time in my kitchen tenure. How different these people were from those I knew in the outside world. They stuck together. And they were fair.

While they were sympathetic to my status as a not-quite-divorced homemaker with a small child, their primary concern was that I fit into the kitchen team and hold up my part of the food-preparation flow. We were a family, working together in close quarters and under highly pressurized circumstances. I was lucky to be a part of it.

It was a strange family though. I was dealing with the kind of people I had never been exposed to before and for whom I was now responsible. They provided me with an education I could never have received in ten years on the streets.

My dishwashers, in particular, were a special breed. Lowest in the kitchen hierarchy, they performed all the scum work, mopping, washing, cleaning, and serving as all-purpose restaurant gofers.

They tended to be a wildly colorful lot. I remembered reading somewhere that, historically, dishwashing has provided the last legitimate economic refuge of the dispossessed. British author George Orwell worked in a kitchen during the 1930s and later wrote about it in "Down and Out in London and Paris." M. F. K. Fisher, one of America's foremost culinary essayists, had also written about kitchen personnel in her five decades of writing about food, its presentation and preparation.

*My* dishwashers, I felt, were more unique than *their* dishwashers.

Of the many who passed through the kitchen during my tenure, I remember three most vividly.

Jesse was the quickest, cleanest, and most streetwise. At the time I met him he was holding down three jobs at three different restaurants in town. It turned out that his early "hands-on" treatment of me was nothing more than a test to see what I would permit as the kitchen boss. I managed

to keep my cool, and the pecking order was quickly established when he discovered that she who controls the food
controls the kitchen.

"Phillips, you make me some 'pa-ghetti and I bring you
some pans," he would say.

"No, Jess," I would counter. "You bring me pans, and
keep your hands off me—then you eat."

His stomach inevitably lost.

I came to fully appreciate Jesse on a Sunday evening,
the second day of a three-day holiday weekend. Arturo's
was packed, with a backup wait in the bar and dining room
of almost two hours. Every burner and bit of oven space
was in use when one of the ovens stopped functioning.
Kaput. No heat. The repairman showed up within an hour,
spread his tools over the floor in front of the malfunc-
tioning unit, and got to work. To say he was underfoot for
four hours was not an exaggeration.

A violent summer rainstorm poured buckets of water
through a leaky roof above the dishwashing station. No
problem for Jesse. He took an oversized garbage bag, cut
a hole for his neck and arms, and pulled it over his head
for an instant rainsuit. Then he fashioned a smaller plastic
bag into a rainhat. He never let up washing the pots and
pans.

The beer lines at the bar clogged, forcing the bartender
to shut off tap service. We ran out of toilet paper for the
rest rooms. Food was flying out of the kitchen. Then the
dishwasher broke a water line, sending two inches of soapy
water over the floor.

None of us even noticed, so intent were we upon keeping up with our respective kitchen duties, until one of the
bartenders came striding through the swinging door to
pull a case of beer from the walk-in cooler. He stepped
through the door and slipped on the soapy water and his
long legs shot out in front of him. Jesse followed with a
bus tray filled with the remains of a dining room full of
dishes. Duck carcasses, salad and vegetable bits, ice cubes,
and Jesse landed on top of the bartender.

Two of us went to their rescue, slid on the soapy water, and landed on top of the mass of arms, legs, and bodies flailing around on the floor. There had to be a better way of making a living, I remember thinking. It was awful— all of us lying there in a heap with food and broken dishes. Then someone started to laugh, and in a second we all were. Even with the indignity of it all, I felt good, all of us pushing and pulling together when outside the kitchen my world was breaking apart.

Jesse crawled out of the mess and stood up.

"Whatsamatta wit you guys?" he exclaimed, shaking himself off like a wet puppy. "Don't you got work to do? All night, lying around, having fun. Get back to work!"

Victor was a friend of Jesse. Tall, with gleaming, polished mahogany-colored skin and brilliant, perfectly straight white teeth, he worked quickly and efficiently. When I gashed my thumb with a chef's knife at the beginning of the dinner hour one night, Victor stepped in and taught me a trick he had learned from his relatives who worked the Cuban sugarcane fields.

"The sugar, put the sugar on the blood," he said, pouring a packet of sugar over the erupting geyser of blood.

I was convinced that his technique was pure folklore, and that a run to a nearby hospital and several stitches would be necessary to ensure a proper closure. But within minutes the bleeding had stopped, the blood began to coagulate, and I was back at the range.

Then there was Ruben, who told me he was studying for a degree in human services at the local community college. His mother telephoned one evening to say that Ruben had had an automobile accident and wouldn't be in to work.

About a week later a parole officer showed up, asking questions. Something about banks and stolen cars and driving into a mailbox while making a getaway. The parole officer was one of several officers of the law to pass through Arturo's kitchen during my time on the line.

When I wasn't concentrating on controlling the kitchen,

I was attempting to mediate the uneasy alliance which existed between the dining room staff and the dish washers. The dishwashers were responsible for keeping the bus pans clear and the shelves stacked with fresh tableware. On particularly busy evenings, the dirty dishes mounted quickly and the bus pans overflowed. This meant that the waiters and waitresses had to carry the trays into the kitchen or had to leave the floor to track down a dishwasher and cajole him into moving the pans. This usually resulted in accusations from both sides about who wasn't doing their job, and it was up to me to step in and stop the argument.

Then, too, somehow the floor staff was always having a crisis.

"You're invited over to my place for a pool party and barbecue," one of the waiters told me, the night after his apartment had caught fire, burned, and been flooded by the rescue squad. "I woke up and thought I was in the middle of the Poseidon Adventure!"

"I have to leave," said one waitress when she arrived to pick up an order during the middle of a shift.

"Why? Are you sick?"

"No. I've been screwing some woman's husband and she just called to tell me that she was on her way over to shoot me."

I watched as she hustled out the back door.

The next evening she was back. The two women had breakfast together and decided to share the husband as long as the marriage remained intact. Harry came along, but he was not the husband. He was a local man, a friend of Suzy's, who had died earlier in the week. Harry's cremated remains rested in an oversized shoe box while the two women discussed the man in their life.

"I had to carry him with me," Suzy explained, "because I don't have a car. Harry would have loved it. I took him to breakfast at the diner and sat him on the counter. No one knew what I had in the box. Gloria and I had our little talk and then I tossed Harry's remains into the river. It was soooo beautiful!"

One night I slipped off a stool I was sitting on during a temporary lull and stepped into a bucket of dirty linens.

"Good thing it wasn't the onion soup," my assistant said calmly, looking down at the frothing bucket of broth standing only a few inches away.

Some nights we could do no wrong. The food was perfect, the customers satisfied. Other nights I felt as if I were the central figure in a Marx Brothers comedy. I came to miss the place on the nights I didn't work, and I would come in early before my shift to catch up on the events of the preceding day.

"You were off last night, weren't you?" my assistant greeted me after a two-day absence from my job. "Did you miss an evening! Even for Arturo's it was a bit much."

Seems that the night shift had weathered a choking (good thing we all had been taught the Heimlich maneuver), a heart attack, a lover's battle, complete with the wife receiving a black eye from her spouse, and a head-on collision in the parking lot. Just another night at Arturo's.

Often, to slow down the breakneck production pace and lift the kitchen tension, we listened to a radio or tape play background music. Only the music never played, it blared, and to make ourselves heard, we would shout at each other above the musical din.

With three different age groups of culturally diverse kitchen workers sharing the same space, the choice of music led inevitably to disagreements. On most nights we compromised, rotating stations or musical preferences on an hourly basis.

One day I persuaded them to leave on the "oldies-but-goodies" station and, as the orders began to be posted, I hummed and sang and be-bopped along with the tune.

"Momma said there'd be days like this, there'd be days like this, Momma said,"* I sang along, tapping my spatula on the counter and swaying to the rhythm. My momma

*See p. xvii for full song credit.

never had, actually, but here they were anyway, days like this, one after the other.

At that, my assistant and our salad maker decided to join in. The three of us harmonized fervently, holding three carrots in front of our mouths as if they were microphones.

Our enthusiasm was dampened by the entrance of the night manager.

"If the three of you have nothing to do but stand around singing," he growled, "I can find plenty of work to keep you busy. Don't you have orders to fill?"

My assistant and I had an oven full of orders, the salad maker was up to her elbows in lettuce. We watched as the manager deftly reached toward the radio, switched channels, and replaced the melodic sounds with a funereal reggae chant.

The three of us looked at each other, looked at him, and looked at each other. Before returning to work we burst spontaneously into one more chorus:

"Momma said there'd be days like this, there'd be days like this, Momma said. Momma said . . ."*

The work became comfortingly routine, a soothing counterbalance to the daytime anxiety of my impending court appearance. I desperately wanted to avoid going to court, but I had no choice. I didn't want to chance that my award would be taken away from me, didn't want to confront Curtis again in what I feared would be another testy financial face-off. The request for a hearing was Curtis's privilege, his opportunity to question the conference officer's decision. Had the tables been reversed, I suppose I would have done the same thing.

Two weeks after I started my nights at Arturo's, I met with Spenser to prepare for our court appearance. I was sitting facing the great wooden desk in his office, waiting for him to stop writing some notes on a legal tablet.

* See p. xvii for full song credits.

"I got a job," I announced.

He looked up in surprise. "Great! Where?"

When I told him his eyes bulged.

"You got a job as a short-order cook?"

"Yes. I got a job as a short-order cook. Look, I can't take another rejection," I said softly. "You told me to get a job, and I did. It's not so bad. It's hard work, but I don't mind."

My attorney said nothing, then: "Does your husband know about this?" I told him I hadn't said anything to Curtis, but that he may have heard the news through the neighborhood grapevine.

Spenser ingested the information. By now I could tell when he was feeding in facts and materials that could be used as tactical points for some future aspect of the case. This was one of those times.

"I can't wait to tell the judge how desperate, how emotionally distraught you were," he said, the words blurting from his mouth, "unable to find work in your field, how you were driven to get a job as a short-order cook, working the night shift."

C'mon, Spenser, I thought. This isn't Perry Mason. But I didn't want to argue with him now. I had a job, finally, and we were soon to go before a judge. Let's get on with it, I thought.

"We have two weeks before the court hearing and an enormous amount of preparation to complete," Spenser said, returning to earth. His tone was brisk, like a military commander issuing orders. I sat, pen and paper in hand, and took down his instructions.

"One. I've had some correspondence with the other side. I told them that we believed the $450 award fell a bit short and that we would be willing to accept $500 a week."

I laughed. That was a dig, a "gotcha."

"Two. I want to go over your financial documents again to clear up this business of the expenses at the inn. I don't want him coming in and claiming unusual expenses on your behalf.

"Three. I want you to get me some bodies that can testify if necessary about your standard of living and your lifestyle. We need to be able to counter his claims of your extravagance."

"Bodies?"

"Bodies. People. Witnesses," he said. "I always like to show up with bodies."

Spenser wanted witnesses who could testify that Curtis purchased my clothing, paid for childcare, was generous in his financial contributions to me, and carried the burden of the household expenses. I said I didn't think that would be a problem.

I had several solid choices: two close friends whose knowledge of me dated from before my marriage, and who had spent many weekends, days, and hours with us, seeing the household from the inside—and who were willing to travel to Connecticut from Boston and New York to testify on my behalf; a young woman who had been Nathaniel's caretaker in my home for the past three years and who had received frequent instructions from Curtis himself regarding the purchase of food, clothing, and household goods. Two neighbors rounded out the body count.

"Are you sure they'll show up?" Spenser asked. "If not, I'll subpoena them." He paused for a minute.

"Yes," he decided, "let's subpoena the whole lot. The bodies. Curtis. Jackie. She was a friend of yours, wasn't she?" he asked, not expecting an answer. "Was she aware of how you lived?"

"Certainly," I said. "We went out together, belonged to the same tennis and swim clubs. She even wore my clothing sometimes." Now she has my husband, I thought.

"Good. She can testify on your behalf. Do you think Stan would be willing to come along too? We won't ask him to testify, but his physical presence will throw them a curve ball. They'll wonder what he knows."

This was something out of a police novel. I had visions of a process server leaping over cars in an effort to nab both Curtis and Jackie and serve them with the subpoena. I was alternately fascinated by the preparations for the "body count," and profoundly distressed at the antics to which we were resorting.

"I guess we have to do this, huh?" I said to Spenser.

But Spenser was already on to his next set of instructions: courtroom demeanor and wardrobe.

"You've got to low-key it this time around," he told me. "Your temporary award was high for this area and I don't want to take a chance on losing it or having it reduced."

My stomach tightened at the thought of having even a penny taken away from me. I had so many bills and expenses to pay. Oil. Electricity. Nathaniel's camp bills. My wages ranged from $86 to $126 a week, depending on how many shifts I could get. That amount didn't come anywhere near covering my basic household expenses.

My anxiety over having the award taken away was only partially soothed by Spenser. "Most often the judge agrees with the recommendation of the family relations officer," he explained. "These people are objective. They know the tricks. The higher-earning spouse—usually the husband—comes in with a low figure. That's why it's important never to accept the first offer when a spouse approaches you with a package. The normal procedure is for the wife to counter with a high figure. Sometimes it's realistic and sometimes it's not.

"Most judges don't believe the husband is showing his real financial condition," Spenser continued. "There are some honest guys who try and do the right thing, but, more often than not, most husbands' figures don't reflect an honest appraisal, so the honest guy is bumped up into the next category. That's pretty much a rule of thumb. It's a game, but you have to play it. We must stick to our position and not back away from the award made to you."

I knew he was right. I remembered that on several occasions during my marriage, sitting over cocktails, business dinners, or out by the pool with other wives at company conventions—I had listened to gossipy tales about

husbands poor-mouthing estranged wives. At the same time
I also heard about the little apartment rented for the girlfriend. Or the business trips to Europe, with "him" seen
in Paris on the arm of a cute young thing. I also knew of
mistresses who had been set up in business by errant
spouses—the twentieth-century equivalent of a kept woman.

Then there were also the stories of the wives who had
grabbed an offer just to get the dispute settled. "I didn't
want to make waves, to make trouble." "I wanted to get it
over with." The standard excuses for giving in, for "settling." The emotional trip was so exhausting they would do
anything to end it. Months later these women discovered
that their "poor" spouses had been playing them for financial fools, and they were the big losers in the divorce stakes.
I wasn't going to do that. Not if Spenser could help it.

On to wardrobe.

"I want you to dress in accordance with your standard
of living, but not ostentatious," he continued. "Something
tailored, but a little out of style. Very little makeup, no
jewelry."

I nodded obediently. Much like an actor who studies
for a part, slowly letting the "character" overtake his real
being, I felt myself being overtaken by a role in the theater
of divorce, uncertain of which person was the living being
and which the creation. By this time I wasn't sure anyway
whether I was the woman playing a role or whether a role
had taken over me. I *was* unhappy and confused, and it
was easier to stay in character and play my part.

"You are to say nothing until I tell you to," he said,
reminding me of my verbal interchange with Rawson about
my résumé. "Be polite, a lady to the fingertips, and don't
interrupt the judge. We are going into a court of law and
the unwritten rules are more stringent than those of a
hearing room."

At home later that afternoon, the process server phoned
to find out where he could find both Jackie and Curtis over
the next few days. I gave him a few possibilities, including

the hours Curtis normally left for work, the hours he returned, Jackie's general tennis schedule, and the location
of a real estate course in which they were both enrolled.

They were cornered and served outside the apartment,
the process server having to leap over a car to nab them,
just as I had imagined. Detective fiction became fact.

I hand-delivered subpoenas to my friends, who were
more amused than insulted.

Spenser continued to make his show of good faith, ini-
tiating letters to Rawson that stated our disappointment
over the loss of momentum in settling the case among
ourselves and suggesting alternate mechanisms of resolving the issues.

At no time did he give Curtis and Rawson any indication of our specific strategy.

"A good lawyer will always let the other lawyer talk
first," Spenser told me. "You want him to reveal his position first. Sometimes you get two good lawyers together
and there is utter silence because they are both playing the
same game."

We had moved forward only an inch on one aspect of
our divorce—the support issue. And that was a temporary
condition, too. A preliminary custody conference, parallel
to but separate from the support process, was scheduled
for the following week. As for dividing our marital property, we had to reach some sort of negotiated settlement
on how the house, the inn, and our other assets would be
split. If we didn't, the whole lot would be given to a judge
who would. If we didn't agree with the judge either of us
could appeal the property split before still another judge.
It was divorce by long division.

Spenser's initial strategy was based on the concept of
"linkage," tying the sale and percentage split of the house,
inn, pension, and profit-sharing funds to the length and
amount of alimony payments. The greater my alimony
award, the more I would be willing to compromise on the
sale and split of the house.

Linkage also affected our custody arrangement. If Curtis turned the inn over to me, I could be assured of a business with a source of income that was also near his home. I would therefore be more agreeable to a more flexible physical custody format because the distances between us would be negligible, causing less confusion and separation anxiety for Nat.

But our inability to find any common grounds of agreement now forced Spenser to shift strategies.

". . . if we could not settle the issues of custody and support," he wrote Rawson, ". . . let us settle the property issues and let the court decide any unresolved issues."

He was determined to try and make some progress toward my financial future by getting Curtis committed to any aspect of the property issues. Curtis wasn't having any of it. He wanted to establish full joint physical custody as a basis for our bargaining. His trade-off was the child versus the money.

The lawyers' cross-correspondence continued. Five years' alimony versus three years. A refusal to pay support if I shared living accommodations with a "cohabitee." An insistence upon an earning plateau. We objected to everything.

For four weeks between the time of our family relations office hearing and the time of Curtis's request for a hearing before the judge, the two attorneys wrote and talked back and forth.

We continued to request a full financial disclosure. They insisted it was forthcoming. Nothing. Curtis refused to give us a full showing of his financial worth.

"Those figures are about as forthcoming as my résumé," I told Spenser.

Curtis claimed he was not responsible for back support because his earlier payments had been voluntary and made without a court order. I insisted upon insurance coverage. The dickering continued by mail and telephone up until the day before our court date. Curtis and I even spoke by phone, with him outlining his willingness to settle and providing facts and figures to back up his case. I listened, wrote down his numbers, and, as per Spenser's instructions, agreed to nothing. We never moved one inch closer to any aspect of a settlement.

Nathaniel's first-grade graduation was scheduled for the morning of our court appearance before the judge. Curtis had refused postponement, so neither of us attended our son's final assembly.

My visiting parents stood in as surrogates. Nathaniel was thrilled to be able to take his Florida grandparents to his school.

"It's okay, Mom," he said as my father tied his grandson's tie. "I'll take care of Grandma and Grandpa."

I hadn't told him where I was going or why I was unable to attend his graduation for fear of bringing up a new set of anxieties. He only knew that I had to attend an important meeting.

"You look awful," lamented my mother as I emerged from my bedroom dressed in a worn and faded lavender linen suit. "That suit must be ten years old, it's baggy and too long. Put on something that makes you look fresh."

"Sorry, Ma," I replied. "I hope the judge feels the same way you do."

The "bodies" and I gathered at Spenser's office to receive final instructions, then walked en masse to the courthouse. The other team had not yet arrived. Spenser cased the entranceways, determined that Curtis and company would arrive by elevator, and positioned our group of six directly in front of the elevator bays so that we would be immediately visible as they stepped onto the hearing-room floor.

Spenser wanted to strike fear into his opponents. My friends really had nothing earth-shattering to reveal. We were hoping that their mere presence would make the other side fear that they might have something to say and thus be more willing to strike a deal.

"Be nonchalant," Spenser told us. "I want you all to look confident, relaxed, like the winning team."

They all looked fine, but I was convinced I had all the

wrong expressions on my face. I was a nervous wreck, running to the bathroom down the corridor every ten minutes and racing back to the group, hoping I hadn't missed the elevator opening. I wasn't disappointed. Curtis stepped out carrying boxes of financial data which I presumed would be used to document his expenses incurred upon my behalf. But I had the living, breathing, warm bodies. The look on his face was wonderful. The look on Rawson's face was even better.

"Who are they?" I heard Rawson ask. I imagined he also wondered what secret information they might reveal. I could see Curtis pointing to each one and explaining the relationship between us. I could get to enjoy this, I thought. If my nerves held out.

Spenser interrupted Curtis's conversation with Rawson, grabbed Rawson by the elbow, and directed his counterpart around the corner, out of our sight. I had no idea what was going on.

The main hall was packed with perhaps fifty other couples and their attorneys waiting for their cases to be heard. We had drawn the only female judge on the Superior Court, a distinguished former criminal attorney, perhaps in her early 60s. We knew virtually nothing of her philosophy or case record.

Spenser suddenly appeared from nowhere, emitting a glow like a magical gnome. He guided me down an empty side corridor.

"I told Mike you had a job," Spenser said. "I told him you were a cook on the night shift of a fast-food joint."

"Oh?" I asked innocently. I knew he had let that bit of news drop to rattle the opposition. "And what did your colleague think of that?"

"He wanted to know how you managed to do that," Spenser said, his eyes sparkling. "I told him you had no choice. I told him that his client has prevented you from going ahead with your business and that you can't write because you have taken the brunt of so much emotional distress. You needed the money. You can cook, so you're working the night shift at Arturo's."

"Well done!" I exclaimed. He had played Perry Mason after all!

"Most of these cases are settled in the hallway," Spenser continued. "Rawson doesn't want to go to court, I don't want to go to court. Get out your notes. We're going to start dealing. I'm gonna do the support shuttle."

Curtis and his attorney were in a corner of one hallway. Spenser and I were in another. The bodies were awaiting us outside the courtroom.

"We're going to try and strike a deal," Spenser said enthusiastically. "It's the bodies. I just know it. We just have to let your husband think he's getting a good deal. We'll give him all the tax advantages."

Taxes. I was convinced that Curtis had never made a decision without considering the tax consequences. I suppose it was smart business and smart financial management: everything—from vacations and dinners to entertainment and my employment—had been considered for its effect on our taxes. Why should this be different?

"Okay," I responded. "I don't need the tax breaks. Give them to him. Let him pay the mortgage, taxes, and insurance directly so he gets the interest and expense deductions. Let him win on that. I'll take more temporary alimony and less child support to give him the tax breaks on that, too, but I want retroactive support, a cleanup payment for what he owes me, and insurance coverage for both Nathaniel and me." I was a little surprised at how quickly I could come to these decisions, but then I reflected that I had been doing, at Spenser's insistence, an awful lot of homework. Now it was paying off. I hoped.

"That's my girl," he said. "Make it palatable for him. Let me see what kind of numbers I can put together."

I wasn't being overly generous or giving in. I was being practical. I had almost no income. Curtis's income was in the six figures. If I took the lump-sum $450 weekly payment I had been awarded by the conference officer, I would have to pay taxes on the entire amount. By splitting the payments, Curtis would be footing a large part of my household payments.

Spenser's feet were practically flying over the corridor floor as he raced between Rawson and me, presenting different sets of numbers to each of us and working up income and expense comparisons in his hand-held calculator. The settlement shuttle continued for an hour, with one of the bodies or Jackie occasionally appearing to check the status of the corridor countdown. Suddenly it was our turn. A sheriff called us for our court presentation.

"He's going for the package," Spenser whispered ecstatically. "I just can't get him to budge on the back support."

Rawson and Curtis appeared and passed us on their way to the courtroom. Neither of them looked at us.

"Remind him about my utilities being cut off in the middle of winter," I said, loud enough so they could hear. "I'm sure the judge would be most interested in hearing about that."

Right there, Curtis agreed to back support.

As we strolled toward the courtroom, Spenser gave me a final briefing.

"We're buying you time and a little financial protection," he said. "If he doesn't keep up his weekly payments, we can cite him for contempt." We entered the courtroom and approached the bench. Spenser was calm; my nerves were jangling from the inside out.

Although the request for the hearing had been entered by Rawson, this was Spenser's geographic turf. He played the role of the genial host, introducing his colleague from the adjoining county to the judge, and explaining that we had come to a temporary agreement which we now wanted entered as a court order. I stood there, my hands demurely folded before me. For some reason I couldn't really look at Curtis. It was becoming clearer by the minute: My marriage was in the process of being dissolved. Over.

Curtis agreed to pay the first and second mortgages on the house, the taxes and insurance, alimony and child support totaling $270 a week, arrears of $1,500, and medical and life insurance. Most of the terms were structured so that he received the tax advantages. It wasn't a bonanza, but we had received a fair deal. It was a *temporary* agreement, to be in force only until a final negotiated settlement was completed.

Curtis could actually skip several weeks of payments before any contempt citation could be issued or wages be attached, but a court order had clout. We insisted the payments be made under court order and through the Domestic Relations Office. The court order was entered "without prejudice," which meant we could change the terms in any final settlement. There was also no limit set against the length of time the temporary court order could be in force.

We thanked the judge and withdrew from the courtroom. The "bodies" were anxiously waiting to hear the outcome and heaved a collective sigh of relief when they heard that a full hearing had been averted and that they would not be called on to testify. They had remained outside the courtroom, engaged in a lively discussion of where to go for lunch.

"Come on," said Spenser expansively, "I'll take you all to lunch."

I knew he must be pleased because he never ate lunch, hated to give up any of his tightly scheduled hours.

"I want to thank you all for coming," he told my friends as we were seated at the restaurant. "I know you gave up work and other responsibilities to be here. I am convinced your presence was essential in our avoiding a courtroom battle."

I should have been elated over the outcome, but I was feeling shaky, more worn out than victorious. I returned home to be greeted by Nathaniel and my parents and told all about his final assembly. When we were alone, I told my parents about the hearing.

"Good work," said my father.

"Never should have married him," said my mother.

"Well, I have Natty," I said weakly. They smiled then.

Curtis had one week to begin his payments; thirty days for the arrears. I had been given some breathing space to consider my alternatives. I had given up considering alternatives for the present. For now, my nights at Arturo's were my only alternative.

# CHAPTER 7

# CUSTODY

We had only one week after the support hearing to prepare for the custody hearing. It was the same procedure. You presented your case before a court official who made recommendations. If you disagreed, you could request a hearing. If either party was still dissatisfied, the case was tried before a judge, who decided the child's fate.

"Settlement is always better than litigation because you are directly involved in the negotiation and can make trade-offs," said Elizabeth Weber as we spoke on the telephone the weekend before my Tuesday morning case. "A judge's decision can be especially arbitrary. Especially in your case, where neither of you are negligent parents. With the financial part of a divorce you have a running chance. It's more black and white. There are comparative figures. Custody is gray."

Legally, Spenser usually handled only the financial aspects of a case. Now he had receded into the background and Elizabeth Weber, my custody attorney, emerged on center stage. I was still somewhat uncertain about her involvement. She was only a year or two out of law school and had been practicing under Spenser's tutelage. (Months later she told me that my case was the first she had ever handled totally on her own.)

Since Curtis had filed the complaint for joint physical custody, he would be taking the offensive to make his case.

"What do you think he really wants?" I asked Elizabeth.

"I don't know, Phyllis," she said, "I really don't." No solace here, I thought.

Curtis was demanding a strict numerical split of days for Nathaniel to spend with each of us. Joint physical custody. Certainly an ideal. Intellectually, I saw the benefits of a joint custody arrangement. Nat would benefit from access to two different homes and two different lifestyles, and from the influence of both parents. Such an ideal, however, is not always practical. I thought it was neither ideal nor practical in our case.

"How can we have shared custody," I asked Elizabeth, "when Curtis and I cannot communicate on *anything* let alone cooperate in raising this child?"

"That's why you have a custody agreement," she soothed me. "Our problem here is we don't know enough about his real intentions and I don't want to set down a written agreement before we are absolutely certain that you are comfortable with the provisions."

As with our financial arrangements during the early months of the post-separation period we had not formalized a custody agreement. Now I was thankful we hadn't. It seemed to me that we all needed time to assess whether the experiment in dual homes would really work for us.

Curtis thought otherwise. He thought I was being deliberately obstructionist. Curtis had placed a high premium on "input" into his son's life, but the two of us could barely speak to each other. We disagreed on everything and those disagreements extended to questions of Nathaniel's welfare, including schooling, activities, and how he should be raised. There was also another, more crucial factor as far as I was concerned. I had shared my reservations with Elizabeth on many occasions, but I voiced them again.

"Just how involved do you think Jackie will be in Na-thaniel's life?" I asked. "Who do you think is really going to be in charge over there?"

What I was really asking her was whether my custody agreement would be with Jackie. With Curtis away from home on business or at work during the week, who was going to care for my child? I was not about to abrogate my child-rearing responsibilities as Nathaniel's mother to her.

"I don't know, Phyllis," Elizabeth said softly. "It really depends on what happens to them and how *she* sees her involvement in this case. We don't know yet what *her* real interests are, so we don't know whether to deal her par-ticipation in or keep her out of the game."

A game! Another lawyer looking at divorce as a game. I hadn't decided whether we were playing Monopoly, the game of life, chess, or Dungeons and Dragons. It didn't matter. I wasn't a very good game player. Not where my child was concerned, at any rate.

While philosophically I believed in dual parenting, in our marriage I had been the "psychological parent," the partner who is the dominant caretaker. That is, I met the criteria used by many judges in determining which parent was "primary"—I had planned and prepared Nat's meals, bought his clothing, taken him to the doctor and dentist, arranged for child care and visits with friends. I had taught him social values and educational skills. Curtis, of course, claimed that he too had been a participatory parent; I couldn't deny that he had taken Nathaniel to the doctor, prepared occasional meals, and chauffeured him to friend's homes. I just thought *I* was more participatory than *he* was. What did Curtis *really* want?

Elizabeth and I talked over possible scenarios, and agreed that the best defensive strategy for us was to "wing it," simply because we did not know what position Curtis was going to take. We decided to stay loose, hear what they had to say, and respond as tactfully and reasonably as we could. Mainly we wanted to prevent a written agreement from being set down. That would buy me a little more time to get a sense of Curtis's real intentions about his parenting responsibilities.

I said good-bye to Elizabeth, hung up the phone, and walked into the television room to check on Nathaniel, who was watching a videocassette of a football game he had taped a few months earlier during the NFL fall season.

"Hi!" I said. "I wasn't aware this was football season. I thought we were into baseball."

Not quite seven, my son was already a sports jock. Every day he read the pages of the newspaper which listed each team's standing. Maybe that's why boys seemed to be more facile with numbers, I thought. I never did that, and my math ability always took a back seat to everything else. Nathaniel's mind raced from team to team, through win-loss-tie numbers and standings with such ease that he could add and subtract in his head easily where I needed a calculator to figure anything.

"It's not," he said, looking at me as if I had voiced an especially dumb statement. "This is the game Dad took Steven to."

How well I remembered.

Curtis had had an extra ticket to a Sunday football game and had taken one of Jackie's sons, Nathaniel's buddy. Going to Sunday football with Curtis was a province that had been Natty's special turf. Nat had stayed glued to the television set that afternoon, understanding little of the action, but searching the crowd for a glimpse of his father and Steven. At halftime he asked if he could telephone Curtis's father, who lived in Denver. I dialed the number for him and overheard my son ask:

"Did you see that play, Grandpa? Do you think my dad and Steven saw that play? They went to the Giants game today."

I knew his little-boy feelings were hurt. I had tried to tell Curtis to go slow on revamping the new family structure, tried to get him to see how his son's feelings might be hurt by the attention paid to another child, but he wouldn't listen. I was interfering in his life, and I was vindictive, he said. It was my negative feelings, he accused me repeatedly, that were preventing Nathaniel's full and complete acceptance of our split. I had to encourage my son's relationship with his father and his new family, he insisted. Curtis was so deeply committed to recreating the ideal family we never had that he was impatient for his child and me to quickly adopt the restructured dual-family environment.

But Nat had had no time to integrate the change in relationships. Brimming over with insights gleaned from two therapists, I tried to make Curtis understand that in his haste to restructure his life, his actions were hurting Nathaniel. But he wouldn't believe me.

Or maybe it was that Curtis didn't want to hear this—or anything else—from me. After all, my motives were suspect.

Joint physical custody, indeed!

Nathaniel had wanted to be with his father during those early months. He missed him deeply. He jumped at every opportunity to talk with him, to see him. He was jealous that Jackie's children, his friends, were living with his father, and was torn between his loyalties to them, his father, and me. It was hard for me not to criticize, not to tell my son what a shit his father was—in my opinion—but the only person harmed would have been Nathaniel, so I held my tongue. I was not about to undermine Curtis's image in Natty's eyes.

The child needed his father. That was the bottom-line issue. As much as Curtis cried denial of access and Elizabeth cautioned me about careful assessment of shared parenting, I had an uneasy sense that, even without a written agreement, the amount of time Nat had spent with Curtis to date measured roughly fifty percent. If that were the case, I had allowed myself to be drawn into a de facto joint physical custody arrangement. Would a family relations officer take that as precedent for our case and arbitrarily set down a joint physical custody arrangement? I didn't know, but I *was* going to raise what in my mind was the $64,000 question: Who was in charge of the child? Me? Curtis? Curtis and me? Curtis, Jackie, and me? Who?

Elizabeth and I arrived at the courthouse expecting to find Curtis with Michael Rawson. Instead, he was accompanied by a woman attorney named Virginia Culver. She wore a wedding ring on her left hand. I thought it ironic that Curtis, who had objected to *my* working during the course of our marriage, condoned it in another married professional woman.

As in the Spenser firm, different attorneys handled the financial and custody aspects of a case. There was no legal reason for the division, but rather personal preference. Curtis's custody attorney was no second-stringer; Virginia Culver was definitely a force to be reckoned with. Tall, with long red hair, and slender fingers capped by ruby-red polished nails, she was an imposing figure—impeccably dressed in a stunning blue-green business suit, with regal bearing and a fantastic legal presence.

Elizabeth stood a head shorter and was the picture of the all-round girl next-door. Freckled and fresh, her light brown hair pulled back off her face, she wore a white linen pleated cotton summer dress and pearls. I looked at the two of them and wished I had the other attorney.

They introduced themselves; each debriefed the other on our respective positions and we entered the conference room. The custody officer curtly greeted us, and began an intake interview: names, addresses, living conditions. We had our first disagreement only moments into the hour.

"Name of child?" the officer asked.

"Nathaniel Ryan Ellsworth," we both answered.

"With whom does the child live?" he continued.

"He lives with me," I said.

"He lives with both of us," said Curtis.

The hearing officer lifted his head from his papers and looked first at me, then at Curtis.

"Where does the child live?" he repeated.

"With me," I repeated.

"With both of us," Curtis said simultaneously.

I was ready to climb over the table and wring Curtis's neck. He was trying to have Nathaniel's legal residence be recorded as dual homes.

The hearing officer looked up again.

"Where is the child today?" he asked.

"With me," I said. I thanked Someone that Natty was in my care.

"Where was he yesterday?"

"With me," I said again.

"Where will he be tomorrow?"

"With me."

Plain dumb luck had placed Nathaniel with me during these days. He was out of school, on summer vacation, and could just as easily have been staying with Curtis.

"Child lives with mother," the official decreed, and recorded my house as Nathaniel's place of residence. Curtis glared at me from across the table. We both knew he had lost a crucial point.

The conference official continued to take down information about our occupations and our respective work schedules, then launched into a lecture as to how we were both obviously intelligent adults, interested and concerned parents, who both loved our child; and how it would be a disaster to move this case into the courtroom. His job, he didn't have to tell us, was to keep the case out of the courts and find a way of resolving the issues. Once he had stated his piece, he asked Curtis to outline what he saw as the issues, why he had requested the conference.

Instead, Virginia Culver took the floor, stating that I had repeatedly denied Curtis access to his child, that I was interfering with his parenting decisions, that he was a concerned and involved parent, and that they had been forced to file a complaint for joint custody in order to guarantee Curtis his rights and responsibilities as a father.

"Sole custody leaves the legal prerogatives to one parent," she began. "That parent is empowered by law to make all the decisions about the child and dictate when the other parent can see the child. We object to Phyllis having the right to deny Curtis access to his son."

I was seething. I had never, ever denied access, denied his rights, his responsibilities. Never. Ever. So maybe I *had* scheduled some activities with his friends when Nat was with Curtis. Was it wrong for me to accept an invitation for my son to attend his best friend's birthday party? Obviously Curtis thought so. But still, I saw that as a misdemeanor rather than a felony. My major concern remained the same as always. What I had done was question who was in charge of the day-to-day welfare of the child. To me, that meant emotional as well as physical welfare.

Raising a child, I felt, was far more than getting him dressed and off to school or taking him to the park for an hour of play. To me, the real issue of custody involved the emotional welfare of the child, the provision of a stable environment—and I was convinced that a child of six needed his mother to provide that day-to-day stability.

In most two-parent households, there was one set of rules, one parent who was "more equal" than the other, one parent "psychologically" in charge of the child. Nathaniel, according to his psychiatrist and school professionals, was showing extreme signs of anxiety and depression over the confusion created by the two sets of masters. Someone, I believed, had to be in charge at this stage of his life.

I was his mother. I was home on a day-to-day basis. And, whether anyone else agreed with me or not, I was not going to give up my day-to-day responsibility for child rearing, not to baby-sitters, not to surrogate mothers, and not to absentee fathers. No, I was Nathaniel's full-time mother and I had every intention of remaining so.

My thoughts turned to Virginia's presentation. She was making a wrenching case. Any minute now I thought her crocodile tears would drop on the conference table.

"Why shouldn't this man have the same rights as a

mother?" she pleaded. "He's a good man, a good father, directly involved with the rearing of his child."

I tried to catch Elizabeth's reaction from the corner of my eye. Virginia could have won an Oscar. I wondered if the hearing officer was buying her case. After letting her make her legal points, he turned to Curtis for his arguments.

"She has consistently denied me access to my child and interfered with my parenting when Nathaniel is in my care," he told us. "I want a court order to ensure my rights and responsibilities as the child's father."

Elizabeth moved ever so slightly. So this was what it was all about. Curtis and Virginia were pushing for a court order to force me into a custody agreement. We had to avoid this at all costs. If a court order was set down, the case would be over, and a precedent set against which it would be difficult to argue. Just as they had tried to force me into accepting *their* terms for a financial settlement, now they were trying to force me into accepting *their* terms for a custodial agreement.

My mind was racing. How could we make an effective presentation to avoid having a court order set down? How could I reasonably object to what we already had? Elizabeth and I would be unable to discuss our options in private, unable to plan what we would say, what arguments we could make. Both of us had to go on instinct and hope.

My thoughts were scrambled, but my brain was sending out sharp signals. Anchors. Base. Security. His home. My home. Their home. Commitments. Child's anxieties. Confusion. Lack of communication. Mother. Father. Key words and concepts flashed before me as I listened to Curtis's presentation and tried to formulate a counterattack of my own. I knew that personality conflicts, accusations, and denials would not be tolerated. Elizabeth had warned me of that.

The key issue was the best interests of the child, and it was up to us to make a case showing that by keeping our custody arrangement loose, flexible, and experimental, Nathaniel's best interests would be served. The only problem was that "best interests" was a vague standard that could be used to justify almost anything.

I had reviewed many times the state's laws on child custody. I had read what literature existed. I had spoken with people who had sole custody agreements and people who had shared custody. The out-and-out consensus among everyone was that there was no right way to formulate a custody agreement. "Shooting the spouse," everyone agreed, was the best means of carrying out a custody arrangement. I had to prove why joint physical custody was not in Nathaniel's best interests. Unless Curtis was a thief, an alcoholic, a drug addict, or certifiably insane, he was considered fit.

Although Curtis's living arrangements, to me, left much to be desired, this would not be considered in the assessment of what type of parent he was, and what kind of relationship he had with his son. The key question that might arise in the future, Elizabeth had explained to me, was "was it harmful to the child?" I couldn't answer "yes" to that issue now.

Still, I was not going to give up my child without a damn good fight. I wanted my concerns and all of the basic joint custody issues on the record in the files of the county's domestic relations office, in case we did have to go to court somewhere down the road. I decided to be objectively unreasonable and make them force me to compromise.

The conference officer turned to me and asked me to respond to Curtis's accusations that I had denied him access. Of all the charges brought up here, in this area I felt on soundest ground.

I pulled a homemade calendar from my stack of papers. I had spent most of the preceding evening making up a month-by-month record of the "time spent with mother" and "time spent with father." Each month was recorded on a separate page. I had colored in "time spent with father" with a brilliant orange crayon. The days stood out sharply.

Nathaniel had spent roughly three weekends a month with Curtis, approximately 50 percent of vacation and holiday time, and had made liberal midweek visits for dinner, sometimes staying overnight.

"Do you agree with her record?" the hearing officer asked Curtis.

He looked over my drawings and nodded yes.

"That doesn't appear to be a denial of access," the official said.

I jumped in, wanting to get my opinion on the record.

"I have never denied, hindered, or prevented Curtis from seeing his child in any way," I said. "But whenever I say that Nathaniel has something else planned, or I voice my opinion over whether it is appropriate for a six-year-old to attend a midweek hockey game that begins at eight P.M., I am accused of denying access. I don't feel that this is an abrogation of his father's rights."

I was testy, argumentative. I wanted everyone to know my position. No one interrupted or argued with me, so I plunged ahead.

"My main concern is the welfare of this child," I said, my voice swelling with emotion. "I am concerned over *who* will be taking care of him when his father is not around. I feel I should have the right to know what kind of supervision is provided for this child. And I don't think that's interference."

I sounded like a bitch, but I didn't care. I wanted them all to know that I was concerned over who was taking care of my child. I was more than concerned. There had been several instances when Nathaniel had been left unsupervised. While the periods of time had been short ones, Natty *was* only six. A child this young should *not* be left unattended. Curtis and I had discussed the issue before. He thought occasional times when Nathaniel was alone while he or Jackie ran to the store or to pick up a sitter built independence. I didn't.

"What do you mean?" asked the hearing officer. "Can you give us any specific examples?"

I could and did.

"Well, I said, "I understand Jackie left the children alone around 10:30 one evening a few weeks ago when she went to take a sitter home. I don't think it's wise to leave three children under the age of eight in an apartment alone whether they are asleep or awake."

They didn't deny my examples.

There was one other item I wanted on the record.

"I also feel strongly that if Curtis says he is going to be with Nathaniel, then he should be with Nathaniel," I said. "I am not entering into a custody arrangement with Jackie. Joint custody means custody with the other parent, doesn't it? If Curtis says he is going to be spending time with Nathaniel, and then leaves Nat in Jackie's care, does that mean Nat is spending time with his father?"

Curtis jumped in, saying that my objections concerned his relationship with Jackie, that I was bitter about the divorce and his relationship with the other woman, and that I had no right to interfere in his child-care arrangements.

I *had* felt a twinge of resentment as the words had spilled from my mouth. Maybe I *was* still angry and hurt over the separation. It was not an agreeable thought; I turned my mind back to the custody issue.

But my concerns, I said, extended to far more than just the actual child-care arrangements. I worked at home. Nathaniel was fully aware of this. If Curtis was not home, or out of town, why should Nat be staying at his apartment for the sake of justifying a numerical split of days when I was available in my house and lived only two miles away?

My fear was that Nathaniel would feel I was rejecting him when he knew I was home and his father was not even around. Was this the basis upon which joint physical custody was decided? A strict numerical split of days when one of the parents was not even present? I raised the issue and waited for an answer. It was quickly forthcoming from Virginia Culver.

"Who takes care of Nathaniel when you are not at home?" she asked.

"I have competent care," I said. "My main sitter is a young mother who has worked for me for three years. A backup is a young nursing student who stays with Nathaniel at night when I am working my shift at Arturo's."

"Does Curtis interfere with your child-care arrangements?" she asked.

"Curtis is fully aware of these support people," I said.

Now it was Curtis's turn.

"How come it was all right for Jackie to take care of Nat when we were neighbors and all of a sudden she's incompetent?" he asked.

I knew this was a point he would raise. I was waiting for it and I opened my mouth to angrily reply that this was a different situation.

The hearing officer jumped in.

"No, these are different rules now," he said. "We're not discussing occasional baby-sitting assistance from a neighbor. We're talking about a custody arrangement."

The tempers on both sides were hot. We were all fiery. The adversarial system, which may have been a suitable way of dividing property and establishing support and alimony, wasn't terribly suitable for determining custody.

"I am more than willing for Curtis to have open, free, and continuing access to his child," I concluded sanctimoniously, "and I feel that I have done so. I do not, however, feel that it is in Nathaniel's best interests for him to be raised by someone else."

We all knew to whom I was referring with my spiteful "someone else."

I wouldn't let anyone else get a word in. I had been so cooperative in the months since the separation, I said, because of Nathaniel's desperate desire to be with his father. I thought I had been doing the right thing for my child.

But now I was possessed by another fear which underlay every other objection. I was *terrified* of losing my child. I was not only afraid that he might be taken from me physically, but emotionally as well. I feared that someone else would be influencing the way he was brought up. Jackie would replace me not only as Curtis's wife but as Natty's mother. I could see the genesis of this in Curtis's repeated objections to Nathaniel's schooling, his friends, his activities. He wanted them changed, neutralized to conform with Jackie's children. He wanted to cut the child's anchors to me. Maybe it was my imagination, maybe not, maybe I was irrational, but there seemed to be some sort of campaign in that direction underway. For instance, these days Curtis no longer referred to me as Nat's mother.

"Phyllis is on the phone," I heard him say when I called.

"Phyllis will be picking you up at noon," he said another time. Not "your mother," or "Mommy." I always referred to Curtis in Nathaniel's presence as "Daddy" or "your father." These kinds of subtle messages had to influence the way a child thought about his parents, and I was concerned that Nat not think I was pushing him away, with Jackie taking over when Curtis was at work or out of town.

I was Nathaniel's mother, and I wanted Curtis, his attorney, the conference officer, and my attorney to know that I was not going to give up my child.

The hearing officer interjected with a question.

"Do you feel Mr. Ellsworth is unfit?" he asked me.

I paused before answering. Whether or not I disagreed with the way he wanted to live and the manner in which he had left us, I could not say he was a bad father.

"No," I said softly.

He turned to Curtis and asked him the same question about me.

"No, absolutely not," he said, deflated.

Well, we had agreed that neither one of us was an unfit parent.

"These issues are not going to be settled in a courtroom," said the conference officer. "You are both intelligent adults and you have both agreed that you are fit parents. What I am hearing is a lot of anger. What is needed is for both of you to begin communicating with each other."

I shrugged. We had never communicated in the marriage. How could we communicate now? We agreed on nothing. I wasn't going to talk to him now. We were at a standoff.

Virginia Culver lunged forward, leaning over the table, both arms outstretched, palms face down in front of her. Her red fingernails glistened.

"I absolutely insist," she said, looking directly into the eyes of the hearing officer, "that a joint physical custody agreement be set out in a court order."

Virginia had grabbed the power of the room, directing our attention to her and forcing us to concentrate on her presence and her words. It was a superb performance. I became even more aware of her physical attractiveness and her smoldering intellectual intensity.

There was a challenge in her statement. She could have written the book on assertiveness training. There was no way I would have turned her down.

"Absolutely not!" I heard from the other end of the table.

Cute, sweet, Southern Elizabeth had sprung to life. She had listened to the interchange for the better part of an hour, saying nothing. Now, she had leaped out of her chair, knocking it over as she rose, and was pounding her hand on the table, emphasizing her objection to the request. Could this be the same demure woman with whom I had entered the hearing room?

I looked at her in amazement. So did the court official, Virginia, and Curtis.

"I cannot agree to a temporary court order," she argued. "This entire issue is part of the greater divorce settlement. Everything is tied together. Whether or not Phyllis stays in the house will affect where Nathaniel goes to school, his activities, the custody and visitation schedule. I cannot, as a representative of the law office of Roger Spenser, agree to a court order *under any circumstances*." She was practically foaming at the mouth, spewing objections to the proposed procedure. "I think we have expressed too many concerns over the custodial arrangements for this child. My client in no way has denied access and I think her concerns are valid. I cannot agree that a court order be set down until some of these issues are resolved."

Elizabeth righted the chair, plunked her body into it, and sat immobile, waiting for an answer.

"All right," the court official said after a moment. "You two get some counseling and resolve these issues. I don't want to see you back here again."

Virginia protested, but the session was over. The conference officer jotted down his decision, collected his papers, and left the room. Elizabeth was breathing heavily to my left. I thought I caught a sigh of relief between pants.

I was concerned about giving away my child. She was concerned about giving away the case. I sat, unable to move, waiting until Virginia and Curtis had departed. I looked at Elizabeth, whose freckled face was glowing with perspiration. She looked up at me, broke into a huge grin, and winked.

"Close call, huh?" she said softly.

The custody conference had resolved nothing. We had no agreement and no summer schedule. Some compromise had to be reached. The hearing officer had repeatedly said that we must communicate, that it was the only way to keep our case out of court and protect Nathaniel from an all-out parental war in which he would be the only victim. I let things ride for a few days and then telephoned Curtis at his office. We were communicating only by phone during business hours. I dreaded the thought of another confrontation. I set one goal for our conversation: a summer custody arrangement agreeable to both of us.

"Yes, Phyllis, what is it?" he said.

"I think we need to set up a summer schedule," I started to say, but he interrupted me. His voice sounded hurt.

"Look, you want to restrict my visits with Natty, restrict them," he said softly. "Fighting you is useless. I'm going to back off the custody suit. I don't want Nathaniel hurt. I'm not going to give you custody, but as long as I don't have custody, and you don't have custody, anything I don't agree with I won't participate in. It's exactly like our marriage."

What did he mean by that? What was exactly like our marriage? I'd have to think about that. But now I had been on the line for only a minute or two and I was exhausted. A sense of overwhelming fatigue had come over me. I didn't want to argue with him. I didn't even want to talk with him. I wanted him to go away and leave me alone. And I didn't want to think about my marriage either. It had to be all *his* fault. Wouldn't I love it to be *all* his fault.

"He wants to be with you, Curtis," I said, trying not to get angry. "You have to let him come to terms with this situation on his own time schedule. Just because you have him for a week or a month does not guarantee that he will feel comfortable. It's not because of Jackie or the kids or you; it's because of the way things have gone the past year."

My words made no dent.

"If you want to restrict my visits," Curtis replied, "just go ahead and do it. If you want to make sure that Nathaniel is here only when I'm here so you won't be able to get the feeling that you don't approve of what's going on, that's fine too."

He sounded as tired as I felt.

"Joint custody is probably not going to work for us," he continued wearily. "You and I can't agree on anything."

"Well, what are you going to do?" I asked.

"I won't give you custody because I don't believe you should have it," he replied. "I think you believe you are doing the right thing for Nathaniel and you do it with all the power within you. I also think you will do anything necessary for your position whether or not you see my point of view. It doesn't matter what I think because you'll disregard it anyway. You believe in what you believe in, period, and you are not going to change your mind.

"It's better not to fight with you," he concluded. "It's just like our marriage."

Just like our marriage. Again, the words, the accusation. He had turned a disagreement over a custody schedule into an indictment of our entire marriage. We had spent almost eleven years in marital union, but had we ever really communicated? I had to admit Curtis was right. Somehow we had missed out on the real meaning of marriage—communication, intimacy.

I sat alone at my desk, and stared at the telephone. It was 4:30 in the afternoon, and I was so incredibly tired, so completely dissipated with knowledge and sadness, that I couldn't even cry. Eleven years of marriage and I barely knew this man; or he me, for that matter. We'd had a life together but we'd never achieved any kind of real intimacy, real committedness. Real intimacy in a marriage had nothing to do with sex. Real intimacy was an ability to communicate, to disagree, to argue, but to talk to each other on common ground. Curtis and I spoke two foreign tongues. I dragged myself from my desk, collapsed in a heap on Nathaniel's bed, and slept through the night.

When I awoke Curtis's words reverberated in my mind like a broken record. I was so certain of my position I was noncompromising.

I had to admit he did seem to have a point. I went the distance for anything I believed in—I always had. Where Curtis and I differed, however, was in our interpretation of my attitude. He thought I was rigid and unbending. I categorized myself as a terrier who never gave up.

So here we were, locking horns again, but this time the issue was Nathaniel. A month away from his seventh birthday, he was insecure, anxious, clinging. He was terrified that something would happen to me when he was at his father's, and angry with his father when he was with me. The nightmares and swollen eyes persisted, recurring at regular intervals.

I really didn't know what Nathaniel's best interests were.

Were his symptoms similar to those of any other child of divorce—or was he different? How could Curtis and I co-raise this child when we were both so filled with hostility toward each other?

If any form of shared parenting was going to work, we *had* to be able to talk to each other. I decided to give the communication and cooperation effort one last shot, picked up the phone, and called Curtis at his office.

I was rung through immediately and didn't open with any pleasantries. *I* wanted to set the mood rather than having to respond to the verbal tenor he chose to establish.

"Curtis, look, from the very beginning I told you that Nathaniel needs you, he wants to be with you, needs time alone with you," I said surely. "He needs a very firm sense of his father. He needs that strong paternal tie so that he will gain a sense of security and accept everything else."

The "everything else," we both knew, was Jackie, her children, and Nathaniel's position as the middle child in Curtis's restructured and extended family unit. We weren't even divorced and I was already thinking of them as a "family." If they were a family, what was I?

"Natty's problems did not start with our separation, Phyllis," he responded emphatically. "They started from the time he came through your birth canal. I've discussed this parenting issue with my lawyer and many psychologists. You've floated in and out of his life, abandoning him to baby-sitters. What he needs is re-bonding."

Re-bonding? I wondered what kind of pop psychology books Curtis had taken to reading. I waited a moment to digest his words and for my thoughts to come together. One of his phrases suddenly hit me: "from the time he came through your birth canal."

"Curtis," I said. "Nathaniel never came through my birth canal. Don't you remember? He was born through Caesarian section."

"Yeah, right," he answered uncomfortably, then: "Damn it, Nat is not dealing with reality, and the reason he's not dealing with reality is that there is no push for him to deal with reality."

"Push for him to deal with reality?" I repeated. "We are dealing with a six-year-old child here—not a labor union."

Damn you, Curtis, I thought. Feelings didn't follow someone else's blueprint for healing. It was hard enough for me to untangle the web of my own conflicting emotions. Imagine how a child must feel.

"You say you want him to have a strong base," he continued, ignoring my comment. "You want me to be a visitor in his life!"

"Curtis, I've gone overboard in encouraging both of you to spend time together," I retorted.

"On *your* terms," he said. "When was the last time you told him that Jackie was wonderful, that she was terrific, and that you wanted him to spend time with her? He doesn't feel that."

"Curtis, I think that's a little much," I said. "While I may not be bitter about Jackie, I'm not ready to tell my son I thought the woman who walked off with my husband was wonderful."

"You know when Nat is going to feel good?" Curtis continued. "When you make him feel good about being here."

"Are you telling me that you hold no responsibility for Nathaniel's feelings?" I asked. "That it's all *my* fault?"

"I suppose you have raised Nathaniel as best you could," he admitted. "I share some of that responsibility, but I'll tell you something . . .

"You have made me wrong all of our married life, from the time Natty was born," he said. "I am the root cause of your feelings. You are in competition with me. The whole divorce thing is pattern behavior."

Pattern behavior?

We were speaking in different languages again. I gave my message one final shot.

"He simply feels he is being pushed aside when he's with you, Curtis," I stated.

"Phyllis, when you drown, you will think you're still swimming," he said.

We finally struck a deal for a vacation schedule of one week on, one week off.

Five days into the summer experiment Nathaniel telephoned, asking to come back. Since Curtis and I had agreed that Nat's preferences for the opposite parent be considered during his alternate-week visits, I assumed his request would present no problem.

Curtis interrupted Nathaniel's call.

"I'll meet you at the shopping center," he said. "I am never going to do this again. Once we agree to a schedule, that's it."

The great proponent of joint custody, I thought. Hah! In principal, joint custody was designed to free the child from artificial schedules and encourage an open and continuing flow of involvement with both parents. Obviously we had hit another snag.

I wondered why Curtis hadn't offered to bring Nathaniel back to the house. We were perhaps five minutes apart. Maybe he thought he would be giving away something by doing that. Or maybe he saw the Acme Supermarket as secure, neutral territory. I plunked myself into the station wagon and took off.

They were waiting for me. Curtis had parked his car, motor running, lights on, parallel to the supermarket entrance. I pulled up to him, the hood of my car head-to-head with his. Just like us, I mused. Head-to-head. I looked through my windshield and into his. Natty, seated next to his father in the front seat, broke into a huge smile as he spotted me.

I opened my door, popped out of my car, and walked the ten steps to where they waited. Curtis didn't budge from the front seat. He said nothing as I opened the door on the passenger side and let our son out. I waved good-bye. He directed his car away from the curb, pulled into the parking lot, and took off.

Natty smiled broadly as he climbed into my car.

"Hi, I'm glad to be back," he said.

"Hi, I'm glad to have you back," I replied. "How come you decided to cut your week short?"

I was trying to pump him for information. I knew that wasn't cricket, but any ammunition I could glean was fair game.

"I just wanted to be with you, Mom," my son said. "I'm just not used to being at that house. The walls are cracked and there's kitty litter all over the upstairs bathroom."

"I see!" I said with a smile. I doubted if either excuse was true. Jackie was a very, very good housekeeper.

We pulled into our driveway, he marched up the stairs, changed into a pair of pajamas, and snuggled under his covers.

"Natty," I said softly, trying to draw him out. "Why did you want to come back?" I wanted to pinpoint a reason, any reason for his sudden return.

"I just wanted to see you and sleep in my own bed."

I was getting nowhere.

"Actually," he said as I studied his face, "I wanted to get away from the smelly shower."

I was trying to take his comments seriously, and was having a very difficult time keeping a straight face.

"Is there anything else you don't like about the place?" I asked.

"Yes," he replied, "it has terrible food. Jackie gives us fake butter with our toast. I think it's called margarine. I tell her I'd rather have peanut butter."

I didn't like to admit it, but I was beginning to think Curtis was right. We had a bit of a manipulation problem here. But I wanted to probe a bit deeper before I wrote off this episode as "child playing one parent against the other."

"How do you think we can resolve these problems?" I asked. Perhaps Nat could come up with a solution himself. He had always been an extremely verbal and logical child.

I gave him a long rope. Even at age six he had a remarkable sense of himself and this crazy family setup. Let's hear his opinions, I thought.

"Well, sometimes when I'm with you, I'd rather be with Dad and sometimes when I'm with Dad, I'd rather be with you."

That was pretty good. I waited for more.

"It's about a fifty-one and a forty-nine," he said. "I mean, on a scale of 1 to 10, six is being here and four is being there."

He wanted so much to give us both equal time, to be fair.

"Go on," I said, "maybe we could work it out that you're with Dad for shorter periods of time, but more of them."

"I want an equal time with each of you," he said emphatically, "but not an equal amount of days. I'll be with you 200 days and Dad the rest. How's that?"

I was so confused by his mathematical calculations I suggested we talk about it again in the morning. Was he aware of what 200 days really were, or was Curtis's insistence upon custody by numbers filtering down to his son? I had no idea. Besides, if he wanted to spend equal time with both of us, why had he come home during his first week with them?

It didn't make sense. Something was missing. Why would Curtis want a joint custody arrangement and then be reluctant to honor its basic provisions? I was certain this bouncing back and forth was no good for any of us. Thank Heaven Elizabeth had been able to forestall a court order setting out a custody arrangement. The summer experiment was just that, and I would have to be shown the benefits of this tennis-ball type of custody before I would ever voluntarily agree to such a committed schedule.

I bent over to kiss my son good night and heard him whisper in my ear that he wanted to put something on the Divorce Reporter. Aha! Mother's intuition. I knew it! I ran for the tape. Something *was* troubling him. I knew all this nonsense was a camouflage against the real issue—and I suspected that I was about to find out what the problem really was.

I took out the special tape, inserted it into the recorder, and placed it before me.

"A couple of days ago I thought my mom was going to stop loving me," he began.

"Why? Did I do something to you?" I asked, bewildered.

"No, it's because Dad doesn't pay any attention to me."

"Give me an example," I said.

"Jackie never checks on me when I go to bed, neither do any of the sitters, and neither does my father," he said. He was articulate and absolutely certain of himself. Or maybe he wasn't.

"It's either that they're not checking on me, or that I don't know they're checking on me," he conceded.

More camouflage. There had to be something else.

"What else? Is something troubling you?"

"I feel like my dad's not going to think about me any more," he whimpered.

I waited for more.

"He doesn't like, love me, because he hardly kisses me," he sobbed. "He only kisses Jackie. He kisses Jackie more than me. I love you, Mommy."

He cuddled up next to me, wrapped his arms around my waist, cried softly for a few minutes and then whimpered again.

"I was worried that if my dad left, then you would leave me too," he said, sobbing softly. "I was afraid that you wouldn't love me and that you would leave me. I love you, Mommy."

My hands started shaking.

"I love you, Natty," I said. "I'm not going to leave you."

He didn't hear my reassurances. By then he was sound asleep. I gently stroked his forehead and felt a tear dribble down my cheek. What had I done to my child?

# CHAPTER 8

# BESIEGED

If I had any doubts that Curtis and I had intense differences over the meaning of joint custody and the manner in which Nathaniel should be raised, they were silenced by a letter to Spenser from Curtis's custody attorney, Virginia Culver. I was (again) sitting in Spenser's office. Almost a year had passed since our separation. Spenser pulled a letter from the stack of papers he planned to discuss with me. It had arrived in the mail that very morning.

"What do you think about this?" he said, passing it to me.

I scanned the letter, skimming the first part which charged that "Phyllis is not giving her full cooperation to the alternate-week schedule." I read the words, open-mouthed. This can't be, I thought. Both of us had been told by the court official in our custody conciliation conference that for any dual child-rearing arrangement to work, a suspension of hostilities and animosities had to be effected between the two of us. Why was Curtis doing this?

Nathaniel was supposed to have input into a flexible schedule. Although the base schedule we had put together was drawn up on a one-week-on one-week-off basis for the summer, if Nat wished to return to the noncustodial parent's home during the alternate week, he had the right to do so. And this is precisely what he had done. It wasn't *my* fault that Natty had asked to come back to stay with me during his very first full week at Curtis's.

But once my disbelief faded, anger took its place. I continued to read the accusations. "In order for any arrangement to work, both parents must be supportive of the child's being with the other parent."

It was easy to read between the lines here. Culver seemed to be charging me with discouraging Nat from being with his father.

I continued reading. The charges shifted into the area of alimony, equitable distribution, and counsel fees. The letter stated that Culver felt she truly did not think that "Phyllis is interested in negotiating a settlement."

I wasn't interested in negotiating a settlement! Outrage began to bubble in my brain. Then I read the next sentence. "I am sure that you have informed her that a negotiated settlement is the best settlement that she will get, but perhaps there is some psychological reason that she wants to continue the fight."

Boom! There was no psychological reason—this was psychological warfare. I knew it. I understood. I knew I shouldn't get angry—but I had.

By now I had shed enough of my original naïveté that I should have known not to take the letter at face value. We had a court-enforced support order and a court official who refused to set down a custody agreement as a court order. As far as anything else went, we were in limbo. Hold on, Phyllis, I thought. Cool down. This is a negotiating tactic. I reread the letter and concluded that the verbiage was an attempt to hardball us into a settlement.

I looked up at Spenser. He had been watching me intently to assess my reaction. I started to laugh and tossed the letter back to him. He smiled and shook his head.

"Now what?" I asked. "They almost had me on that one. Can you believe it?"

"They're blaming you for everything," he grinned. "It's much easier to claim that the wife is vindictive rather than trying to settle the tough issues. They're throwing the kitchen sink at you."

The remainder of the letter had also claimed I was harassing Curtis at home. How, if he was out of town or out of the office, was I to reach him, other than at home to discuss last-minute pickup, delivery, or scheduling changes related to school or sports? It was all so ridiculous, so petty.

Maybe it *wasn't* so ridiculous, I thought. It had almost worked.

"By the way," he continued. "I saw Michael Rawson at a state bar convention last week. He thinks you're dragging your feet about not getting a real job."

I laughed and shook my head. I *had* a real job. I was working at Arturo's—it sounded to me like Rawson wanted me out of the kitchen.

"Oh really?" I waited for Spenser to continue.

"Mike says you should give up being a writer," Spenser deadpanned. "I told him you were doing the best you could, that you had a drawer full of rejection slips, and that it wasn't easy to break back into that career track.

"So you know what he said to me?" Spenser continued, without waiting for a response from me, shaking his head in amazement as he recalled the conversation and repeating the words of Curtis's lawyer emphatically. "Maybe she should try something else?"

"Maybe I should try something else?" I repeated, shocked at Rawson's cavalier dismissal of my career.

"What did you tell him?" I pressed Spenser.

"I asked him if he'd say the same thing to a forty-year-old man," he said. "This is your profession, after all."

Bless Spenser, my protector. I *had* tried something else. Remember? I had given up writing to become an inn-keeper and how far did that get me? It prepared me to be a short-order cook making $42 a night. Was I supposed to work as kitchen help the rest of my life?

I had no doubt about my eventual ability to find work. Just where and how and for whom were still a blank. I was trying to break back into the free-lance market, and had completed one small magazine article, but it had been a laborious process. My writing skills were rusty. I knew it would take time to get them in shape and my concentration back.

For now, I just couldn't think straight. I wanted to get the whole thing over with, to sign off forever on this period of my life. But on the other hand, I was also determined not to give in to Curtis's financial and emotional sanctions. Hold out, I thought, go the distance. I had to think of it like a race, or like swimming laps—look up, catch your breath, and push, push, push. You can do it. Just push, push, push. As hard as I tried to keep my spirits up during these days, the real truth was that I wasn't competing in a race at all—I was treading water, and barely keeping my head above the surface at that.

More months in limbo. No movement on anything, and a change in season from the racy red hot of summer to the chilling frostiness of late fall. Another lonely weekend was sneaking up on me. Of course I had no social plans. Since Nathaniel was at his father's, I had agreed to work an extra shift at Arturo's. I would work Friday, be free Saturday, and not have to report back to the restaurant again until Sunday evening. Then off two days, until my next two-day shift. I sat in my office playing with my Rolodex and thinking about what to do during my two days and evening off. I hadn't seen Meredith in a while, but she was away. I had a few other local woman friends, but this was Friday afternoon, my friends were all married, and weekends were for their families.

I thought about *my* family living 1,500 miles away. I could have used a dose of tender loving care, about now.

You could get that from most families. No questions asked, just welcoming arms. A place to be; people to be with.

"There is nothing so sad as a woman in the throes of divorce with no family around," Spenser had once said to me. "If you have family you know you at least will have someplace to go for holidays, or someone to talk to when you're feeling down, but for the single woman without family nearby, divorce can be devastating."

I didn't tell him that my family was in Florida. I had passed the point of wishing that they were closer to help me out, but at times like this I would have loved to have someone close whom I could just ring up to say, "Hey, what's for dinner? Can I come over and be with you?" You just didn't do that with friends, at least I didn't and couldn't with most of my friends.

My friends. Now *that* was an interesting subject. I looked at the names passing before me as I continued to flip through my Rolodex looking for someone nearby I could go out with. I had friends from years ago that I was still in contact with, but they lived hours away. I was looking for someone locally to share an evening of food and conversation.

How I had lived in a community for so many years and had developed so few real friends was baffling to me. Or perhaps it wasn't. Maybe I hadn't exerted enough of an effort, or maybe I was perceived solely as Curtis's wife, not as a "woman person." God knows I hadn't participated in the community except as a wife. Now that I was no longer a wife, there didn't seem to be much of a place in the community where I *did* fit in—except for the volunteer civic work I was, at Spenser's behest, careful to keep up. But socially, my current status in the community, I knew, was typical of that of other divorced, separated, or single women living in a suburban family-oriented locale: sort of Modified Pariah. We were odd women out, the type you could invite to a large cocktail party where no one would notice your singleness or find you threatening to their husbands or beaux. Rarely would we be invited to a small gathering. If you had an escort, that was something else, but an invitation would almost never be extended to you alone.

Occasionally if a husband or boyfriend was out of town I would hear from the woman half of a couple, suggesting that we get together for a drink or meet at one of our homes, but rarely would we go out. *Never* would we go out if the male partner was around. A few longtime friends sometimes suggested dinner with *them* as a couple, but these occasions were few and far between.

Of course there *was* the cadre of gossip mavens who only called to get caught up on my divorce dirt. I had no interest in spending time with them now—or ever again.

I did hear a lot of excuses. At the grocery store. In the bookshop. At the bank. Or the gas station.

"I should have called. We had a few friends in from out of town. I just plain forgot."

"I thought about calling you, but I never thought you'd be around."

"We went out on the spur of the moment and were going to call, but . . ."

"Call me. Let's get together."

When I did, it was never the right time. I knew the right time would never come, the invitation would never be made. Maybe the words made the person uttering them feel less guilty. I didn't know. After a year, I had stopped caring whether they called or not. At the same time, I stopped calling them.

Nathaniel's school friends and their families provided an interesting counterbalance. Since they were in another town, I saw them less often, but they had—en masse—provided an extended family-at-large support system for me through our children's school and play contacts. And although I was not part of their geographic community, I felt myself to be a member at large. Of course, I was also not a visible daily reminder of their marital mortality either.

I once discussed my lack of social contacts with Spenser.

He had initiated the subject. "Are you going out at all?" he asked. It was an awkward question coming from my attorney. I felt shy, uncertain how to respond. I wasn't sure if he was testing me, since he had told me from the beginning I could be denied support if Curtis could prove "marital misconduct," or whether he was honestly concerned about my social life. *Technically* I couldn't be caught going out with a man. It was downright silly. I decided to be straight with him.

"I don't like the singles scene," I told him. "I never felt comfortable doing the things single people are supposed to do. I'm not a bar type, I don't like organized activities, I don't have the money to travel, and whatever friends I do have don't seem to think of me when there *is* something going on."

Spenser had looked at me appraisingly, then his face softened.

"Phyllis," he said, "everyone probably thinks you're able to cope so well that they think you don't need them!"

I looked at him in surprise. I hadn't realized I gave off that kind of an impression. They should only know, I thought wryly.

He paused, then went on. "I bet you scare men off because they think you're so capable."

"Oh," I said, now thoroughly deflated.

"I know you're approachable, Phyllis," he continued kindly, "but I think it would probably take a special man to see that."

Spenser certainly never minced words. But if I were not at least somewhat capable, I thought with a flash of resentment, I'd be walked all over. Since I was capable, no one called. I wondered if I would ever be able to reach a median stance. Or at least let people see me as I was.

I turned my attention back to my Rolodex. Four-thirty on a Friday afternoon. Forget it, I thought, it's not worth the effort.

I was about to leave for my shift at Arturo's when the phone rang. It was an invitation to come to dinner the following evening. I barely knew the host and hostess, a couple who had recently moved to the area from the South, but I did know one of their neighbors who had just suggested they give me a call as an extra body for a visiting gentleman. Yes, I'd be delighted to come, I told them. Maybe the weekend wouldn't be so bad after all.

The Friday night shift was going to be fast and lively, I thought, as I pulled into the restaurant parking lot. The bar was packed with weekend revelers, and, as I entered through the kitchen door, tossing my sweatshirt under a counter, pulling a clean apron over my head, and tying a tea towel over my hair, I spotted a free phone. Nathaniel was spending the weekend with his father. Better call and check in before things get really hairy around here, I thought, before I have no time to think.

I dialed the apartment phone number, leaned against the kitchen wall, and waited for someone to answer. The waitresses were pulling dinner rolls from the warming trays, butter pats from the cooler. The dishwashers were backed up from the day shift. Typical weekend kitchen chaos. The produce man stepped around me and over the crates of vegetables he had unloaded from his truck and which currently were stacked on the floor, waiting to be rotated into the walk-in refrigerator.

"Hello?" a woman's voice answered my call.

"Hi, Jackie," I said above the din. "Is Nat around?"

I waited, expecting to hear my son's voice. Instead, Curtis picked up.

"I spoke with Nathaniel's therapist today," he said. "She says he's depressed because he never sees his father."

Keep your temper, I told myself sternly, but as usual I couldn't.

"Never sees his father?" I exploded. "What kind of crap is that?"

These days, every time I spoke with Curtis, he made some statement that set me off. Now, again, I blew up right on cue. It took days before I came back to earth. A lot of my quick temper was the result, I think, of my increasing sense of frustration over our seemingly never-to-end standoff. I was constantly exhausted, panicked about money, and, perhaps worst of all, lonely—very lonely, miserably lonely.

"You are not the custodial parent," Curtis said sharply. "You have no right to make arrangements for Nathaniel. You are not physically in charge of him."

Again, the who's-in-charge question. I was not to say yes to birthday parties on his weekends with his father, or to visits to friend's homes. We had a custody standoff.

But no one at Curtis's home was really in charge and, in the absence of a someone, I had taken over. Why not? Why shouldn't I? Curtis was never around anyway.

"Nathaniel is insecure and anxious," Curtis was saying, "and he's that way because he doesn't see me enough."

"He's that way, you fool," I screamed back, "because you are undermining my authority and management of this child's life. You are trying to take my son away from me! I won't allow you to do that!"

I slammed the phone down, not realizing that I hadn't gotten to speak to my son. I sounded like an irrational nut—even to myself. Every pair of eyes in the room was focused on me, silent and embarrassed. I picked my way through the supplies and debris littering the floor as the kitchen help worked madly to store the fresh food. As I took my place on the line before the range, my hands were shaking. He had done it again. I had played right into his hands.

I turned my attention to the food, and immediately tipped over the first order of cheese-encrusted onion soup into the bottom of the searing oven. Flames and smoke surrounded me as the smoke detector buzzed loudly. I knew the ringing would stop when the cheese burned off the bottom of the oven. I reached for my kitchen tongs and pulled a duck from the backup oven, swiftly tipping the ironstone plate which held the partially cooked fowl over the garbage bucket to pour off the excess fat before saucing the bird. In my haste I dumped the duck into the garbage.

"Where's my cranberry duck?" cried a waitress. "Table six says they ordered it an hour ago."

"The duck is in the dump," I said frostily. "Tell them it's on its way."

I set up another duck and sent the waitress back to the floor. It was going to be a long, hard night. I felt like a zombie and settled into a wordless blue funk as I cooked, speaking to no one, thinking, just thinking.

Eight hours later, after I'd fed what must have been every mouth on the East Coast, my assistant threw me my sweatshirt.

"Go home," he said kindly, placing his hand on my shoulder. "I'll break down the kitchen for you. You've had enough."

The eldest child in a family of six, he was only twenty, but displayed a maturity and sensitivity far beyond his age and experience. In fact, he had never traveled farther than the immediate locale. He had dropped out of high school at age sixteen, going to work to help his parents support his younger brothers and sisters. He had progressed up through the kitchen ranks to cook's assistant and was studying for his high school equivalency exam in order to enroll at the local community college next semester.

He was right. I had had enough. I thanked him profusely, marched out to the parking lot, and got into my car. The held-back tears came as soon as I got on the road. I had known I couldn't let anyone see me disintegrate. It was too revealing, too personal. I didn't want anyone to pierce the veil in which I had shrouded my emotions. I didn't want them—the townsfolk—or Curtis—to know he was getting to me.

I drove along the winding country road toward my home with tears streaming down my face but determined not to give an inch. Curtis was not going to have any indication that he was gaining ground in his attempt to break my spirit. I would *not* give in.

Still, inside my head, I *had* given in. I was high-strung and anxious. I worried constantly about everything. Money, Nathaniel, me. My car payment was due next week. My salary from Arturo's didn't come close to covering even one of my expenses. My court-ordered alimony check had been late this week and my electric and phone bills had gone unpaid. It wasn't the first time. Even under a court order my support checks were frequently late. Was it deliberate or was it due to the inefficiencies in the county Domestic Relations Office? I complained bitterly once to the office, only to be told that Curtis had missed a payment or two but that he eventually caught up and that I might have to wait for as much as six weeks of missed payments to file a formal complaint. Utilities, however, didn't want to hear about the check not being in the mail.

In addition to these bills, every part of my house seemed to be disintegrating at once. The washing machine leaked, the dryer needed a new heating element, the toilets needed new valves. The screens were filled with holes, allowing swarms of unidentified insects to enter the house. I couldn't afford repair bills or exterminators. I used the local laundromat and kept cans of Raid within easy reach. The driveway had developed massive craters, and to plug up the potholes required a complete resurfacing of the hill. Estimated cost: $5,000. If my car accidently plunged into one of these gaping holes, damage to a tire, or, worse, an axle or the front end of the vehicle was inevitable.

Every piece of Nathaniel's clothing seemed to be wearing out at once. Shoes, jeans, sweaters. The day I decided to hit the discount children's store, he was invited to three birthday parties—the money that should have gone for shoes went for gifts for his friends.

To top my frustration, Nathaniel's school had called that very week, the headmistress expressing concern over my son's excessive anxiety.

"Is there anything we can do to help you, Phyllis?" she asked.

I was grateful for her show of concern but could offer

no suggestions. Tell my husband to make me a reasonable offer, I wanted to say.

I had only one year of tuition set aside for Nathaniel in a separate account and applied for financial aid. But *both* parents, I was told, had to fill out a financial statement showing need. I was below the United States poverty level; Curtis was in the highest income bracket. *Together*, we didn't qualify as a needy couple.

The school was used to dealing with two sets of parents, but could not interfere with the actual relationships between the families. That, they felt, would be unreasonable and inappropriate. They could and did send two separate mailings to each parent when schedules, activities, and report cards went out. They did schedule separate parent-teacher conferences and suggest psychological assistance when necessary. *But* they certainly couldn't tell one parent how to behave toward the other.

As I drove home I thought about the most recent episodes in a series of slights. Nathaniel's Hannukah pageant. All the parents were invited. I was talking with one of the class mothers and looked up, only to see Curtis walking in to the assembly with Jackie on his arm as if she were Nathaniel's mother. How humiliating! The three of us together at a school assembly. I couldn't stomach it.

"C'mon," said the class mother, guiding me to a row up front so that my back would be toward them. "Let's take our seats."

Afterward I barely made it out the door before my torrential rain of tears started to flow. I knew that Natty's psychiatrist had told Curtis not to bring Jackie just yet to school functions or other events where I would be present. Get the divorce settled, she said, give him time to accept the new arrangement, it was embarrassing for Nat to have to explain to his friends who this woman with his father was. (Not to mention how his mother felt.) Wait awhile, the psychiatrist told Curtis. When you get married, then she can be labeled a stepmother—it's better for the child to have a label. But Curtis had done it anyway. I didn't care that they had come, I told myself over and over; I just felt like a fool, a damn fool.

Nathaniel's monthly Cub Scout pack meeting. Usually it was held on Friday nights when Natty was with Curtis; but on this occasion I was attending to watch my son be awarded a special badge. He was sitting on my lap waiting his turn to be called to the stage when his den mother approached and introduced herself.

"Hi, I'm the den mother," she said, extending her hand. "Are you a relative of Nathaniel's?"

"I think so," I replied. "I'm his mother."

The woman was visibly distressed.

"I'm so sorry," she said. "I had no idea he had a real mother. Are you in for a visit?"

"In for a visit? I live here!"

Embarrassed, she explained that when Curtis had signed Nat up for scouts there had been no mention of a mother. Neither my address, phone number, nor name had been offered.

"Why don't you add my name, address, and phone number to your contact list?" I suggested pointedly. "I can assure you that I am alive, and well, and kicking."

Her mistake really hurt. Badly. I wondered: if others were not aware of Natty's connection to me, how would he absorb the exclusion of references to me, his real mother? I had a continuing fear that Curtis was trying to blot me out of Nathaniel's life—and might just succeed.

I was unsure whether my resentment was warranted, so I told Spenser all of this.

"No, Phyllis, you're not being overly sensitive," he said kindly. "I think that's cruel and unusual punishment."

Then he quickly moved to what by then had become standard instructions.

"Be a lady," he counseled. "Never let him know he's getting to you. Never let him think there's a chink in your armor."

"What can we do to solve these problems?" Curtis repeatedly asked Nathaniel's therapist.

"You have to first understand why the problems exist before solutions can be applied," she replied.

I knew the mother-child bond was strong, but I didn't think I was strong enough emotionally to withstand the psychological pressure I was being subjected to. I was rabid with fear that my child would be taken away from me. My terror alternated with a desperate resolve: Natty was *my* son, *my* baby, and I would *not* let him be taken away from me.

Occasionally my fears were given vivid illumination.

"I'm making a lineup for my football team," Nat told me one Saturday afternoon while watching a college game on television. "You're going to be the middle linebacker. Okay?"

"Okay," I shrugged. "What does a middle linebacker do?"

"She protects the center."

I knew from my days at a Big Ten university that the center hiked the ball.

"Okay. Who's the center?"

"Jackie."

I winced. The two of us were teammates, playing together. What was Nathaniel really thinking? What could I do to make him certain that I would stick by him all the way?

I tossed and turned during the few hours that remained of that Friday night, brooded most of the next day about my blowup on the telephone with Curtis and my horrible night at Arturo's. Lighten up, Phyllis, I kept telling myself. You'll cope better as time passes. Only time seemed to be passing so slowly and with no progress at all.

What a stroke of luck that I had that dinner party to go to. A diversion! I needed that now. I decided to put the conflict and the custody issue behind me and have a good time. I put on a dark blue sweater, a matching skirt, and boots, and threw a paisley scarf around my neck. I didn't feel chic, but I didn't feel out of style either. My clothing was tailored and in good taste.

I arrived at the house and glanced through the windows as I made my way up the porch steps to the entrance. The room was full of people and everyone seemed to be listening to a man gesturing animatedly and seated in the center of the couch. I knew that this had to be the single man my hostess had referred to when she extended the invitation the previous night.

He *was* attractive, perhaps in his late forties. Nice blue eyes. A prematurely grey full head of hair spilled over his collar. He was dressed in tweeds and boots. Gentleman farmer or academic from nearby New Haven, I thought.

He was gesturing as if he were conducting a lecture. Academic, I decided. Yes, a college professor, full of confidence in his specialty—whatever that was—and holding forth before a rapt audience of admirers.

It had been a long time since an attractive single man had crossed my path. I was nervous. I wondered if I could cut the social interaction. I considered going back home and telephoning with an excuse.

But before I could even turn around, a couple came up behind me, rang the door bell and the three of us were all welcomed in together. As the couple moved to hang up their coats and mine, the hostess scurried off to get us drinks. There were ten people in the room listening to the lecturer with rapt attention. No one noticed my arrival. I lowered myself into a straightbacked chair in the corner of the room and listened.

"I am not amoral," he was saying, "I don't like being promiscuous, but you take a woman out three times and she's ready to get married. So I take them out three times and go on to the next one. Fucking isn't done with a lot of forethought and commitment today. It's like going out to get ice cream when you were in high school, same kind of emotional commitment."

I sat motionless in my chair, initial enthusiasm now

extinguished by his words. We were being treated to a one-man monologue on the art of being a single male. A rather unpleasant monologue at that.

"There's this woman passing through my life now," he went on paternally, noticing me and giving me the "don't bother" once-over. I recognized the signal. No interest here.

"She's thirty-six and horny," he said, dismissing the unnamed woman with a wave of his hand. "She doesn't know how to kiss and she's a lousy lay. I tell her I'm not interested and she keeps calling. I never call her, I don't encourage her, and she's crazy about me."

A real Mr. Macho, I thought. What an evening this was turning out to be!

"She's no different from all the others. The lines are all the same. 'I've never met anyone like you, it feels like we've known each other forever'—they're all the same."

The bottom line was that he spent a lot of time going "out with the guys."

"I like being with them," he concluded. "With a woman, you can't just take her out and have a good time. They're always looking to get married."

Macho creep, I was thinking. For this I gave up a quiet evening alone with my VCR? The men in the room were practically salivating.

"Women are like racehorses," he continued. "You begin training a two-year-old and by the time they're four-year-olds, you've got yourself a decent horse. Same thing with women. You can't start training an old mare and expect it to become a champion."

It was obvious to me that the last thing he wanted to do was spend an evening with a "not-quite-divorced female nearing forty."

"Speaking of old mares, Phyllis," said my host, in a comment I suspected was meant to be taken as flip, "how's your case coming? Are you divorced yet?"

All eyes turned toward me.

"Status quo. Nothing's happening," I said evenly.

"What's the holdup?" my host asked. "It's been over a year, hasn't it?"

I didn't want to get into a discussion with this crowd, didn't want to justify my reasons for not giving in. I decided a simple explanation would be best.

"We have not been able to agree on a division of assets according to the equitable distribution provisions of the state's divorce code," I said.

Kill 'em with legalese, I thought, hoping to kill this line of conversation.

"What's equitable?" asked the charming Mr. Macho, leaping right in. "Marriage is a fifty-fifty proposition. Joint assets should be divided equally."

"Equal may not be equitable," I said, starting to explain the ten categories of the state's property-distribution standards.

I could feel the tone of the room turning sour. Not one woman said a word.

"You could have worked," said the host. "Weren't you going to open a restaurant?"

"Sure, but—"

He cut me off. "Does your husband own his business?"

"No, but—"

"So you're dealing with property and salary," he continued. "You lived in the house together. That's fifty percent. You're capable of getting a job. I don't think you have a right to expect any alimony. You're a young woman. You can work."

Every woman in the room shifted uncomfortably in her seat. I felt not a shred of sympathy from them toward me. It was as if I had brought about my own demise. I had been criticized by at least one of these women, behind my back, for being terribly "aggressive" in the past. Maybe she thought I had slammed a tennis ball too hard one day. No one uttered a word that could even remotely be considered to be in my defense.

"You're the same as every other divorced female I meet,"

chimed in Mr. Macho. "Self-absorbed, raping the husband's pocketbook. You women wanted equality. Now that you've gotten it, you're complaining that it's not enough. What's this poor guy paying you now?"

"Maybe $20,000 a year under a court order," I volunteered, failing to mention that my husband made more than $100,000 a year or that he had many times that in deferred compensation, stock, and other assets.

"You're not exactly poverty-stricken," he sniffed.

I bristled, debated whether to take him on, and backed off. I wondered if *he* could live on that amount of money while sustaining a large house. My yearly expenses—excluding the mortgage, taxes, and insurance—came to $16,000 a year: $150 a month electricity; $184 a month oil; $84 a quarter garbage; $163 a month car payment; $700 a year car insurance. Vet bills, lawn and yard care, repairs. Taxes on the alimony portion of my support payments. That was without food, gas, or clothing.

I couldn't sell the house because it was jointly owned. I couldn't leave the house because I would be prejudicing my property rights. If I didn't pay the household bills and expenses, my credit rating would be shot to hell. I realized none of these excuses would have meant anything to these men. I was a greedy bitch, out to get everything I could from Santa Claus.

"What are you holding out for?" asked my host. "Give in already. You've cut yourself off from everyone. You have to start opening up and seeing the other side, Phyllis. Divorce is nothing more than a business deal. If you're a man, you see it as economics; as a woman, emotions. Give in, cut your losses, and get on with your life."

A *business deal*? I thought numbly. Here it was again. For the rest of the dinner I was quietly participative. I couldn't take being in the witness box both at the behest of Curtis and others like these people whom I barely knew.

It was bad enough being a participant in my own divorce, but now this criticism was coming from outsiders. What right did they have to criticize me? Those self-satisfied men with their six-figure salaries! And their wives! Not a word of support or understanding! I asked myself repeatedly what these women would do if they had been left as I had been.

In spite of so-called women's liberation, divorce as a social phenomenon these days was only mildly different from years past. It was more acceptable, easier, and there was less "who's at fault" mentality; but it was not so different in the pocketbooks. I knew that at least one of these women's husbands had an income in the seven-figure category. I also knew at least one of them held no property either jointly or in her own name. At least my home, our property, and my car were in joint names. Curtis could not sell anything without me. Eventually I would be awarded my equitable share of our marital assets. Just *how* equitable depended on how long I could hold out.

These women were partners in long-term, relatively satisfactory marriages. Each, I was certain, never considered the possibility of divorce entering her home. But it could at any time, especially these days, and if it did they would be totally unprepared.

After dinner, one man drew me aside as the hostess offered around cordials and brandy.

"My wife owns nothing," he bragged. "And she wants to own nothing."

"What if you leave her?" I asked, argumentatively. I was more willing to get into a one-on-one discussion than take on a roomful of people.

"I'll make her what I think is a reasonable offer and she'll take it," he said. "I know what she needs to live on. Nothing more. She never worked. I've supported the family all these years."

Same old argument. I'd heard that one before.

"Yes," I agreed with him, "and she also made it easy for you to be a success. You had nothing to do but get up, go to the office, and come home. She did the cooking, the shopping, the arranging. She raised your children, entertained your business associates, traveled with you, and supported you. She was your emotional partner. Isn't that worth something?"

"Not in the open marketplace," he said.

He was so proud of himself, strutting and carrying on like a peacock.

The woman had signed away all of her rights to what, under the divorce laws, could be deemed marital property. And, if he died, she could be without any rights to these assets if he willed the property to someone else. Was she aware of her actions and what they meant? Her name was not on any bank or brokerage account other than a low-balance joint checking account. Even her husband's mail went to a post office box to which she had no access.

I was astounded that this well-educated, sophisticated woman could allow herself to be placed in a position of *total* financial dependency. She could bleat that her marriage was one of trust and equality, but if that were so, why all the financial secrecy? If her spouse walked out the door she would have an impossible time following his financial trail. More importantly, I wondered what she would live on if her husband did to her what mine had done to me.

Yet I was the one at center stage during the course of the dinner, castigated over my intransigence, my motives and actions questioned by almost total strangers. It occurred to me then that maybe these women were so silent and so nonsupportive because they saw only too well what might happen to them. Don't make waves, don't question. Accept the status quo. Maybe it will go away. Stick your head in the sand and everything will be all right.

Not for me, thanks. My dinner partners were not going to change my course of action. I felt sorry for myself, but sorrier yet for those ostrich wives. For years I too had lived in a never-never land. And when reality hit, I was totally unprepared. No more.

I could hardly wait for the earliest appropriate moment to thank my hostess and (reluctantly) my host and beat a hasty retreat. I excused myself, saying I was working the early shift at Arturo's and had to be at the restaurant the next morning. I knew they'd never know the difference. Arturo's opened at noon.

For days afterward I didn't move from my house other than to work my shift at Arturo's and take Nathaniel to and from the school bus. My host's words had merely stung at the time, but later on I felt as though I had been knifed. And I was still bleeding.

By now I was pretty much up against a stone wall as far as people were concerned. My day-to-day interactions had been reduced to a minimum because of my nights at Arturo's. Working the night shift was my way of avoiding a world I couldn't deal with. I slept during the day and retreated into my cocoon in front of the restaurant range at night. I concentrated on the physicality of my job because I was totally incapable of concentrating on anything else. My major source of social stimulation was talking with the sales staff at the Video Palace about which movies to rent. I must have seen hundreds in those months. For $2.50 I could get three films on a two-day special.

I watched movies on weekends to fill in my evenings and also when I came home from my night shift at two A.M., so keyed up from the evening's activities that I couldn't unwind. I watched them in the mornings when I arose. I saw everything. Clint Eastwood. Truffaut. Mel Gibson. Marvelous Mel Gibson. I had my own Mel Gibson retrospective. *Mad Max. The Road Warrior. Tim. Gallipoli. The Bounty.* Then there were rock videos, MGM musicals, science-fiction epics. I watched them all.

When I wasn't watching movies, I was sleeping, curled up in my son's bed among his stuffed animals, safely hidden from the world in a warm and comforting nest. I had stopped sleeping in my own bedroom shortly after Curtis's departure, taking up residence in the guest room, next to Nathaniel's, so I could hear him when he called out in the middle of the night, bound quickly out of the spare bed, and soothe his nightmares. My son's room, however, had become my daytime anchor.

It was here that my tears would flow freely where no one else could see me and where I could allow the hurt, the anger, and the pain of my inner core loose. This was private time for me. I tried hard to project an image of strength to the outside world, of "coping" with an unsettling, troublesome, unpleasant condition, but in my son's bed, holding onto his panda for protection, I could cry bitterly at what my life had become. A statistic, another divorced housewife, with no career, no money, no relationship, and half a child.

I was pulled in so many directions at once, I felt as though I had lost my ability to cope rationally with anything. I was coasting along, responding to the words and actions of others—principally Curtis's. I had no control over these; in my legal battle I responded defensively, in my emotional battle, not at all. It was easier, frankly, to accept the status quo and not to cope at all. If I "coped" I would have to begin making some decisions about my future, and I was not ready to do that. I was frightened and afraid, so I did nothing but withdraw further into my head. Just as my body could do nothing more than prepare meals for hungry diners, so too my mind was unable to connect with any plan of action for my future.

Phyllis, get it together, I kept telling myself. Maybe tomorrow, I thought. But with each ensuing week I felt myself sinking deeper and deeper into an emotional stupor from which I couldn't seem to escape.

During my bedtime hours, if I wasn't sleeping or watching movies, I lay in bed thinking. Heavy thinking time. I wasn't thinking about anything special, about my future or anything in particular, I just spent a lot of time contemplating everything and nothing. The overpopulation of squirrels in our yard. Whether or not to talk to Nathaniel's teacher about his negative attitude (again). Why I hadn't been able to see how unhappy and alone I had been during my marriage, and why I was so unable to break away from Curtis myself (again and again). Occasionally I would drift off into heavy thinking time when Nathaniel was around.

"Mom, Mom, can't you hear me?" he cried once, shaking me to see if I was all right. I had been concentrating so intently that I was not aware of his presence.

"I'm just doing some heavy thinking," I told him.

Later he would laugh at me if I lapsed into deep concentration. Heavy thinking time. No action, just a way of keeping everything on hold.

"You're into heavy thinking time, huh, Mom?" was his cue to break both of us up.

Or, "I'll see you later, Mom, I've got to do some heavy thinking."

He would inevitably trot off to the bathroom.

I thought about lots of things, none of them very productive. A recurring preoccupation was about how people treat you as a divorced woman—mostly like a leper. The friends who don't call because you're no longer a couple. The ease with which most people assume you can slip back into a normal life—they'd rather not assume otherwise. The lack of offers of help—real help.

There were many who extended the vague and polite "if you need . . ." offers of help, but in a time of emotional depletion and financial panic, those offers hurt more than they helped. "If you need to borrow money, let me know . . ." was one I heard a lot. I could never bring myself to ask.

The one time I *did* ask, I was rejected.

"I'm in a cash flow bind," I was told. That was enough for me.

Most people, I rationalized, made the offer, never expecting it to be accepted.

Only once did one person hand me $500 and say "Pay me back when you have it." It was Stan, the other spouse. I paid him back within weeks.

"If you needed money, why didn't you ask?" a distant acquaintance said to me shortly after I began my night work.

"Why didn't you offer?" I snapped.

I couldn't understand whether money made people crazy or whether they thought I was lying about not having any. I was not talking luxuries, I was talking basic essentials like toilet paper, dog food, and coffee filters.

My neighbor Meredith and her family were wonderful, for weeks on end calling at the last minute to invite Natty and me for dinner. I realized much later on that on these occasions she had had us plugged in to their plans all along, but didn't want me to think she was making assumptions about my activities, or lack of them. Her generosity was such that I never felt obligated or patronized.

Occasionally a female friend called wanting to go out. Usually I declined, partly because I did not feel up to it, but more often because I had no money to split the tab. They could not understand why I could not put aside an "extra $10" for an evening out. I didn't have the "extra $10."

At the same time, the neighborhood "ladies" never tired of passing the news that they had seen Jackie and Curtis at this restaurant, at this theater, at a friend's home—and how happy they looked! Technically I couldn't even accept a date if a man wanted to take me out. Since I was still legally married to Curtis, Connecticut's divorce laws specifically stated I could be denied alimony on grounds of "marital misconduct." These grounds, however, did not apply to the husband, only the wife.

How I resented Curtis's and Jackie's freedom to do the things I had done so freely once before and was unable to do now because of my severe financial crunch! I decided I was a failure in every part of my life. I hadn't "made it" in any kind of career, and I sure hadn't made it as a "wife." Instead, I had been rejected for someone prettier and softer and nicer.

I was in limbo and I hated myself for being there. I wanted so much to break out of the deep rut in which I had buried myself. I'm not ready, I kept telling myself. When would I be? I asked. I delayed thinking about my future. There wasn't much I could do about it at this point anyway. Besides, it was so much easier to sleep away my days and work away my nights. I told myself I needed time to heal, but time was running out for me. One day it occurred to me that if I didn't get out of my bed soon, I would probably go under completely. I "heavy thought" about that for a very long time.

The next day I took the first step toward climbing out of my emotional ravine by registering with a placement service run by a professional writer's organization to which I belonged. It was a passive membership. I had not written a word in more than a year. But I received a referral almost immediately. An accounting firm in Hartford needed a ghostwriter to help an executive with a piece on mergers and acquisitions. Would I like the job? The fee was negotiable.

I knew absolutely nothing about accounting, and even less about mergers and acquisitions. The placement service had categorized me as a business writer because of past articles I had written about the workplace for several women's magazines. I was also the only Connecticut-based business writer on their roster. I accepted the assignment anyway. Christmas was only two weeks away and I had no money to buy presents for Nathaniel.

I didn't even know what women wore in the business world. It had been eight years since I had had any contact with a corporation. I decided on a black gabardine suit, somewhat out of style, but serviceable. I looked horrible. Pasty white face, shoes in need of new heels, ratty hair, no makeup, and an hour's drive to boot. Some reintroduction into the workplace.

I met with two cordial female executives. If they had any reservations about my outfit, they kept them to themselves. They explained the assignment and we calmly negotiated the fee: $20 an hour. I worked forty hours researching and backgrounding myself so that I could write a decent piece which should have been completed in ten hours. I billed them for ten hours. They were pleased with the result. If I would check in with them in another month, they might have another assignment by then. I called Meredith to celebrate.

"Let me buy you lunch. I can afford hamburgers," I told my friend. "I'll come by and pick you up."

"Great, I need a break," she responded.

We were parking the car outside the local hamburger joint when Jackie drove past us. She was driving her black BMW, her blond hair flying around her against the open car windows. I couldn't see what she was wearing, but I knew it was an "outfit" rather than a pair of jeans and a sweater.

I continued to stare out the window past Meredith long after Jackie had driven from sight.

"You can't be something you're not," Meredith said, looking straight into my eyes.

I knew what she was telling me. There was nothing I could have done to save the marriage. God knows I had tried hard enough—but in my fashion. And it certainly hadn't meshed well with Curtis's fashion. That was the rub. Meredith was right. Neither of us could be something we weren't. Curtis had pretty much remained himself. I had tried to be someone else. It hadn't worked, but I hadn't wanted to see it. Curtis had. I tuned back in to my friend.

"I think people should be able to appreciate the differences, the individuality of the two people in a marriage," Meredith said as she opened the car door, and then continued her words as we crossed the street to the restaurant. "That's what keeps a relationship dynamic. It's the ability of two people to change and complement each other's change that makes a marriage work. The hard part is that you never know before you get into it whether it will or won't work."

We were seated, we ordered, and were served. I felt good being able to take my friend out to lunch.

Her words made sense. Marriage *was* the process of accommodation. Neither Curtis nor I had accommodated the other and the marriage had fallen apart.

"You changed the game plan, Phyllis," Meredith continued as the waiter placed our coffee cups before us. "Most marriages have an unstated bargain, an unconscious set of rules or expectations. I think you and Curtis operated under different philosophies. You had different expectations of what you wanted from a marriage. Intellectually, you were very different."

I stared at her. How could she know all these things? We had barely been in her company at all over our years together as neighbors. It must have been obvious to everyone. Everyone but me. The wife is always the last to know.

"What do you think really makes a marriage work?" I asked.

"Growth, survival, the ability to change," she said, running her finger over the rim of her cup. "You have to like each other, respect each other, but you can't build yourself around someone else's expectations."

Her words sank into me. Deep. I remembered hearing a woman in a supermarket talking about her ex-husband.

"He thought I was overweight," she said, "so I went to aerobics for weeks. My body was so tight. Then what happens? He runs off with a dumpy blonde."

I empathized with her. Her firm body could not keep her marriage together. All my cooking and entertaining on behalf of my marriage didn't work either. Obviously we lacked the real glue, the right stuff. We lacked intimacy and understanding. At this point it was all too clear to me that I had never known what intimacy meant. Not sexual intimacy, but emotional intimacy, the kind of relating to another person that gets you inside his head and under his skin, the kind of feeling and understanding that comes from sharing a life together, not just existing as two separate parallel parts. I had never been able to develop that kind of closeness in our relationship. Maybe I never would in any relationship . . .

I'll have to give this some heavy thought, I told myself, suddenly feeling close to tears.

The opportunity came up sooner than I anticipated. Christmas Eve surfaced with Nathaniel at his father's. I was alone. My parents were away for the holidays. Not one person called. No gifts. No goodwill. No spirit. No company. Nathaniel would return tomorrow and we would open the few presents I had for him then, but for this evening I was alone. The weather sank to five below, with my hilltop blanketed with snow. Some time during the night the pipes froze, leaving me with no water or toilet facilities for the weekend. The heater refused to kick over. I retreated to my son's bed and, feeling like a character in a Charles Dickens novel, slept away the holiday. Tomorrow, tomorrow I would confront reality. Maybe this was what reality had become for me.

I had spent more than a year focused on changing my life and Nathaniel's life as little as possible. Now I knew that would be impossible. Curtis had created a mythical image of his future and was actively pursuing it. I had created a mythical image of mine, but it had more to do with living in the past than in the present, let alone planning for the future. Our marriage *was* over and while my future was uncertain, I knew that some changes would have to be made.

Meredith's words were solid. She was right. Her advice was finally sinking in. I couldn't be something I wasn't. I had to learn how to reach out to others, to have real as opposed to phantom relationships—in love and in friendship—and I had to start exploring a career and a lifestyle that made sense for *me*.

What *was* certain was that joint custody was not going to prevent our divorce from changing Natty's life, just like my misplaced pride was not going to prevent the divorce from changing *my* life. I was completely on my own. Maybe I would marry again. Maybe not. But I had to take steps to begin providing for myself. No one was ever going to "take care" of me again. It was time that I started taking care of myself.

# CHAPTER 9

# BREAKING OUT: A LURCH OR TWO IN THE RIGHT DIRECTION

I didn't know where to start. Work, friendships, my house, the community. Nothing was right. I was living in the wrong place doing the wrong thing with the wrong people. It wasn't them. It was me. I was out of synch in this lovely country atmosphere. During all my married years I had tried to fit in, but ultimately I couldn't. The limbo years. I lived a "balanced" but passionless life. Bland jobs, bland marriage, bland feelings.

My marriage was bust, but I couldn't move off dead center in divorce. I knew how to "cope," to put on a strong face, but I didn't know how to do anything else. I didn't even know how to talk with people, men and women alike. I was isolated from the world at large, professionally obsolete, and totally absorbed in my day-to-day survival. It was time to get out and to change, but I didn't know how.

A partial answer came from my lifeline, the telephone.

"Phyllis! I'm having some friends for dinner. Come on over," said the caller. "You've got to start getting out."

I didn't recognize the voice, but I knew it didn't belong to a regular caller. As I listened to the directions to a "bar-be-cue," I remembered that a friend of my aunt's had purchased a summer place nearby. It was Ellen, on her first country escape weekend.

"How are you doing?" she asked sympathetically. "Estelle tells me you've been having a rough time."

Estelle was my aunt. She knew everything and usually *told* everything. I adored her. I'm sure she suggested Ellen call me, to try and cheer me up. That was more than okay by me. I liked Ellen and I appreciated the offer. It felt fine to have someone being nice to me.

I said I would come, and hung up. I had never been particularly fond of "nights out" with the "girls," but Ellen was a vivacious, personable woman I had liked immediately from our first introduction many years back. She too was in the throes of a divorce. A soulmate. But with a difference: as an executive of one of the nation's largest advertising agencies, her professional and social contacts were many and varied. Her friends would probably be an interesting group. It might be a start at moving into a more "normal" existence.

I arrived at around six to find Ellen and a decorator friend picking colors for her dining room walls, two women weeding in the garden, and another spearing chicken and vegetables on skewers for kabobs to grill outside.

The chicken skewerer was a commercial real estate agent, the garden weeders were a photographer's representative and a lingerie designer.

A sudden thunderstorm focused our attention on the outside. A door blew open and two more women whooshed into the kitchen. Samantha and Jane, a teacher and a financial analyst. They had just returned from a shopping trip where they had acquired beach chairs and a rubber raft for the empty pool—a house gift for Ellen.

"Hi," they said together. "You must be Phyllis."

I wondered whether Ellen had briefed the group on my status and condition. I was still uncomfortable about being semi-single and still a little embarrassed about how

I had been cast aside. I wondered if they knew. I doubted if they cared.

Squooshed into the tiny kitchen, and with little room to manuever and limited counter space upon which to prepare the food, I found myself jostled repeatedly between the bodies which remained in perpetual motion. I retreated up the stairs to an alcove at the far end of the kitchen and plunked myself down on the landing. From my perch I could watch everything, but stay removed from the tumult.

We were all within a few years of each other, but there was an ease about each of them that made us seem years apart. I felt old, worn, run-down. They were relaxed, confident; I was awkward, gawky. They even looked different. I was wearing jeans and a polo shirt. They were wearing everything from bathing suits and boots to tube tops and shorts. One had a shoestring tied around her neck as a necklace. I felt improperly dressed and improbably out of place—I wished I had never come.

I scoped out the scene, trying to find something to help out with or some shred of conversation I could relate to. Give it a chance, Phyllis, I kept telling myself. You're new at this and they seem nice.

When I volunteered to set the table, they seemed delighted to have me join in and help out. The chicken was served, accompanied by sautéed zuchini and a fresh green salad. Everything tasted wonderful. Or maybe it tasted wonderful because someone else had done the cooking. This was my night off and it felt grand not to be in front of a hot oven.

As we savored our meal and sipped our wine, I began to feel the alcohol untie our tongues and spirits. I felt myself loosen up. One of the women passed around a joint. Grass! I hadn't touched the stuff since the 1960s. When my turn came I debated whether or not to indulge—for about three seconds. Then I inhaled, choked, and took another drag. The smoke brought back sharp memories of my years as a single woman working a beat for a political magazine in Washington. My job had been exciting, my friends spirited. Hardly a week went by without a common dinner sparked by a jug of the grape and lively conversations. We solved (over and over) the problems of the Vietnam war, racial crises, and women's issues. At Ellen's house we dispensed with the world's social problems and, over dinner, dug into our own.

*Men.* The subject everyone wanted to talk about. How to meet them. What they wanted. What *we* wanted. Relationships.

As Ellen poured coffee we talked about the difficulties of meeting men and establishing any sort of friendship, committed or otherwise. Girl talk. Gossip. I hadn't had a session like this in years. Two of us were separated, two were divorced, two had never married. We represented a large city, the suburbs, and a small town, but we were bound by a commonality of experience.

"Men have never ever had it so good," said Pat. "Anything goes. They can just walk out the door, set up housekeeping with someone, and if that doesn't work there is another body, usually someone younger and more nubile, waiting in line."

Her words were not said with any bitterness. She was merely stating a fact.

Look at me, I thought. I was a living, breathing example. It was one thing for a relationship to turn sour or dissolve, another for formerly unacceptable behavior to have become acceptable. Men treated women badly because they could get away with it and they could get away with it because women made too many excuses rather than call men on the carpet for ill treatment. Maybe that was why the divorce rate was so high. Fifty percent! I had heard so many women, single and married and in every walk of life, excuse bad behavior with an "It doesn't mean anything . . ." "He didn't call because . . ." or "He doesn't know what he's doing." I'd done it myself. But, damn, it *did* mean something!

"You think the women's movement changed anything?" I heard Barbara ask.

"No way. It was all rhetoric. Men are still the dominant sex. How many women do you know who have been treated really well by the men in their lives? What happened to good old-fashioned courtship? A guy doesn't have to do anything. Women are so desperate. They feed these guys, sleep with them, wash their clothes, and comfort them. And what do they get in return? Vaginal infections, that's what!"

"It's like a business deal," I chimed in with my newly acquired awareness of negotiation tactics. "Women don't really know how to deal in business. Men go for the advantage. And when they can get it, they take it."

"Women don't know how to play that game," agreed Pat. "Our involvement is totally emotional. If a man is, say, trying to make a sale, he'll go after three customers rather than one. That way if one doesn't come through, he's still got the possibility of two others. Same thing with dating. On the other hand, we expect a man to devote his sole attention to us."

She was right. What woman didn't want to be the center of a man's attention and affections? I certainly did—some day.

I suddenly understood the behavior of a man I had recently been fixed up with. He seemed to like me and we had gone out a few times. Then he started calling every so often to "touch base," as he called it, but not to ask me out.

At the time I didn't understand the telephone business, I was so out of synch with today's dating manners and mores. He would call to talk, touch base, and that was it. After I had wandered around the house sputtering after receiving one of these "touching-base" calls, Nathaniel had a comment.

"It means he likes you enough to talk to you, but not enough to take you out, Mom." Even as a little boy, he knew the signals. I had to be educated in order to decipher the code.

"Actually, the touching-base routine is a pretty good sign," said Pat. "That's a sales tactic too. You know, you call a client to say hello, keep in touch, see what's going on. Maybe nothing happens, but maybe it will."

The old business-deal routine again, I thought.

"You can't take anything a man does personally," said Jane, the financial analyst. "You can't categorize things in black and white anymore. If a guy is interested enough to call you to talk, talk with him. Establish a telephone relationship. He's stringing you along, you string him along. Maybe he's got a friend, maybe you'll need an escort one day. Maybe you need an extra male at a dinner party. It's a fallback. You want to keep the contact so you have a stable of male friends."

I still hadn't learned how to develop male friendships. Nonsexual friends. Most of these women had a stablefull. I'd have to work on it. I did have one—Stan.

"One thing I've learned since I've been single," added Barbara, the teacher. "To men, women are interchangeable. Unless they are crazy hot for you, as often as not they just want somebody to be with rather than wanting to be with some*one*. *That's* where women are different from men."

"You're right," said Pat, "but I think that's because men in general are more multidimensional than we are. They spread themselves among work, family, wives, loves. And *that's* why *we* fall apart when a relationship ends and *they* don't."

I was a case study of the satellite wife. In spite of my attempts at a career, I had invested so much time and energy in satisfying Curtis's needs and desires, that virtually every decision I had made revolved around him. He had his work, his family, his house. I had *his* work, *his* entertaining, *his* house, and very little of anything of my own. And that was why, I suddenly realized, when our marriage broke up, he could pick up and go on with his life—because his life was already in place. Mine was splintered into tiny fragments and I had to first patch up the pieces before I could start over again.

"So Phyllis," Barbara said. "How does it feel being an almost divorced woman after being married all those years?"

"I don't know," I said. "Sometimes I don't mind. Other times I do!"

"Divorced women get a bad rap," injected Ellen. "Everybody thinks we're out to cut out the husband's heart and liver. Nobody sympathizes with the woman. She's the one everyone calls a bitch."

"Have you experienced the 'drop your divorced women' friends game yet, Phyllis?" asked Samantha.

I thought a moment, trying to figure out what she meant. Then it clicked. There were few couples who wanted a single or separated woman around. We were dangerous. The wives all thought we were going to steal their husbands. The husbands were uncomfortable around us. I had been encouraged not to attend social events without an escort. That's when I had stopped trying to re-enter my former social circle as a single.

Ellen had been strangely quiet during this exchange. Now she spoke.

"Listen, you guys, there are no hard-and-fast rules in the war between men and women. It's the times. It's them. It's us. And with divorce, it's the laws, too."

I knew what Ellen was saying. The new divorce laws had given men the go-ahead to trash women. They could leave their wives high and dry. Walk away from supporting their children. Refuse any financial responsibilities toward their families. And many women, rather than fight for their rights or proper financial allocation, accepted this victimization because they didn't want to make waves—or because they wanted it "over with." The very laws so many women had fought for under equal rights legislation were now causing women to be treated inequitably.

"What do you mean?" asked Barbara.

"Let me give you an example," said Ellen. "My husband moves out of the house and into a place with a girlfriend. That's bad enough. A few months later I'm talking on the phone at eleven o'clock at night and I hear a key in the door. Sure enough, it's him."

All eyes and ears are on Ellen.

"I ask him what he's doing and he tells me this is his house, this is where he lives. I get upset and angry because we've already filed for divorce, then I calm down because I think maybe he's just trying to harass me a little."

I smiled at her. Curtis had threatened to do the same thing with me.

"The next day I call my lawyer and she tells me that he's within his rights and that because we both own the house, he has complete access to it, and there is *Not one damn thing I can do about it!*"

"To make matters worse," she continued, her voice pitched about three octaves higher, "I go away for the weekend and find out that he's not only been in the house, but he's slept with his girlfriend in my bed and taken a bath with her in my bathtub. My bathtub, can you believe that?"

"It's the equitable distribution provision of the divorce laws," I said quietly. "When both names are on the deed to the house, you both have access to it no matter who's living there and who's not."

"How was it before?" Susan asked.

"Before, if a woman's name was not on the deed, she had no claim to the house. She got zip." I told her.

"Progress," said Barbara.

I knew exactly how Ellen felt. There was never a complete assurance of privacy, no guarantee against intrusion, and certainly no way of preventing any husband from showing up one day and removing every piece of furniture, every personal belonging. It wasn't a question of having an ex-spouse possibly intrude upon a sexual encounter; it was, rather, the constant feeling of being on tenterhooks, never knowing that your physical integrity was secure. I knew of women who had returned home from work and had found their homes stripped.

"How did you know about the bathtub?" I asked curiously.

"I found a note from his girlfriend during one of my garbage runs," she said, as though it were the most natural event in the world. "Once he moved back in, I started going through the garbage to see if I could generate any evidence. I went through his papers, too. That's how I found out about some property I never knew he had."

I had tried that, too, but Curtis had been too clever for me. Our files were cleared out way before I even thought to search them. Checkbooks, too. I found nothing.

"Did he ever do the midnight negotiating routine with you?" asked Samantha. "You know, that's when they call late at night and try to talk to you about knocking down a settlement. It's very disorienting. That's why it's done—to try and get you to agree when you're not really thinking right."

"Yeah, I went through that," said Ellen.

I was mesmerized. Curtis always called late and wanted to talk about settlements. I was usually too tired to talk about anything.

"It's mind games," Samantha continued. "They try and get you all riled up and emotional so you don't think straight. That way you'll agree to what they want. Took me a while before I figured that one out."

"Enough." It was Pat standing before us with a pot of coffee in one hand and the game of Trivial Pursuit in the other. "Enough of men and divorce and phone calls and baths. Anyone want to play?"

"Yes!" we all agreed. I would have agreed to anything at that point. I was enjoying the evening. They really were a nice bunch of women. They weren't particularly satisfied with their loves, but they seemed satisfied with themselves. They seemed to be doing all right. I wanted to be like them.

Another glass of wine. Another joint. A little coffee and we were ready for Trivial Pursuit. As we began to roll the dice I asked a question I had wanted an answer to all evening.

"How do you meet men?" I asked. They laughed. The cosmic question.

"Direct access," Pat replied. "Work, business, outside interests, friends. Forget the health-club stuff. You want day-to-day contact. Get yourself into something where you meet people informally. There's less stress. There are dry spells, but it works, it really does."

"How do *you* meet men out here, Phyllis?"

Now *I* was under fire.

"Mostly through friends," I replied. In the flush of wine and marijuana I found myself recounting my first few social experiences. Even though Spenser had warned me that I could lose a potential support award if Curtis could prove "marital misconduct," I had decided to accept occasional dates. I limited where I went, however, to public places like restaurants, movies, or friend's homes.

As I thought back over the five or six men I had dated during my first year of being single, I was somewhat shocked at my remarkable lack of judgment. What I thought had been interesting then was terribly embarrassing to me now. What an odd lot they had been. A minister. A jock. An apple grower. I had had *nothing* in common with any of them. Friends had fixed me up "to have someone to go out with." After a while I decided I preferred my own company and stayed home. But in the early months of separation, anything male that professed interest in me looked good. This, my friends informed me, was typical of women going through a divorce. "The Year of Bad Judgment," Ellen intoned mock-solemnly.

I thought about the curious mix of men in my life and started giggling. They started giggling too. Maybe it was the wine, the grass, or the good feelings, but I couldn't stop giggling as my mind raced again through the list of men I had gone out with during my first year of being single. How could I have gone out with these men? And how could they have gone out with *me*? I thought again.

Argh! A shiver ran along my spine. Too bad there wasn't a course training you to be single.

"What did you see in the jock?" asked Ellen. I knew she was baiting me but I went along with her. She knew my athletic interests were limited to walking up a flight of stairs.

"I didn't have to share the Sunday papers with him," I deadpanned. "He took the sports section and gave me everything else."

My new friends laughed warmly at my comeback.

I thought this might be the time to ask these veterans of the shifting social scene for some practical advice. I felt comfortable with them, so I didn't feel embarrassed at asking these, to me, very basic questions.

"How do you get a guy to leave?" I asked them.

"Drive your own car," said Barbara. "Especially on the first date. That way if he turns out to be a dud you can always leave. If you let him come to pick you up, you are asking for trouble. Tell him you'll meet him. It strokes his ego that you don't expect him to pick you up. And it's safer too. You don't want a guy in your home if you don't know much about him."

That made sense. I resolved to drive my own car the next time I had a date. At this point it seemed like an occasion that might never materialize.

"Another thing," Barbara was continuing. "When he puts the make on you at the end of the evening, tell him you can't because you have to go home and walk the dog."

That sounded good too.

"What happens if you don't have a dog?" asked Ellen.

"If you've driven your own car and you just want to get away from him, why does he have to know if you have a dog or not?" explained Barbara. "It's your getaway."

I filed that one too. I had a dog.

"Tell me something," I asked of the group. "What do you expect from a man?"

We were getting looser and looser. I felt I could say anything now.

"Oh, flowers, dinner, a nightcap," said Samantha with a toss of her head.

"I just expect him to show up," said Barbara.

Pause, then the punch line.

"Of course, I'm usually disappointed," she added.

I could barely catch my breath. The one-liners were coming so fast. Men, I thought. They should only know the way that women talk about them.

"I don't expect anything," said Jane. "In fact, my social life has been so bad lately that the only telephone call I've had in three days was from a breather."

"Well, your social life is looking up," I commented drolly.

They laughed uproariously, clapped, and raised their glasses toward me. I had been admitted to the club.

We polished off another round of wine. Another joint. I heard my name and looked across the table.

"Phyllis, here's a trivia question for you," said the woman opposite me as she held up a card.

My turn already? I had just named the capital of Ghana.

"What are three two-letter words for small?"

I thought for a while. That question had never come up during previous Trivial Pursuit games. I was stuck.

"I give up—what are three two-letter words for small?"

I waited for a reply. My new friends looked at each other and waited. Then came the answer.

"Is it in?"

My tablemates collapsed into laughter. They were beside themselves. They had obviously pulled that one on others. I grinned stupidly. We had disintegrated into a college-dormitory all-nighter. The easy banter and camaraderie made me feel bonded to these women. I had a new appreciation of why men enjoyed spending an evening with their friends at a poker game or a sports event. If only more women could understand the need for cordiality rather than competition with each other, I thought. It was fun being with my new buddies.

It was almost morning before the party broke up. I was

wide awake. I felt like I had shed a skin, like a snake
slithering out of its protective covering as a new one emerged
to take its place. I was ready for a change.

"Thank you," I said, as I was leaving, "thank you all."

Ellen drew me aside and gave me a big hug.

"Phyllis, she said kindly. "Do something about the way
you look. Men size you up real fast. Appearances are important. Good luck. Keep in touch with us."

My new friends were right. It *was* time I did something
with myself. My night out with "the girls" had made me
realize how out of style, disheveled, and scruffy I was. The
image staring back at me from my bathroom mirror showed
a haggard and unkempt woman.

A vivid reinforcement of my negative image also came
from the videotapes of my cable show, now in rehearsal.
My face was lined, exhausted, and drawn. My hair was
shapeless, brittle, and dull. The color had even faded from
a deep brunette to mousy brown. There was no chance of
my being perceived as anything other than a woman under
stress.

Two unexpected birthday checks, one from my parents, another from my mother's sister in California, started
the ball rolling.

"Spend the money on yourself," said the note accompanying my parent's gift.

"This is for *you!*" said my aunt's.

The birthday gifts, I decided, would go for a new hairstyle.

I walked gingerly into my former hair salon.

"Where on earth have you been?" cried my stylist. "I
thought you had moved. What have you done to your hair?
I've never seen it like this."

I briefly explained the events of the last year. I had
neglected my appearance so thoroughly that I had had no
idea how dowdy I looked. I was barely aware of any change.
Besides the erratic growth of my hair, months of bending

over the hot ovens at Arturo's had singed the edges, leaving them burnt and uneven. I looked and felt like a worn-out dishrag.

"You could probably use some color," said my stylist. It was more an order than a suggestion. "We need to put some life back into your hair. Let's talk to Walter."

"How much is this going to cost me?" I asked nervously. I had only the money from the checks plus a few extra dollars. I thought how lucky I was to have found a free parking space on the street rather than having to pay for a garage.

"Not much more than a cut," she assured me.

"If we do this," I said uncomfortably, "I don't think I'll have enough to tip you."

"It's okay—you need this more than I need the tip."

They were putting life into my hair, I was reinjecting life into me. How appropriate!

She moved me to Walter's corner and he took over.

"Let's take the color up a few shades," he suggested. "Your facial tones are too fair for you to be a brunette."

Me, light hair? I had always been a deep brunette, a natural brunette, or so I thought giddily. What the hell, I figured, let's do it!

Walter went to work, gently pulling strands of my hair through tiny holes in the plastic shower cap which covered my head. The formula went on, the cap came off and I waited for the revelation. Nothing showed on my wet hair. He ran his fingers through the wet strands.

"Looks pretty good," he said. "You have just become a blonde."

He placed a towel over my head and led me back to the stylist.

"Blond!" she gasped, as she removed the towel. "Blond! You've gone blond!"

I still couldn't see the color, but, as she cut and dried, the shading emerged. She stepped back, admiring her craftsmanship. I couldn't believe my reflection in the glass. I looked like a completely different person.

"Now you need new makeup to accent your new look," said Walter, appearing to study the final result.

I rarely wore makeup, partially because Curtis had preferred a more natural look and partially because I was too lazy to fuss with it. The attractiveness of my hair provided an incentive.

"Do it now," Walter called as I left the shop. "If you don't, you'll have time to think about it—and you won't do it. Get yourself a new face while your hair is fresh."

I did. I marched straight in to the closest department store, took a quick turn around the makeup counters, found one offering a special sale, zeroed in on a palette of colors that looked appealing, and let the saleswoman do her stuff.

She knew she had an easy mark, so I let her cover my face with her products, listened to her pitch, complimented her on her skill, and told her I would take one tube of lipstick.

"I do get the special promotional package too, don't I?" I smiled as innocently as I could.

She knew she'd been had, but she was a good sport, tossing eye shadow, blush, mascara, and a small container of foundation into the bag with my lipstick.

"Come back and see me when you need the works," she said. "That's when I'll really show you how to do your face."

I laughed, thanked her, and told her I would. Definitely.

From no face to a vibrant face. The change was dramatic.

The first response was the best.

"Mommy," said Nathaniel, when I picked him up from school, "you look so pretty."

"You look so good I didn't recognize you," I heard so often I began to wonder how bad I had looked before. The makeup stayed.

"It wasn't that you were unattractive," said a friend. "Your hair was always nicely styled, but the color was mousy. You never did anything to enhance what you had."

The feedback and encouragement were amazingly uplifting. I hadn't realized how far down my confidence had sunk. I was like a child, responding to any bit of praise and encouragement.

Why do people tell you things after the fact? Why hadn't anyone said anything to me during the months before when I *really* needed it? The positive reaction was all the incentive I needed. That, and a comment from my son, propelled me on to big change number two.

I had an early morning job interview in a nearby town; Nathaniel had school. To avoid a last-minute rush in the bathroom by both of us, I had risen early, dressed, and then gone to awaken him.

"C'mon, get up, sleepyhead," I said, bending over and kissing him gently on the forehead. "I have a job interview this morning and you have to go to school."

He looked sleepily up at me.

"Are you going to work dressed like that? It looks like something you slept in," he commented.

I was dressed in a plain beige woolen shirtdress. It used to be what I called classic. Even my son saw it—and worse, me—as frumpy. I was a country mouse, out of touch with what women were wearing these days. If my son saw me that way, I wondered how I would come across to a potential employer.

I dropped him off at the bus stop, went to my interview—for work as a community relations coordinator (another "Don't call us, we'll call you")—and decided the next thing to change would be my clothing.

That evening I ransacked my closets, which were an amalgam of dress-for-success bows, blazers, and country jeans. Every piece seemed ill-fitting and out-of-style. The colors were wrong, too. I had loaded my wardrobe with beiges, browns, and rusts. Against my blond hair and revamped facial tones, these colors appeared washed out and jaundiced.

New threads were in order, but my Arturo's paycheck would not support a Bloomingdale's shopping spree. I could barely pay for my new hairstyle. My luck held out. Arturo's owner was going on vacation and asked me to work his shift. It was a mixed blessing. I worked four double shifts, a total of 64 hours. My wages: $336.00, enough for some new clothing.

I hesitated. Money was so hard to come by. What if I had an emergency? What if Nathaniel needed something? I decided to allocate half for clothing. It didn't leave me much, but then I didn't need much, just a few things to wear on job interviews or social occasions (if I were lucky enough to be invited to one or two) until my divorce was over and I was back on my feet again.

Here fate, in the guise of Meredith and her sister, took me in hand and brought me to a women's discount clothing store. As I automatically pulled more of what I already had in my closet off the racks, they put my selections back and pieced together a softer, more feminine look. A purple sweater set, silk skirt, silk blouse, unlined jacket, all at end-of-season super sale prices. I spent $150 of my pay from my "doubles" (as the back-to-back shifts were known) and had a season's worth of clothing. The fabrics felt sensual against my skin, the investment made sense to my pocketbook. Where had I been all these years?

If I needed any further encouragement, it came from an unexpected source. I had been invited to speak about the trials and tribulations of being a writer before a group of women at the local library—the monthly brown bag literary lunch—and was sharing the program with a prominent woman author. I was amused and honored that we were on the same program. Although I had a book coming out soon, I hadn't published anything else in years. My colleague was the real thing, with more than twenty books to her credit, running the gamut from cookbooks and biographies to historical novels and juveniles.

She was a large woman, conveying a formidable presence, her gray hair pulled neatly into a bun at the base of her neck. I had looked forward to meeting her and trading shop talk.

We were introduced and she bent over as if to share a secret with me, slightly out of earshot of everyone else.

"That's a beautiful shade of lipstick you're wearing," she said. "Whose is it?"

I had to think a moment, so unprepared was I for her question.

"Lipstick?" I fumbled. "Oh, my lipstick. I'm not sure. I got it on one of those special deals. You know, you buy something for $7.50 and get $40 worth of makeup samples."

I found myself telling her the story of my makeup encounter, my hair, how I was in the middle of a divorce. She expressed concern and asked how I was doing. Then she continued her line of personal questioning.

"Where do you get your hair done? Where did you buy the blouse?" she asked.

I told her about my transformation and how the little things meant so much to my growing sense of self-confidence.

"Good!" she said, patting me on the back. "You're doing okay."

Her face changed slightly. It was maternal, concerned.

"What have you done about your underwear?" she asked.

"My underwear?" I thought of my lingerie drawer filled with basic white and beige. No lace.

"My dear, to catch a fish you need surface lures," she whispered confidentially, "but you also need to troll."

I stared at her in surprise. Her face was beaming; her eyes alive. There were hidden fires here. Obviously, she knew what she was talking about.

A few days later, I repeated this conversation to my friend Sandy. We had grown up together in the suburbs of Chicago. Now we lived over an hour away from each other, and only spoke by phone every few months, but the bonds of teenage friendship were still strong. When I confessed what my underwear wardrobe consisted of, she was aghast.

"*Quel* boring!" she exclaimed. "No wonder your marriage failed."

"Oh," I said. Those clothes were just so practical, I was thinking.

There was a discount designer lingerie outlet in her neighborhood, she said. If I could not find the time to outfit myself, she would go for me.

Sandy is a size 16; I am a 6. I ran for my car keys. I could not believe that I was getting into my car and driving over an hour to buy underwear. Even discount underwear.

The shop was located at the top of a flight of stairs over a set of run-down storefronts in a Connecticut beach town. We arrived just before closing on a warm May afternoon and were the only customers in the place.

"My friend's husband walked out on her, she's single again, and she needs some things," Sandy announced authoritatively to the saleslady, a dour woman who appeared to be in her mid-sixties. "See what you can do."

"What did you have in mind?" the woman asked calmly. She acted as if she had heard this pronouncement many times before.

"Something alluring," Sandy answered.

I looked around the room. There were racks of teddies, loungers, camisoles. I didn't know the difference between any of them.

Sandy and the saleswoman took over, pulling undergarments in various shades, styles, and sizes from the racks. Once they had an armful I was marched off to a fitting room.

The two of them sat in judgment while I tried on piece after piece. They eliminated anything white, anything that made me look too bony on top and too hippy below. At one point the saleswoman left, only to return a moment later with a cornflower-blue silk and lace teddy cut high on the thighs. I was stunned at my image in the mirror.

"Save that for a special occasion," said the saleswoman, a smile actually flickering in the dour face. "It's a knockout."

By the end of the session I had also acquired a peach silk appliquéed camisole and tap pants, a black silk and lace camisole, one chocolate Grecian-style teddy, and a peach at-home lounger. I had no idea when or where I would wear the goods.

"What about panties?" asked the saleswoman.

I agreed that a few more bikini panties couldn't hurt. We took two in purple, two in black, two in peach.

"Take a yellow," the saleswoman advised.

"Yellow panties?"

"They're supposed to be lucky."

When she totaled my bill, I learned that I had spent $161.78 on lingerie. I charged it to my Visa card, which had arrived in the mail that very day. I hadn't the vaguest idea how I was going to pay the bill.

"See, this is what friends are for," said Sandy.

The two of us spent the rest of the evening sharing a bottle of wine and, mindful of my purchases, to keep me slim and trim, a fish dinner at a nearby restaurant.

It had been a perfect day. I knew that a new hairdo and clothing and even new underwear would not change my life, but I was taking a lurch or two in the right direction. I giggled as I thought of the yellow panties. Well, maybe they *would* bring me luck. I would take all the help I could get. It was about time I started making some changes in the rest of my life.

# CHAPTER 10

# FINAL MANEUVERS

A new look and new friendships were not about to erase the frustration of a life still stuck in limbo. Curtis and I were no closer to any kind of a solution on custody or finances. Almost two years had passed. Our six-year-old son was now almost eight.

I still refused to believe Curtis when he said he had no "extra" money. He continued to take his Caribbean vacations and suggest that Nathaniel be removed from private school and relocated to the public school. At the same time, Jackie was conducting interviews to take her children out of the public school and put them into Nathaniel's private school. I was furious at this turn of events, because I assumed Curtis would be taking over *all* these financial responsibilities, when in the end it was Stan who provided for *his* children's schooling. Our lawyers continued to exchange correspondence. I continued to work at Arturo's. None of us made headway on anything. When would it all end? I wondered.

Suddenly, in the midst of this void, we received notice that Curtis was pressing for a full custody hearing.

"For what?" I demanded of my attorney. Curtis and I had both been told that the custody issue would not be settled in a courtroom. We had been advised to get some counseling. We had tried an experimental schedule of joint physical custody. Nothing had worked. Curtis wouldn't negotiate and wouldn't communicate. What did he think a court would do?

"What's going on here?" I asked again. "What does he want?"

Elizabeth ducked the question. "I don't know what's going on here, Phyllis, but I know I've got to buy us some time," she said. "We've got to keep this case out of the courtroom."

"What do you suggest?" I asked.

"I think you're going to have to counterclaim for sole custody," she said.

Earlier she had told me I couldn't win a battle for sole custody. Now she was telling me to go for it. I didn't want to fight. I'd had enough conflict, enough confrontation. I wanted to go home and crawl back under my covers. So much for my newfound confidence.

"It's a delaying tactic," Elizabeth said. "I'm hoping they'll bounce the case back into a conciliation conference and a full-blown custody study rather than schedule a full trial."

With two conflicting motions before the court, each side had an opportunity to present its case before a conciliator. Curtis had had his chance to press for joint physical custody. Now it was my turn to press for sole. It was a tactical move to avoid moving ahead with a full custody hearing. We took a chance and filed a new set of papers. Our gamble paid off. The trial was delayed and soon we were back before the court's custody conciliator.

"Weren't you here before?" he asked, looking from Elizabeth to me and from Virginia to Curtis.

"Yes," we all answered sheepishly.

Elizabeth and Virginia had had a go-round in the hallway and came close to a first draft on an agreement for custody. This time new terminology was used. Rather than the red-flagged "joint physical custody," both attorneys agreed to re-label the custody issue. It was now termed "shared custody," and had a somewhat different meaning. It was a point for our side, a concession for theirs. We were moving away from a straight fifty-fifty split of days and into an area that involved "decision making" regarding Nathaniel's life. I could live with that, but I wasn't going to agree to everything just then. Curtis wasn't either. Curtis objected to any clause using the word "primary" in it. Primary residence, primary custodial, primary anything raised a red flag. To him, primary meant "sole," "mother" and no father. He wasn't having any of it. My concern was about who had the final decision regarding the care and welfare of the child. Again. At that point the family relations officer arrived and we marched into his quarters.

Elizabeth had taken the precaution of having me retain an outside psychologist as my professional expert should I ever have to fight a real custody battle before a judge. She wanted an outsider prepared to testify as to my fitness and emotional stability. So I had spent a few sessions with Dr. William Samuels, formerly chief forensic psychologist at the county's largest hospital. Samuels was exceptionally well respected and a skilled courtroom witness. According to Samuels' tests and his opinion, I was emotionally fit. Not that I had had any doubts. However, the irony of still being covered under Curtis's medical insurance plan and having my custody defense paid for by Curtis's company was not lost on me.

"You're seeing Bill Samuels," asked the conciliator. Curtis and his lawyer looked surprised. "Are you going too, Mr. Ellsworth?"

"No, I'm not," said Curtis. "I'm seeing Lyndon Smythe."

It was our turn to be surprised. Smythe was head of one of the area's foremost university psychological study centers and a vocal proponent of joint custody. We had been lining up our troops while they had been lining up their troops.

"Nice," said the conciliator, testily. "His and her therapists.

"Whom does the child see?" he went on.

"Dr. Lilyan Dean," I said. "She was recommended by the school. She's been seeing him for over a year, but she won't testify because she feels she is Nathaniel's advocate and cannot align herself with either of us." I was beginning to be overwhelmed by a massive sense of the stupidity of it all.

"I want a temporary court order to guarantee access to my child," Curtis interrupted.

"Denied," said the court official. "I told you two to get some counseling and I meant it. The only person who is suffering here is Nathaniel. Now get some help. Both of you."

Case dismissed.

This time around I had been a bit more certain that a custody agreement would not be set down in a court order, but I hadn't been prepared for the conciliator's hostility. He was absolutely outraged that we could not resolve our differences—major to us but small potatoes to him.

As objectionable as I found Curtis's choice of psychologist, so he found mine. The only solution we could agree on was to set up a four-way session between the two of us and our respective psychologists. No attorneys allowed. As long as we had his and her therapists, might as well use them, I thought.

Both Samuels and Smythe would, if necessary, wage a courtroom battle for us, but neither was wildly enthusiastic over the prospect. Each had told us individually that Nathaniel had strong feelings toward *both* of us, that he was equally comfortable in each of our homes, and that each of us was a decent person and fit parent. The words "better" and "best interests" were banned from discussion.

I was disappointed that my own psychologist would not judge me to be a better parent than Curtis, but I was also secretly relieved that if we ever did go to a full hearing, a judge would be unlikely to find Curtis "better" either. What we had to do was hammer out a schedule and agreement that would work for both of us. Either that or go to court.

We met in Smythe's office. Our goal was to outline the parameters of a custody agreement by finding areas we could agree upon. As we worked our way toward the tougher issues, our differences would be aired before two trained professionals. Whether Curtis and I wanted it or not, we had become participants in an exercise in custody mediation.

I had huddled with Elizabeth the hour before the four of us met. She had cautioned me not to give away anything and to lean on Samuels for input. Nothing was sacred, and everything was subject to revision and review by the two attorneys.

"Curtis is hung up on lingo," she advised. "Give him the semantics. You go for the substance."

Elizabeth had insisted that I outline my priorities regarding "time spent with mother" before the session.

"What's your bottom line?" she asked.

"Bottom line?"

"Right," she said. "What's really important to you? You won't get everything. What do you really want?"

I thought a moment. I had no objection to equal time for vacations, holidays, and weekends. My major desire was that Nathaniel be based with me during the school year, that he leave for school from one home.

"I want Nathaniel with me during the school year," I said firmly. "It's the major influential portion of his life."

Elizabeth looked at me and nodded her head.

"Negotiate everything else around that item," she said. "It's a big ticket." With all this clear in my mind, I entered the lion's den.

Both psychologists agreed that my request was reasonable. They also said it would be best for Nathaniel's sense of security that he leave for school every day from one home. Had he been older, they said, this might not have been so important. Curtis nodded, then insisted that Nathaniel participate in activities, including sports, Cub Scouts, and religious training in the community in which we lived. I agreed, but also refused to be held to a chauffeuring schedule since I was uncertain of my work schedule. When Curtis objected, both psychologists, his and mine, said that if he felt strongly enough about Nathaniel's participation, then *he* should provide transportation. I wasn't objecting to my son's participation. I was objecting to being *the* only carpool parent.

We agreed to keep Nathaniel in his school, each of us contributing proportionally toward tuition costs. And we agreed to select a psychologist who would mediate any future custody disputes.

The sticking point came when Curtis insisted I agree to a full shared custody agreement in writing. I objected, saying that our discussion still had not covered what for me was the primary issue—who was in charge of day-to-day parenting issues.

The room tensed. Curtis was staring straight at me.

"You agreed to joint custody," he asserted. "Now you're backing out again."

"I agree in principle to shared legal custody." I said, "and I would be willing to sign an agreement that says 'I agree in principle.' I won't agree to anything else until I see how it really works.

He bought it. He got his semantics and I got my substance. The two words "in principle" undermined the validity of the entire document, just in case we ever had to go to court. Just in case.

"Hi, Mommy, it's me," said the voice on the phone.

Nathaniel's words were soft and teary. He had been with his father for the weekend. It was nine A.M. Sunday morning. I wondered what was up now.

I waited, hoping for a clue, wondering if he would open up without my having to dig.

He didn't waste any time.

"I have to stay here alone with a baby-sitter all day,

Mommy," he cried, breaking into tears. "Jackie and Daddy are going away all day. Why can't I come and stay with you?"

Natty was sobbing, uncomprehending. Jackie and Curtis had plans for the day and had made arrangements for a sitter to stay with Nat. This enraged me. Why did my son have to stay alone all day with a sitter when I was only two miles away? It didn't matter that I had occasionally left him with sitters. To me, this was different turf.

"Don't you want me to come home and be with you, Mommy?" he sobbed.

I chose my words carefully.

"Natty," I said slowly, "please try to stop crying and listen to me."

"I want to be with you, Mommy," he said. "Why do I have to be with a baby-sitter all day?"

"Nat, I would love to have you with me, honey," I told him, "but the rules say that you are with your dad this weekend."

I had explained to him many times before that there were different rules for different situations. He knew that Curtis's house was run differently than mine.

"I know that, Mommy," he said, "but why can't I come and stay with you? I could come back here when Jackie and Daddy come back tonight."

Children always have an alternate way of looking at a situation. Nathaniel's suggestion was a logical solution to a thorny issue. Still, I had given my word to Curtis, his attorney, and the custody mediator that I would not interfere any more with arrangements for Natty when he was in his father's care.

"Nathaniel, I would love to have you with me. I just don't think I can break the rules."

The custody mediator had been quite specific in my being held accountable for any potential interference with Curtis's plans. Nathaniel accepted the decision.

"Okay, Mommy," he said, dejected. "I love you."

"I love you too, Natty."

I gently hung up the telephone, went to the bathroom, and vomited.

I sat for a while, pulling myself together. Then I returned to the telephone and dialed Curtis's apartment. Jackie answered.

"I have just spoken with Nathaniel," I stated in a calm, neutral voice. "He is very upset. I am aware that I have agreed not to interfere with your arrangements, but I feel that as his mother I had to call."

Jackie said nothing. I continued.

"I do not feel that it is in his best interests to stay alone with a sitter when I am here and available. I would be more than happy to have Nat here with me during the day—you can consider *me* the sitter if you like—and he can return to stay the night with you."

She said nothing for a moment. After all, we were adversaries, not allies.

"Curtis is at the store," she responded finally. "I'll have to talk with him when he returns and get back to you."

We said nothing more. I hung up and waited.

Less than three minutes passed before the phone rang again.

"I've made the decision," I heard Jackie say. "There is no reason Nathaniel shouldn't be with you today. We'll pick him up when we return late this afternoon."

"Have you discussed this with Curtis?" I asked.

"No," she said. "I'll tell him when he returns. Natty is very upset and he's right—he should be with you."

A mother's instinct, I thought. I knew she would have felt precisely the same way if her two children had been in a similar situation. Maybe we weren't adversaries after all.

From the beginning, Jackie and I had skirted each other with excessive courtesy. We waved as our cars passed each other as we drove our respective children to soccer and school; we talked briefly at the supermarket. Once we had even arrived at a local restaurant at the same time. I was with Meredith; Jackie had arrived alone and was waiting for a friend to join her. Meredith and I were seated in the front of the restaurant; Jackie in the back.

"Who do you think she's meeting?" I whispered to Meredith as soon as we were seated. Meredith could see her; I could not.

"I don't know, but I think you should go talk to her," my friend said conspiratorially. "You never know when you'll need her to be the go-between between you and Curtis."

"I've kept the lines open with her," I assured my friend. "I don't want to use her help until I really need it."

Meredith agreed that was a good idea and we returned to our burgers and beers.

Now I was certain the ice was really broken. Curtis and I were at a standoff, so locked into our individual positions that we could not see the other side. Jackie was in the middle. She had a vested interest in resolving the conflict. They wanted to get married, get on with their lives. By placing Nathaniel's welfare ahead of the possibility of incurring Curtis's wrath, she proved to me that she could be an objective third party. The issue was not who was wrong and who was right, but how we could work out an agreeable arrangement. Maybe she would even be willing to come to our mediation sessions. Maybe she could kick some sense into Curtis, or at least sit on him.

The best way to keep a custody conflict out of court, according to Elizabeth Weber, was to encourage a relationship with the other parent. Who would have ever thought that the other parent's new love would become part of the communication process?

I shivered with excitement at the possibility of this logjam breaking up. But if Jackie's help meant that I could finally go on with my life, Curtis could go on with his, and she with hers too, whatever that was or would prove to be, I was all for it.

That Sunday Nathaniel spent an ordinary day with me

and was picked up by Jackie and Curtis shortly before dinnertime. I walked my son to the car, kissed him good-bye, opened the back door for him. As I slammed his door, I moved forward to the front seat. Jackie's window was open. I bent slightly, intending to suggest to both of them that a three-way mediation session might be useful for all of us. I glanced at Curtis. His expression was not encouraging to me. I altered my words in midsentence, directing them to Jackie only.

"I think it might be useful for us to get together and talk things out," I said, pausing. "Would you be amenable to a mediation conversation? We could perhaps talk in the presence of a third party, maybe Lyndon Smythe. Why don't you think it over and get back to me?"

With Curtis looking on and listening, she agreed to think it over. That evening I received a telephone call from her; on the surface, the subject matter was Nathaniel's upcoming schedule for the month.

"I think a mediation conversation would be helpful," she said at the end of the call. "Would you like to call Smythe or should I?"

"I will," I said. She had bought it. I was amazed, pleasantly amazed. I wanted to remain the initiator. "I'll get back to you as soon as I reach him."

I called Smythe first thing the next morning.

"You want to have a custody mediation session with Jackie?" he repeated. It was the first time he had received such a request. "Does Curtis know?"

Elizabeth and Spenser were equally amazed, but gave me few instructions other than to be aware of potential two-on-one influence. Smythe, after all, was "Curtis's psychologist." My antennae were finely tuned, sensitized to any undue father orientation.

The meeting took place within two days. Fearing a loss of momentum or, worse, a change of mind, I had insisted we get together as soon as possible. We met at 6:30 on a rainy humid Tuesday night. Jackie arrived first. As always, she looked cool: she was neatly attired in a white cotton shirt, black pants, and white clogs. How this woman always managed to look neat and collected under the most oppressive conditions escaped me.

I was a wreck: my hair drenched, my clothing soaked. When I entered the room my shoes squished with water. No wonder Curtis preferred her, I thought with a *slight* loss of confidence. In spite of my new look, I hadn't gotten it quite all together yet. Not like Jackie, anyway. I probably never would, I thought, with a sudden surge of self-confidence: I was, after all, a different kind of person. Jackie greeted me cordially, but not excessively so, and we took seats at opposite ends of the reception room.

Our psychologist mediator motioned for us to enter his inner office. Both Jackie and I had had previous sessions with Smythe, so his approach and demeanor were not unfamiliar. He sat behind his desk facing us, bouncing ever so slightly as he leaned forward and then backward in his chair. His hands were folded in his lap. He looked at us, smiled warmly, and made a brief introduction about how unusual a situation this was, but that he welcomed any alternatives toward resolving the conflict.

"Who wants to start?" he asked, tossing the initiative to us.

We looked at each other. Might as well jump in, I thought. I reviewed the events of the weekend and how we had arrived in his office. I started to have second thoughts midway through my explanation. Until then I had been pumped up with excitement over the possibility of a breakthrough. Suddenly it hit me. I was mediating my son's future with my husband's intended.

"What are we trying to accomplish here tonight?" Smythe asked.

His voice was soft, soothing and disarming. He was Curtis's representative, but I felt sympathy and objectivity toward me, too. He was clever, asking what we were trying to accomplish rather than asking for a delineation of our problems. He was encouraging solutions, not a continuation of our standoff. Well, I was here; she was here. Perhaps something *could* come out of this session.

Jackie offered her opinion first.

"Curtis is afraid that Phyllis will withhold Natty from him," she said. "Without an equal agreement for full joint physical custody, he is afraid that Phyllis will retain full control over Nat and he feels strongly about having input into Nathaniel's life."

"Do you think I have denied access?" I asked. I wanted her opinion out, on the line, in front of a third party.

"No!" she said, without even pausing to consider.

"Well, why do you think he feels that way?" I asked. I wanted to know the answer myself.

"Because of what happened in the beginning," she said. "When you wouldn't let Nat come over and be with us."

I saw red immediately. It was all I could do to keep my temper. Fortunately, Smythe stepped in, saying that he didn't think it was my intent to deny Curtis access to his child, and that perhaps a strict numerical division of time did not serve either of the parties well. I sat back, telling myself to cool down.

Smythe reminded us of the basic tenets of the shared-custody concept.

"What we're talking about is the balance of power," he said. "When the power balance is equalized, conflicts begin to resolve themselves because neither party is going to have the child to use over the other. When neither party has power, the only alternative is to cooperate with each other."

Smythe's words made a lot of sense. They made even more sense when I considered my relationship with Curtis, in my marriage and now. Maybe it had all been a power game. Just like in business.

"I feel strongly that Nathaniel should be with me during the school year," I said, restating the position I had always taken. "I will give in on vacations and holidays and be flexible other times, but I will not agree to him bouncing between us."

"Okay," was her answer.

They were giving in on a numerical split of days. We were making progress. Now it was her turn. She accused me of interfering with their arrangements and arbitrarily making plans for Nat without considering their schedule. Smythe suggested that a formal agreement would help structure Nat's times with each parent, thus eliminating some of these concerns.

"Curtis makes a big pretense out of Nathaniel being in his care," I said defensively, "but he's always dumping him off on someone else. Why shouldn't I interfere?"

"My position is that I have three children to make arrangements for," said Jackie. "You cannot arbitrarily accept invitations for Nathaniel to go to birthday parties or anything else when he is with us without even checking to see if we have anything scheduled."

I saw her point. She was right. Actually, she wasn't so bad. I knew she had taught Nathaniel how to ride his bike the preceding weekend. Both Curtis and I had failed miserably in the same task, each having tried repeatedly over the course of several years.

"You're right," I said. "I'll try and do better and check with you before I schedule anything. She just looked at me. I felt my face redden. "Or, maybe I shouldn't schedule anything when he's with you."

"Maybe you shouldn't," she said mildly.

I pressed the point about leaving Nathaniel with me instead of a sitter. For the time being, she agreed that it was probably better for Nat to stay with me—as long as he be allowed to return to them as scheduled for the evening or overnight just as he had on Sunday. I agreed.

The session was almost up. One final category remained. Activities. They wanted Natty to participate in local activities. Little League. Cub Scouts. Religious training. I didn't see what the problem was here. I had already agreed to participate. Her eyes widened in surprise. Maybe someone hadn't told someone else everything.

Smythe deftly guided us toward a conclusion, saying

that it appeared we seemed to be thinking pretty much along the same lines and he saw this as a mechanism for us to keep the channels of communication open. If we could continue to talk like this, perhaps we could have a good extended family relationship in the future.

By the end of the hour we agreed: the document that had been developed in conjunction with Smythe, William Samuels, and the two attorneys essentially represented the substance of a shared custody agreement that both of us could live with. I would *not* sign, however, until Curtis's good faith and intent were shown by his completing the negotiations for a full financial settlement.

"Mothers sometimes understand each other better," Smythe observed at the close of our session.

We both nodded in agreement.

"The main sticking point here appears to be the financial settlement," he summarized. "Jackie, is there anything you can do to move Curtis on resolving the standoff?"

I sat and waited for her reply.

"If Phyllis will get me a list of her demands, I'll take care of it," she stated.

I tried not to show my amazement. Jackie had agreed to mediate the custody issue. Now she was taking on the financial side as well. Did she have the authority to do this? Had she discussed this tactic with Curtis? Smythe was as surprised as I was.

"Are you sure you want to put yourself in the hot seat?" he asked incredulously.

She replied that if her participation would be useful, she would be willing to put herself on the line.

"Will Curtis go along with this?" was Smythe's next question.

"Yes." Her reply was firm, deliberate.

I said nothing. Obviously, she had a lot more influence with Curtis than I had *ever* had.

"Are you willing to negotiate with Jackie?" Smythe asked me.

"Yes."

"I guess the next step would be to set up another session," Smythe said. It was set for Thursday, two days hence.

Spenser was skeptically pleased when I gave him a rundown of our session the next morning, but refused to go along with providing them with a list of our demands.

"I'm supposed to come up with a list of our financial demands," I said. "What am I demanding?"

"You're not going to give them anything," he said. "Our position all along has been for them to make us a realistic offer and we would respond. You tell Jackie the same thing."

"I have to show up with *something* in writing," I protested, but Spenser was firm. His strategy from the beginning had been for *them* to make the offer and for us to respond. He didn't want them to know what our bottom line was, what our base point for the negotiations would be. That's why he insisted that *they* set the offer and *we* counter. No written anything from us.

I was saved the trouble of explaining why I didn't have anything in writing for our meeting because the meeting never came off. Thursday afternoon I received a telephone call from Jackie.

"Rawson and Curtis met last night," she explained, "and they are sending a letter to Spenser with a full offer for a complete settlement package. This negates our reason for meeting tonight, but perhaps we could use the letter as a basis for communication and talk after you have a chance to review it."

I thanked her, and told her that I would respond as soon as I reviewed the contents of the communication with my attorney. I was elated that I wouldn't have to lose face and ecstatic that we were *finally* receiving a decent, reasonable offer.

Spenser called me on Monday.

"Can you come over here and pick up a copy of their newest offer?"

The tone of his voice was more a command than a request.

When I arrived at his office, he was in court, but a package of papers was waiting for me. I pulled them apart, scanned the contents, and stood in his reception room, open-mouthed with dismay. This was no move toward a settlement. It was more like the initial salvo in a full-fledged war.

Totally dismayed, I went on to the specifics: a substantial reduction in every aspect of Curtis's initial financial offer. Every category offered less than his opening gambits of months ago: 40 percent of the house, no alimony, no medical coverage, and on and on.

The packet also contained a notice of a full custody hearing, to be held one week from that very day, along with a notice for a full-fault grounds divorce trial.

What was going on here? I had played right into their hands, both sets of them. The weeks of mediation sessions, the emotional compromise, had meant nothing. I really thought we had made progress, that my mediation session with Jackie was moving us closer to a conclusion. This letter told me flat out that I had been set up. I had really been played for a fool. Business deal, I muttered to myself. Why had I let myself forget?

With the custody hearing scheduled so soon, I didn't have adequate time to prepare my case. And a fault trial! I would have to defend myself against the silly accusations made in the cross complaint filed a year ago. Abandonment of my child. Unstable woman. I knew the accusations were false, but could a judge be convinced? I had been so certain that we were making a breakthrough in the logjam! Had I completely misjudged Jackie's intentions? Her willingness to serve as a go-between? Or had Curtis simply decided to play hardball?

My head started to spin, my ears began to ring. I was headed into a full-scale panic attack. Unfortunately for my deteriorating state of mind, both Spenser and Elizabeth Weber were unavailable for nearly twenty-four hours. I called both their offices repeatedly to see if they had returned from their respective court hearings and was told politely but firmly that my messages had been delivered. Finally, I received a conference call from both of them.

By then I was convinced Curtis would get Nathaniel and I'd be cut off without a dime, forced to spend my life working at Arturo's cooking steak sandwiches, making marinara sauce, and feeding Jesse and all his friends.

"Why haven't you returned my calls?" I blurted into the phone. "Have you seen this latest communiqué? What the hell is going on here?" I was frantic. Spenser and Elizabeth were calm.

I couldn't come out and confront them directly with ignoring me, but I was definitely accusing them of abandoning me in what I saw as a period of great personal need. By then I should have known better: lawyers give legal advice, not personal support.

"This guy is trying to bust your chops," Spenser said almost conversationally. "It's a last-ditch effort, a typical negotiating tactic where the opposition lowers the offer to make you think you are not going to come out with anything—and where they hope to frighten you into accepting anything. It's just a game." His tone told me I should have known that by now. Mentally I swore at myself. I had once again reacted emotionally. I should have known better. Business deal, I reminded myself. Nothing personal. Hah! It was as personal as anything got!

Spenser's logical explanation had cooled my anger. I waited for him to continue.

"I've contacted Rawson and suggested an all-day Saturday negotiating session," he said. "We have to try and come to terms. We cannot let this case go to court. If it does, you may lose on an arbitrary set of decisions about the issues in your case. Decisions about your child and your life will be made for you."

Elizabeth was on the speaker phone.

"We're also going to pressure Rawson and Curtis for a delay on the custody hearing," she chimed in. "We simply cannot allow them to hold that chip over our heads. I don't want you to go into a Saturday settlement with the loaded gun of a Monday hearing held to your temple. Besides, I have two other trials scheduled for Monday."

I knew what Elizabeth was telling me. If we didn't get a postponement, we would be under almost coercive pressure to settle the property issues Saturday to avoid a custody showdown on Monday. With two other cases scheduled for the same day, Elizabeth's ability to prepare fully for my custody trial was uncertain.

"Monday is not so good for me, either," I said.

"Why? Are you working?" she asked

"Not exactly. My cable project has a meeting in New York. We're trying to drum up some funding for programming." My colleagues from my League of Women Voters cable television show and I were going to talk to an executive at one of the national cable networks. I had been planning to let my co-workers go ahead without me.

"Do you have a letter?" Spenser and Weber asked simultaneously.

"Of course," I replied.

"Bring it over," Spenser ordered.

My attorneys intended to ask the court for a postponement of the custody trial based on my being out of town on a previously scheduled appointment.

Before hanging up, we scheduled a prep session for the Saturday meeting. We really were facing a loaded gun. The custody trial was now only six days away. Curtis was out of town and wouldn't be back until Friday night. Rawson was in court all week. Saturday was the only day we could all meet, so Saturday it was.

When I met with Spenser two days later in midafternoon at his office, I brought the letter from the cable television network's headquarters in New York. The contents of the letter expressed great interest in the League of Women Voters cable television project. The executive was looking forward to a meeting with us Monday at 10:30 A.M.—half an hour before my scheduled court appearance—to further explore the possibilities of joint programming ventures between volunteer organizations and commercial cable television networks.

"The League of Woman Voters is meeting with cable television?" Elizabeth's voice and expression were more than doubtful. "I don't think a judge will consider that a legitimate excuse."

"Give it a try," said Spenser to Elizabeth. "Why don't you walk the letter over to the judge's chambers?"

Elizabeth agreed to make a quick run to the courthouse. Spenser and I settled in to plot our approach for the Saturday session.

Taking each of Curtis's categories one by one—the house, pension fund, the equity on the inn, alimony, child support, medical and dental coverage, college, insurance provisions, joint assets—we reviewed his proposal, comparing the percentages he had suggested in each category against the average being awarded by our county's judiciary in cases brought to trial. It was precisely to the letter of the law. Leave it to Curtis, I thought. Book value, the lowest offer possible.

I complained about every category. Everything I had been fighting against, all the inequities, the lack of adequate time to rebuild a base for my future, the undisclosed assets, surfaced in his offer to me. He was hoping I would agree to his lower figures because I feared I would lose everything in an arbitrary assessment by a judge of how our assets should be equitably distributed. Curtis was counting on me buying the old adage: "A bird in the hand is worth two in the bush." The only problem was that the bird Curtis was offering was scrawny and underweight, with very little meat on it. I was hungry, but not for scraps.

The June temperature and humidity permeated into Spenser's air-conditioned office. I thought of Jackie and Curtis enjoying themselves on the beach. It was her birthday and they had taken off for a three-day lovers' midweek retreat. I wanted Spenser to agree with me, back me up, tell me I was right. Instead, I heard . . .

"What are you willing to give up?" Spenser asked flatly, without looking up. He sounded unusually cross for him, almost as if he thought I was a troublesome, annoying, unrealistic bitch. He wanted to settle the case fast, I thought, he was bored with it. He had carried me for almost two years without any money but my initial payment. There wasn't all that much in it for him. My lawyer was throwing in the towel. I couldn't believe my ears.

He looked straight at me. His blue eyes were emotionless. "You will get sixty percent of the house, fifty percent of your son," he said. "Don't fight the system. It's time for compromise."

I couldn't believe what I was hearing. I had followed his advice for more than a year and a half, been patient, a lady to my often chewed fingertips, had held out against the harassment and intimidation, and now my attorney was telling me to give in?

"What's going on here?" I blew up. I was a raging bull. "You've been telling me to hang on for months, now all of a sudden you're telling me to give in? No way. He's got everything, money, liquidity, assets, earning power! All I have is a court order for $270 a week!"

Spenser looked exhausted. The temperature that afternoon was close to ninety, the humidity intense. I knew he had just returned from visiting his wife in the hospital, where she was bedridden with a broken hip. I glared at him, trying to assess his motives, and getting more suspicious by the minute. I searched my brain for the proper words, desperately trying to find the right way to convey my dissatisfaction.

"Have you cut a deal with Rawson?" I blurted out accusingly. "Are you selling me out?"

The minute the words left my mouth, I wished them back. Too late. Great, Phyllis, I thought. Subtle, real subtle.

Before I could say anything else, Spenser abruptly stood up and dismissed me.

"Phyllis, I want you to go home, cool off, and come back tomorrow night at eight o'clock ready to talk reasonably," he said, his voice subdued but strained. "I want you to list your priorities and everything you are willing to give up to get them. Start thinking realistically. We have one last shot to settle this out of court."

He didn't even walk me to the door.

I spent the remainder of the day fuming but obediently making lists of "if this, then that," "if that, then this." Basically, I was unwilling to give up anything. I was stubborn, immovable, uncompromising, and irrational. I was also terrified, terrified to confront Curtis directly and terrified that Spenser had given up. I felt that I was getting a raw deal and, worst of all, that someone that I had trusted implicitly was suddenly and for no apparent reason turning on me. It's not so, I told myself, and tried to believe it. It took me until the next morning before I did, and then I began to wonder if Spenser would forgive me.

I appeared at Spenser's office promptly at eight Friday evening. The intense heat wave that had blanketed the area had not yet lifted. I was dressed in a simple, feminine black and white flowered summer shirtwaist, my legs covered with white mesh cotton stockings. I wanted to appear neither businesslike nor casual, but wanted my clothing to portray me as a "woman" rather than a "client" so that for a few moments business could be set aside and we could make up as people. I also wanted to convey to Spenser that, although we had disagreed, I knew that it was okay and that we could still like each other.

Spenser was rested and in good spirits. So was I. We greeted each other with sheepish smiles. Spat or no, we were still in this together.

"Have you thought about what you are willing to give up?" he asked.

"Yep."

"Well?"

"I'm not going to give up anything," I said. "At least, that's the approach I'm going to take. Nothing. Nada. You, Rawson, and Curtis will have to convince me to give up part of the pie. My stance will be that I am not giving one inch after holding out against his unfair offers and unreasonable intimidation."

"I thought that's what you'd say, Phyllis," he laughed. "So I've come up with a new game plan. Get out your pencil and paper. We've got a lot of work to do tonight."

Now *this* was my attorney! We shook hands and shook off our differences.

"We're going to change our approach from defense to offense," he said. "We're going to throw out Curtis's plan, ignore the percentages, and present them with a totally different package, a fresh approach.

"It's a risk, a complete gamble," he continued. "They may not go for the new rules, they may walk, but they may also be willing to play the game to wrap this case up." He paused, raised a quizzical eyebrow at me. "Are you willing to roll the dice?"

Spenser's eyes were lit up. I knew he had cooked up something grand. "You bet!" I said.

"I knew there was a reason I thought you were a good client," he said.

We worked three hours straight. I had reams of paper detailing our positions, outlining my dialogue, cues, and theatrical gestures. I was on the make, on a gambler's high. I was certain we were going to beat the system.

"Phyllis, go home and get a good night's sleep," Spenser gently said, as we finished our preparations. "I want your mind razor-sharp tomorrow."

# CHAPTER 11

# DRAW—NOTHING PERSONAL, ONLY BUSINESS

I woke at six, unable to sleep any more. Blinding sunshine flowed through the windows of the master bedroom. I had returned to our—now *my*—first floor bedroom about a week ago. Staggering out of bed, I let the dog out through the sliding glass doors which opened on to an outside deck, then quickly retreated back into the coolness of the house. The heat wave had not let up and I was gasping for breath from the heavy oppressive air.

While Nathaniel slept I pulled clothing from my closet, organizing apparel and accessories as I organized my thoughts. I had slept restlessly, but, although I had awakened physically tired, I was mentally alert. My adrenalin was pumping overtime as I tried to remember all of Spenser's instructions.

I showered quickly and started to dress for my starring role in the theatrical production which would begin in a few hours. We were going totally professional today. I wore a black linen suit set off by a pink, lace-trimmed blouse, Chanel pumps, and stockings. Stockings, in this weather! My briefcase was packed with legal documents. I painted my face with a palette of colors, tamping down the perspiration with a never-before-used powder puff. I tossed my compact and a lipstick into my shoulder bag, blow-dried my hair, and gave it a few passes with setting gel. As an afterthought I threw on a string of pearls, then added a pair of matching earrings. Surveying myself in the bathroom mirror, I was pleased with the results. I looked feminine, but also assertive and slightly intimidating.

Nathaniel stumbled downstairs from his bedroom. He was only half awake.

"Where are you going?" he asked. "I thought you had a lawyer meeting."

"I do. How about some breakfast?" I cut off his questions, not wanting him to know how important this session was. If our strategy failed, we would have to start all over, and I didn't want Natty to be disappointed if a settlement didn't come through. I made him breakfast, drove him to a friend's house, and returned home to begin the final countdown.

I entered the house, went straight for the phone, and called Curtis's apartment. Jackie answered. It was 8:20.

Good, I thought. I had been hoping to get her and not Curtis.

"Jackie," I said, my voice warm and conciliatory, but firm, "I am calling to tell you that I am going into this negotiating session with a mind-set to settle. I am coming in good faith and in a spirit of cooperation. I truly hope we can work things out in a manner that is equitable and fair.

"I want you to know," I continued, "that Spenser has hired a court stenographer to be available to take down what we agree on today so that it can be entered as a court order on Monday. I want to continue with the same type of openness we seem to have reached with the custody issue.

"We have begun to re-establish a relationship, we have similar goals, and we seem to be able to communicate," I said, pausing briefly before I concluded my speech. "If you feel comfortable about attending this session today, I want you to know that I have no objection to your being there."

I knew they had just returned from a three-day mini beach holiday celebrating Jackie's birthday only hours earlier. She was relaxed and pleasant. But then, she was always relaxed and pleasant. A morning person, she—like Curtis—flew out of bed the moment she awoke, fresh, alert, and ready to go.

"Curtis and I talked about my being there," she said confidentially, "but I'm not sure of my time schedule yet. We just got home a few hours ago. I just don't know."

I thanked her, hung up, and rushed out to the car. I was ten minutes late for our nine A.M. departure from Spenser's office.

"Did you reach her?" was his first question.

"Yes, yes. That's why I'm late. I was on the phone with her."

"Is she coming?"

Our entire strategy hinged on her presence. We were both keyed up, trying to second-guess her decision.

"I don't know. I think I caught her off guard."

"Good," he said. "That's exactly what I want. I don't want her to have too much time to consider the pros and cons of her participation."

Spenser was relying on an impulsive decision to participate.

He looked me over and appeared satisfied with my apparel. Actually he had no choice. We were already late in leaving.

Elizabeth Weber emerged from the office, grabbed me by the shoulders, and gave me a bear hug. I had become very fond of her during the course of my case. She had become a friend. Her spontaneous show of affection showed me she felt the same. She had also shown herself to be a fine attorney. Still, dressed in shorts, a T-shirt, and sneakers, her hair pulled back in a pony tail, she looked like something out of a Pepsi commercial. I returned her hug.

What was she doing here on a Saturday morning?

"Your custody trial has been postponed for a month," she said. "The gods must have a wicked sense of humor —or perhaps think there is a great future for the League of Women Voters in cable television."

I was stunned.

"Rawson finally agreed to a postponement," Elizabeth announced gleefully. "That buys us a month to prepare for a custody trial if things don't come off today."

Spenser had disappeared. He suddenly reappeared streetside driving a large maroon Mercedes. I knew he also had a royal blue Mercedes two-seater. Was I paying for this maroon bomb?

"Your car is ready, madam," my attorney said from the driver's seat. "A Mercedes car dealer paid my fee with this one," Spenser said, laughing as he answered my unasked question. "Let's get moving."

Elizabeth gave me one last peck on the cheek, wished us luck, jogged alongside the car for a block, waved, and turned a corner. We were on our way. We rehearsed dialogue and reviewed stage directions during the drive.

"Remember, act like a bitch when things start heating up," he said. "I want you to appear unreasonable so that I can get you to agree on specific points. They must think I am leaning on you to agree to a settlement."

"I know, I know," I said, "and when I feel a kick under the table I'm to get up and leave the room in anger."

We had been over the scenario dozens of times. I was rehearsed out.

We pulled up to Rawson's office, located on the first floor of an apartment building in a posh Connecticut shore suburb, and traversed the parking lot looking for Curtis's car as we made our approach toward the building's entrance. His car was parked nearby.

As we entered the lobby, Spenser patted me on the back, but said nothing. The gesture was confidently paternal. As we approached Rawson's suite, the door to his office opened. Jackie stepped into the lobby, stopping in front of us to say hello.

"I'm going on a coffee run," she said. "Can I get you a cup?"

We both accepted graciously, and waited until she left to nudge each other. Spenser was practically squealing with delight.

We entered Rawson's office and I was struck immediately by the difference in opposing teams. Spenser, dressed in a summerweight gray pinstriped suit, and I in black linen, looked like a team of bankers paying a call on a client. Rawson was the casual weekend attorney, garbed in a light beige knit jacket, beige pants, and brown knit shirt. Curtis, wearing a polo shirt and Levis, and Jackie coming back in, dressed in white pants, a purple shirt, and white clogs, looked like a pair of successful weekend yuppies. I had noticed Jackie was also wearing a set of beautifully designed silver drop earrings set with semiprecious stones. On her wrist was a matching bracelet. I assumed they were Curtis's birthday gift to her. My birthday gifts had once been as romantic; in the last several years they had evolved into things like Cuisinarts and capuccino makers. Well, I guess that was a clue, I thought ruefully. I pushed these thoughts aside. We had a settlement to negotiate. None of this "down memory lane" stuff.

We trooped into Rawson's conference room and sat down, with Jackie and Curtis facing Spenser and me. Rawson sat at the head of the table. Jackie passed around our coffees and set a box of donuts midway between us. We all dug in. I felt the donut sink immediately to my hips. I knew the calories would never dare show themselves on Jackie. Why did the "other woman" *always* look better than the wife? Weren't there any ugly "other women"? It wasn't fair!

Spenser waited until the cups had been opened, sugar packets disposed of, and donuts selected. Then he began.

"We are meeting today in good faith in an attempt to

effect a settlement that is fair to all," he said. "I want to thank Jackie especially for being here."

What a setup, I was thinking. Does she have any idea what is going on here?

Once his opening remarks were completed, he moved to the main presentation.

"What I propose is that we approach the division of assets as a judge would. This means we put everything in the marital pot and divvy up. We'll start."

He hadn't given the other side a moment in which to comment. I waited for some objections from Curtis. From Rawson. Nothing. Absolutely nothing was said.

"We have one major requirement," Spenser continued. "We want the house. The entire house and that is non-negotiable. We're willing to compromise and work around this one point."

We were ignoring the percentages. We were also moving away from the wounded wife routine and getting tough. Thanks to Spenser's coaching, I was ready. I sat immobile, with a blank expression on my face. Just as I had been instructed.

Rawson said nothing, Jackie said nothing. Curtis, however, immediately protested and restated his position that we should sell the house and split the proceeds. He needed his share to buy another house, he explained, because of the tax advantages which come from home ownership as opposed to renting an apartment.

"I am sympathetic to your position," Spenser said calmly, "but the plain facts are that you make a lot of money and your wife makes nothing. Your current earnings and future comparative potential are totally unbalanced and we must equalize the marital assets."

Rawson still said nothing. Spenser continued.

"It's not my fault that you make a good living, Curtis, or that you are heavy in deferred assets," he said compassionately. "Phyllis needs liquidity now. The house gives her that. You need an ability to earn a living and provide for your future. You get that by only having to provide rehabilitative short-term maintenance rather than long-term alimony, and by keeping the bulk of your assets. We can't take that away from you. We want to be fair."

Curtis's expression remained sullen. Jackie's fingers rested gently on his forearm.

"Ask your attorney if you don't believe me," Spenser said. "This is the way it's done in court."

Rawson nodded his verification.

"Give the house up," Jackie said encouragingly to Curtis. "Let's get on with this."

Spenser prepared a list of our joint assets, then drew a vertical line down the middle of a piece of paper, writing *W* for wife at the top of one side, and *H* for husband at the top of the other.

I had said nothing as yet. I just watched, a polite, interested, but coolly detached look on my face.

"We'll start," Spenser repeated. "The house goes in the wife's column. What do you want? Pick whatever you want."

"I'll take my company stock," was his reply.

That was an interesting revelation. Curtis was the number-two man in a family business. Privately owned, the stock would become valuable only if Curtis's company went public. That was a possibility, but wouldn't happen for years. It did, however, give Spenser and me some insight into Curtis's cries of poverty about the condition of his company—and therefore his job stability and ability to come up with a reasonable level of short-term support.

It also revealed an interesting gender difference. I went for the home, my security, my base; he went for his work, the substance he valued most. I didn't feel that I had lost anything. That was rightfully his.

"I'll take the $15,000 equity in the inn," I said, selecting my second choice. If I couldn't have the building itself, I rationalized, I might as well take the equity. At least I could comfort myself with the argument that all those years of restaurant training had not totally been in vain.

We continued until only the furniture and the pension and profit-sharing funds were left. It was Curtis's turn.

"This is a joke," he said sharply. "She's entitled by law to fifty percent of my pension and profit-sharing fund. That leaves me with the furniture."

"Why are you upset?" asked Spenser in polite surprise. "That furniture is worth quite a bit. After all, you yourself valued it at $44,000 on your financial statement. That's a rather tidy sum in your column."

I could barely keep a straight face. There was at the most a few thousand dollars' worth of furniture in the house. It had remained largely unfurnished because of Curtis's continual insistence that he had no funds to allocate for a decorating allowance. What we had was an amalgam of pieces collected over many homes and apartments during the past decade. Nothing matched, nothing really fit. The only items worth anything were my wedding gifts, which I had selectively preempted earlier in this session since they had largely been gifts from my family, and a few paintings. I gave him the paintings.

Spenser kicked me under the table. It was time for me to be unreasonable.

"I don't think you should take the furniture," I burst out accusingly. "It's not fair. Are you going to cannibalize the house in which your own son lives? You have a beautifully furnished apartment. Are you going to take the beds we sleep in?"

Curtis looked at me, trying to figure out where I was coming from. "But the furniture belongs to me," he said defiantly. "It's my choice."

I was sure he suddenly had to have the furniture because I said I wanted it.

I turned on Spenser.

"How could you do this to me?" I cried, near tears. "I'm going to have a bare house. What am I going to tell my son? I don't have the money to refurnish an entire house. We'll have nothing but empty rooms to live in."

I stormed out of the room. Spenser rose to run after me, then turned and spoke to the others.

"Let's take a break," I heard as I sailed down the hall.

"This is trying for her. I'll attempt to calm her down and knock some sense into her."

I continued on down the corridor, found an empty office, lifted myself onto the edge of a desk, and waited for Spenser to enter. He knocked and opened the door gingerly, peering around the opening to see if I were there.

"Wow! Good temper," he said, closing the door. "They think you really want the furniture."

"He can have the damn furniture," I said. "It's old, worn, and worthless."

"He doesn't want the furniture," Spenser said. "Neither does she. Trust me. You won't be living in an empty house. I just want the $44,000 listed in his column so we can up the ante on alimony and child support. We'll have a higher figure against which to negotiate the final equalization of assets. How do you think we're doing so far?"

"Pretty good," I told him. "Jackie's keeping him in line." She *was* keeping Curtis under control. So far he hadn't really blown. Her participation had been an ameliorating factor. I was so glad she had come.

"Ready to go back?" I asked my attorney.

"No, not yet," he said. "Want to yell a bit? I want them to think I'm really leaning on you to be reasonable. How much alimony do you think we should go for?"

"Five years, but I don't think he'll go for it."

"I don't either," he said. "How about pushing for five, settling for three?"

"Okay. That's fair."

"Let's have a little shouting and screaming now," he said.

When we returned to the conference room, I tried to show anger in my face.

"My client gives up the furniture," Spenser stated. End of discussion. "Shall we move on to alimony and child support?"

We dickered back and forth on alimony. We insisted on five years, they insisted on one, and after I angrily threatened to walk out—again—we compromised on three.

We agreed to specify a figure for an initial four years of child support rather than an open-ended "up to the age of eighteen years" amount, giving us room to negotiate in the future rather than include a locked-in provision for a cost-of-living increase. I was taking a chance on Curtis's good faith toward supporting his son, but I believed he would do right by Nathaniel. Clauses for college and school tuitions, orthodontia, medical insurance, and summer camp were agreed upon. The costs in these categories were to be split between us. I had no idea where I would get the money to pay my 50-percent share.

Only one category remained: payment of my legal fees. Curtis balked. Now it was his turn to storm out of the room. Jackie and Rawson hurried after him.

"This is usually the hardest part for any husband to swallow," Spenser said. His eyes twinkled. "No husband wants to pay an attorney for representing the woman he's divorcing."

"What are we up to?" I asked. My initial $2,000 retainer had been devoured long ago. I estimated we had racked up somewhere around $15,000 in hours billed.

"I'm not sure," he said. "I didn't break down the numbers before we came."

"What if he refuses?" I asked.

"We refuse to sign the agreement," said Spenser. "That's why we did everything else first. We have placed a very large carrot before him."

Curtis, Jackie, and Rawson returned. Curtis agreed to pay on one condition: That we would not leave the room until we had a written signed agreement.

I shrugged. I wanted to appear just a *little* bit unreasonable, but not enough to blow the whole deal.

"Okay, if you insist," I said ungraciously.

Actually it was to my advantage to have a written agreement. Maybe he thought I didn't know that. The two attorneys hastily dictated and wrote out the agreed-upon provisions in longhand. Spenser never called in the stenographer he had had "on call." When it was finished, we initialed each item.

I tried to be nonchalant and removed from the signing. I wanted him to think I was not quite satisfied with the outcome. I thought I had become a pretty good bluffer. Then I felt a smile begin to spread over my face. I excused myself and ran to the ladies' room, where I sat for five minutes trying to recompose my face. We had a settlement! Soon the whole terrible nightmare would end. I was coming out okay. Not great. Not bad. Okay. I could start a new life.

Within days Spenser sent a typed copy of the agreement to Rawson and Curtis for signature. Three weeks later we received their reply—pages of changes, modifications and insertions we had neither discussed nor considered.

This time it was Spenser's turn to hit the ceiling. My turn to soothe my attorney.

"What the hell is going on here?" he was screaming at me over the telephone. "What kind of fast one is he trying to pull?"

"It's his MO, remember?" I said. I had known something like this would happen. "He's got to get in the last lick. Set up a meeting with them and we'll go over the objections. Just find something for him to win."

It took a month for all of us to get together. Spenser was on vacation. Curtis was on vacation. I kept on working at Arturo's. Finally, a month after our Saturday settlement meeting, we all met again.

Rawson could not attend and sent in his place a young associate who tried to explain the changes to Spenser. These included funding Natty's education from a newly established trust fund Curtis had set up for him. At that point it contained only $37.

"How do we know there will be funds in there when it comes time to pay the tuition bills?" Spenser snapped. "You want to specify that all education monies are to come from this fund when there is only $37 in it? What are you trying to put over on us?"

The young associate stuttered that it was a beginning, that when it came time to pay Nathaniel's college tuition, funds would be there.

They wanted a hold-harmless clause involving the inn when the property had been bought and already transferred to our partners. This meant I was holding Curtis harmless for any liability claims to the building from potential customers or residents even though he was not an owner any more. I wasn't an owner any more either, but I had received the money from the sale. Spenser assured him that once the property had transferred—as it had—he had no further involvement with it, no matter *who* received the proceeds from the sale.

He wanted to remove his name from the mortgage on my house.

We objected vehemently because of the possibility that the bank could call the loan and I'd be left hanging without a mortgage—or be faced with a substantially increased interest fee.

All these clauses were nit-picking details meaning nothing. Stupid, I thought. Give in on the small stuff. This means nothing. Let Curtis have his way. There is no substance to any of this. I wanted the damn thing completed and signed. Now it was me who wanted out. I'd had enough.

I turned to Spenser.

"Why can't we just give him what he wants?" I asked.

"I was coerced into signing an agreement I didn't really want," Curtis sniffed. "I want to assure that I am protected here and I want these issues solved today. I'm willing to sit here until midnight until we have a signed document."

Another of Curtis's union-busting tactics. Wear down the opposition through fatigue so they'll give in. By now I was well versed in these moves. So was Spenser, and while Curtis may have been willing to stay there until midnight, Spenser wasn't. He finally blew.

"I have to be in court at eight *a.m.* tomorrow morning,"

he screamed. "*You* were the one who wanted everything settled a month ago, now you show up and want all these changes on the minute. No way! I am not going to be pressured into anything. We need time to go over the ramifications of these details and I am not staying here one minute after five o'clock."

At that point it was 4:15.

Curtis, the associate, and I looked at Spenser. He was livid.

"And if you don't like my attitude," he turned and snapped at me, "you can find yourself another attorney."

His face purple, my attorney stormed out of the room. This time I went after him.

In the hallway, he spun around and grabbed my elbow.

"I'm not angry with you, Phyllis, believe me," he hissed apologetically. "But these are tiny details which may affect your future. I want to explore every one of them to see how they could affect you years down the road. I want to make damn sure this guy isn't putting something over on us."

When we returned to the conference room, Curtis's second-stringer agreed to prepare the changes with his client and then submit them to Spenser for approval. Everyone agreed. We would meet again in another two weeks. Enough, I kept thinking. Enough already. Let's close the deal and get it over with. My frustration level had finally matched Curtis's. Enough. Get it over with.

I had to put some space between myself and these proceedings—just to break the tension. But with my every penny going into day-to-day survival, there was no way I could afford a vacation. I had had two years of unrelieved stress and it was all beginning to get to me. What could I do that didn't cost any money?

With my limited funds and lack of travel time, a mini-weekend seemed the only viable solution. Perhaps I could combine the need for a getaway with a heavy dose of quality time with my son. Nathaniel had spent the summer bouncing back and forth between two homes like a tennis ball. With the arrival of Labor Day his base had now shifted to my home. He would be starting school within days. Summer had slipped by us, with practically no special mother-son time spent together. Nathaniel had been asking to visit the Port of Baltimore and the National Aquarium for months. This was the perfect opportunity. I could make the drive easily in less than a day and, with weekend specials on hotel rates, the expense wouldn't be too great.

"I really didn't want to go," my son said within fifteen minutes of our departure. "I just wanted to see the fish."

"I could have taken you to a fish store," I countered.

Giggles from the back seat. It was the start of our normal front-seat-back-seat on-the-road who-can-verbally-best-the-other relationship. We had spent so many hours in automobiles driving to and from his school and every other place we had to go that the two of us kidded around a lot to break the monotony of the drive.

"Just kidding, Mom," he said. "I'm glad we're going away together.

"What do you call a bird that's run over by a lawn mower?" he went on.

"I don't know, Natty," I answered, in my best "straight man's" voice. "What *do* you call a bird that's been run over by a lawn mower?"

"Shredded tweet!" he roared.

"Got me again," I laughed. He never ran out of jokes, puns, or questions these days. It was good to see him being happy. He seemed to have adjusted fairly well to his new family setup.

We arrived at our hotel during the height of the evening rush hour. I had hoped to avoid the traffic, but my miserable sense of direction had caused us to circumnavigate our destination several times before Nat spotted a sign for the hotel.

"What if we just spend two days driving around Baltimore?" he asked as we passed the same shopping mall for the third time.

I knew he was tweaking me. We had managed to get lost in what seemed like every city, small town, and community along the Eastern seaboard over his years as my backseat passenger. He loved to travel and was used to my frequent stops, starts, and searches for directions.

The trip had left me exhausted. Some R and R, I thought. I badly needed to crash for an hour, after which we could regroup and have dinner. I checked us in as Nathaniel checked out the soda and ice machines, and the cable stations available on the TV in our room. Nap time for Mom. The last half of a baseball game for Nat. I collapsed into a deep sleep. I felt as if I could have slept for months, like a bear hibernating until spring.

After what seemed like a minute I heard a voice from the next bed.

"C'mon, Mom, I'm starved. You can't go to sleep for the night. Get up. You have to feed your kid."

"Okay, okay." I have to feed my kid, I thought, as I shuffled around the room, trying to inject a measure of energy into my body. I looked out the window and into the night. The lights over the harbor twinkled like a carnival. It looked inviting. Nathaniel was sitting on the edge of his bed, pulling on his sneakers. Feed me, feed me. *Peep, peep*, like a little bird. Okay, let's move it. Food time.

Baltimore's Inner Harbor lives up to its advertisements. Cheap, accessible, and fun. It's a great place to take children. It was a perfect destination for us. We walked around the shops, the malls, and the food hall, picking, choosing, and nibbling on a variety of finger foods. I had intended us to have a decent dinner in a restaurant, but Nathaniel wanted to sample a little of everything. Nutritionally the mix of chicken wings, chocolate chip cookies, and ice cream left a lot to be desired. What the hell, a little garbage food wouldn't hurt either of us.

The spontaneity of our evening stroll revitalized my body and my mind. I didn't want to break the warm and gentle sense of mother-son affection that flowed between us. As we sat on the bench overlooking the harbor, savoring our ice cream cones in the muggy September air, I couldn't help but think how Natty had changed.

He had been a six-year-old child when Curtis and I split, not much more than a toddler. Now, two years later, at the age of eight, he was a little boy, an active, involved, small-sized human being. I wondered how the events of the last two years would affect his relationships in the future, how he would relate to women, how he would connect with Curtis, Jackie, and me as he passed through adolescence into adulthood. I could only hope his emotional development would continue with the degree of stability he seemed to have attained. I rested my hand on his shoulder, tapping my fingers lightly to signal that it was time to leave.

"Let's go," I said, "we're both pooped. We'll get up early tomorrow and see the sights."

He offered no objection, taking my hand and holding it tightly as we walked through the hotel lobby toward the elevators that would whisk us to our room. He still wasn't too old to hold his mom's hand. I knew he would soon outgrow this, but tonight I was grateful that he still needed the physical connection to his mother.

"I need to talk to you, Mom," I heard him say from his bed across the room after we had shut off the lights and turned in for the evening.

"What about?"

"When is the divorce going to be over?"

Damn, I thought this getaway was going to be a distraction. We were more than 400 miles from home and still the subject hovered over us.

"Soon. Why?"

"Cause then you and Dad will stop fighting."

Years of conflict could not be erased by an overnight getaway. Every counselor we had seen stated repeatedly that it would take two to three years after the divorce was finalized for some semblance of normalcy to return. I really didn't want to think about it.

"We don't fight now," I told him.

"Yes you do. I wish you would get remarried."

The fantasy again. How could he think that? Neither Curtis nor I had ever given him any indication that this was even a remote possibility. But I knew that even children whose parents had been divorced for decades often dreamt of a reconciliation between the two parties.

"That won't happen, Nathaniel," I told him firmly. "We don't like each other much."

"Are you sure?"

I knew he wanted a "maybe" answer from me. I wanted to put a stop to any fantasies here.

"Yes." My voice was tightly controlled.

There was silence for a few minutes.

"Are you ever going to get married again?"

What was this child driving at? Was he trying to tie things into a bow, settle me into a marriage according to a traditional family lifestyle, or find out if I had someone in mind for a stepfather for him? I decided to waffle on the question.

"I don't know. Maybe."

"I don't think you will," he told me assuredly.

"Why not?"

"Because you never date. Wouldn't you like to go out? The last time you went out was about four months ago."

I was amazed at how much his little mind took in. I wondered how much else he had observed over the years.

Tears started to trickle down my cheeks. I was glad the lights were out so Nathaniel couldn't see. I was crying, not for the lack of a love interest, but for the sensitivity expressed by my eight-year-old child.

"Sometimes I go out when you're with your dad," I said, trying to keep my voice steady and unchoked.

"No you don't," he replied accusingly, "because if you did you would tell me about it."

"Well, I'm awfully busy now and it's hard to meet people where we live."

"I know. How can you meet anyone in the middle of the woods?"

I smiled. Even he sensed how isolated we were.

"I think it's time for you to go to sleep now," I said, trying to end the discussion. He was quiet for another minute or two.

"Mom, how much money do you have?"

"Enough. Why?"

"Because if you need some, I'll take it out of my bank account and give it to you. I don't need it."

I had tried not to let Natty know how tough things had been for us financially. But he had picked up those signals as well. The tears were now streaming from my eyes. I sobbed silently.

"That's okay, Nat," I gulped. "But thanks for offering."

"Really—take it," he said. My son was offering the entirety of his $220 savings account.

"No, that's okay. I'm fine. Really. Thanks anyway." I was trying to be convincing. He wasn't buying any of my words.

"C'mon, go to sleep," I said. "We'll talk in the morning."

"Okay, Mom." He knew the discussion was over.

He stopped talking, then I heard his voice once again. "Mom, I love you."

"I love you, too, Natty," I replied. "Now, go to sleep."

He fell into a deep sleep almost immediately. I was up all night, tossing and thinking of my son's words.

I was in a state of semiconsciousness when he awakened the next morning, chipper and alert.

"Hey, Mom, get up, let's order room service." The digital clock on the bedstand read 6:30 A.M.

I closed my eyes. "Go look at the menu and decide what you want," I croaked, barely moving my lips.

For Nat, room service was the ultimate. He had discovered it at age two during one of our Florida grandparent visits. You made a telephone call, placed your order, and, presto, someone appeared with it at your door. Just like magic.

"They don't have pancakes or French toast," he announced. "That's what I wanted." He was propped up in his bed, intently studying the menu contained in a huge book of hotel services which covered his lap.

"Let me call and see if the kitchen will make up an order for you," I told him.

My nights at Arturo's had taught me that chefs were usually willing to accommodate special requests if the kitchen was slow. Twenty minutes later a waiter appeared with our order.

Nathaniel's face beamed over the impending feast and my initiative in procuring the French toast, then fell as he removed the silver cover which kept the food hot.

"Raisins! They made the French toast with raisins!" he howled. "I hate raisins! You know that!"

The offending platter looked wonderfully tempting, garnished with powdered sugar, butter curls, tiny bottles of maple syrup, and a pink carnation.

I looked at him disapprovingly. I was certain, no matter how much he disliked raisins, that the cause of his outburst was not the raisins.

"I guess I'll just have to cut around the raisins," I said, ignoring his ill temper. He calmed down.

"There won't be any toast left," he said, watching me try to cut around the raisins. I had never seen a piece of bread studded with so many raisins.

Nathaniel inhaled the food.

"Actually, it's pretty good," he said. I was used to Nat's sudden outbursts. I suspected he never spoke with Curtis in this manner, but I was glad he could show his emotions, not keep his feelings trapped inside.

"I'm ready for the next piece, Mom," he said. "Could you try and do a little better job on the raisins this time?"

I sat across from him, slowly drinking my coffee and wondering when the unconscious unease of the divorce process would go away. Curtis and I had been separated almost two years and still I felt emotionally unsettled and anxious—and *I* was an adult. Could I expect a child to heal quicker than me?

By ten o'clock we were out of the room and on our way to do the tourist run. We, and a cast of thousands, visited the National Aquarium, the harbor, the Museum of Science and Technology, tramped in and out of old ships and new ships. Wherever we went, there were hordes of people. I felt as though I were an extra in a Woody Allen movie. By late afternoon we were both museumed out.

I couldn't afford more than the $85 it cost for an overnight stay. When I suggested an early departure, Nat offered no resistance.

"It was a great trip, Mom," he said as we pulled into our driveway hours later.

"I'm glad you had a good time," I said as I turned off the ignition. "What did you like best?"

"The raisins," he said.

The final signing of the divorce documents took place two days later. Curtis was once again accompanied by his attorney's young associate. Once again we were in Spenser's office. We began with the custody agreement. Spenser lifted the first set of papers from the stack set before him and offered them to Curtis.

Curtis took the documents, reread the provisions, signed the forms, and passed them to me. Nothing had changed from the agreement devised with the two psychologists months earlier. I signed. Then the two attorneys signed.

We moved on to the financial papers, Spenser reviewing once again the provisions and listing the specific items requiring signatures.

"Do you have the quit-claim deed to the house?" he asked Curtis. This meant Curtis was giving up all rights to what would become my property.

"Yes," he said, reluctantly. I felt that he regretted giving up the house to me, and waited for a last-minute hitch. There was none.

We continued to pass documents around the table. Life insurance, interim medical coverage, the property settlement. The process took less than half an hour. It was a pro forma signing with no surprises. I was ecstatic to be done with it.

"All right," said Curtis crisply, upon the final turn of the round-robin paper chase. He was back to business. "When can the divorce be finalized? How long do we have to wait?"

We had agreed to a ninety-day no-fault divorce, but we all knew that the court backlog prevented a true ninety-day dissolution. Curtis wanted an estimate of how long a ninety-day no-fault would really take.

Spenser looked at him. "You want a divorce? I'll get you a divorce," he said tartly, picking up the telephone.

We watched as Spenser dialed. "Can anyone hear us today?" he asked the party on the other end. Looking at us, he nodded his head. "The court can hear us right now," he said. "Let's go, Curtis." And my attorney whisked my husband out the door. The associate and I sat and waited, trying to make small talk. It was impossible. Forty-five minutes later Spenser and Curtis returned.

"Here's your divorce," said Spenser, tossing a set of papers at me.

I thought Spenser was kidding, but he wasn't; the papers had been signed by a judge, stamped by the court, and registered in the official files. I was stunned at the speed of the unexpected processing. Relieved to have it done with. Then thrilled. I was free!

"May I use your phone?" I heard Curtis ask my attorney. Spenser handed him the phone across the table. I thought Curtis was calling his office to tell them he was on his way in.

Instead, he had dialed Jackie. With me and the two attorneys sitting there, we heard him say:

"Hello, darling, want to meet me for lunch? I just got divorced."

Spenser and I looked at each other with embarrassment. I shrugged and leaned back in my chair. He was all hers now. And boy, she was welcome to him.

I had wondered whether I would feel let down. No

way. I felt wonderful, almost giddy. I stood up and wished Curtis well, shook hands with his attorney, gave Spenser a warm hug, and walked out the door into the warm September air. Almost two years had passed since I had heard Curtis's words, "Phyllis, I'm leaving you."

I wanted to show Spenser how much I appreciated him, how much I had learned from him, but somehow suggesting lunch didn't seem appropriate. Neither did a gift. Yet I wanted my attorney and his staff to celebrate with me.

That afternoon I bought a case of champagne, earmarked a few bottles for Spenser and Elizabeth Weber and the rest for the staff.

"Please celebrate with me," my note said. "It was a long two years, and a wonderful relationship."

I also finally said good-bye to Arturo's. My co-workers had known I would be leaving as soon as my divorce came through, and we had already said our farewells. But I wanted to resign in person to my boss and to give him adequate notice so that a replacement could be found. If necessary, I would stay until a new relief chef was trained.

I walked into the kitchen, expecting to find my usual crew. Instead, a flurry of activity was taking place, in the center of which was a husband-and-wife cooking team I recognized from another restaurant in town.

My boss emerged from the bar.

"Phyllis, you know Sid and Joan," he said. "They've decided to buy Arturo's. We worked out a deal last night."

"Great!" I said. I knew that two of Arturo's three owners had wanted to move on; the third would remain with the new team.

"I was coming in to resign," I told all of them. "It's time for me to move on, too."

"All divorced, are we?" said my boss.

"Free as a bird," I said.

We wished each other good luck, hugged. "Well, this is it," I said. I felt kind of funny. I was glad to be leaving, glad to be finally getting on with my life, but there was a lump in my throat too. I had been part of a family here, had gotten some badly needed support (both financial and emotional) here, and I would miss it.

My boss—now former boss—walked me to my car.

"What are your plans?" he asked.

"I'm not sure," I told him. "I've got a few possibilities in the works. What about you?"

"We're thinking about taking a little place at the beach for the summer," he said. "Nothing fancy. Steak sandwiches, chicken Parmesan, spaghetti marinara."

I hugged him once more, got into my car, and started to drive off.

"Hey Phyllis," I heard as I was pulling out of the parking lot. "If nothing pans out, you can spend the summer cooking with us."

I flashed him a thumbs up and took off.

That evening, Meredith and Ellen took me to dinner to celebrate. We ordered a bottle of Piper-Heidsieck.

"To relationships," we said, toasting each other.

Ellen took a small box out of her purse.

"A little something for your future," she said.

I carefully opened the wrapping and peered inside. I felt my face redden as I withdrew a minimal pair of lacy black panties.

"To freedom," Ellen said, lifting her glass.

I lifted my glass and touched hers, then started to laugh. "To freedom," I said.

To say I had a hangover the next morning was an understatement. I had managed to make a pot of coffee and crawl back to bed when I heard Nathaniel bouncing down the stairs. He sat down on the side of my bed, gave me a big kiss, and started to list his plans for the day. Soccer at noon. Football game at three, sleep over with a friend that evening. We were interrupted by the telephone. He looked at me and saw that I had no intention of answering the grating ring. He reached for the receiver. I didn't intercept. I watched as he listened to the caller, and waited for his response.

Looking at me he said, "I'm sorry, my mom will have to call you back. She's not functional yet."

Whether my child was referring to the state of my body or the state of my mind, he was right, on both counts. I was not quite functional yet.

But I would be.

# CHAPTER 12

# GETTING FUNCTIONAL

Curtis married Jackie about a month after our divorce was finalized.

"I went with Daddy and Jackie to get their wedding license." Natty told me conspiratorially. "And after we got the license we got a free gift."

I wanted to appear disinterested.

"Oh? What kind of gift?"

"Scope, detergent, and hand lotion."

"That's nice," was all I could manage.

One week later, I heard through the neighborhood grapevine that Curtis had bought a house. The price: $260,000. I also heard that his company was booming. A new office had opened in Boston and a major expansion was in the works locally. I walked around for days, feeling like a fool, chastising myself for ever giving him the benefit of the financial doubt.

I didn't begrudge him his new house, nor did I feel cheated out of an indeterminate amount of assets. I was sullen and resentful because my fears had proven accurate.

The house and his booming business were the final nose-thumbing. I had been humiliated, intimidated, harassed, and forced to wage a bare-knuckled fight for what was rightfully mine—and he had had his share carefully salted away all along.

I was angry that I had been played for a sucker, but *very* glad that I had held out and not given in to my self-doubts nor to Curtis's polished performance of bluff and bravado.

It was late on Sunday morning. I was performing another round of postmarital autopsy, alternately musing, dozing, and reading the Sunday papers. I reached for my coffee cup, skimmed "The Week in Review," and tossed another section of *The New York Times* onto the pile of magazines and newspapers sprouting from the rug next to my bed. My weekly "casting of the sections" had been a habit Curtis abhorred. Now I threw each one down with a carefree spirit.

With Nathaniel upstairs engrossed in a pregame television football special, I was selfishly enjoying my morning laziness. The noise of a car crunching the gravel on the driveway interrupted my Sunday in bed. I looked out the window. Curtis was walking toward the house.

I had forgotten he had made arrangements to begin removing his $44,000 worth of furniture. I hastily slipped out of my robe and pulled a sweatshirt over my head. I was on my way to the front door when I realized I was wearing nothing beneath the sweatshirt except a pair of panties. I retreated to my closet and pulled on a pair of Levis. I had been married to this man for more than a decade, yet suddenly felt an intense sense of propriety. I had to cover my behind.

Spenser was only partially correct about Curtis's ultimately rejecting the furniture. Entitled to all of it, he walked through the house, casing each room to see if anything looked salvageable. The only major things he wanted were my dining room table and a baker's rack. He referred to a shopping list he carried with him.

"We need a sugar bowl and cream pitcher," he said, "preferably crystal. What do you have?"

Questions like this no longer fazed me. Somehow I had accepted that it was perfectly in character for him to act like this.

I had an extra sugar bowl and creamer. Nothing so small was worth arguing over, in my mind. The papers had been signed, I was free, two years of trial-by-divorce had ended. How they could bring themselves to use the things I lived with was a mystery to me, (*I* wouldn't be able to, in their position) but I wanted all the loose ends settled, wanted to wrap up this part of my life, get moving. I didn't know where I wanted to go or what I was going to do, but I needed to get out of neutral and into gear. I gave him the crystal creamer and sugar set.

"I want all the camping equipment," he said. To me, roughing it was a weekend at the Plaza. He could have *all* the camping equipment. Every bit of it.

We descended to the boiler room. He pried open the steamer trunk which had remained untouched since our first year of marriage.

"Oh, whew!" I said, recoiling from the stench. "You can't be serious about wanting this stuff, can you?"

He was serious. He took the air mattresses, propane stove, cooking equipment, lantern, plastic egg-storage container, and tent stakes. He left me the trunk.

He stored his booty in his brand new Saab. He had previously driven a Chevy. The hidden assets are surfacing, I thought to myself. I smiled pleasantly.

"I want the plants," he said, motioning to the dozen or so planters scattered around the house.

"The plants?" They were terminal. I wasn't a plant person—they'd been neglected for two years.

"And the clay pots." Stacks of unused plant containers lined the boiler room steps. We loaded these in the Saab also.

"I'm giving you two bags of potting soil as a bonus," I offered.

He took them.

On a second pass, he took half a set of dishes, a few utensils, and most of his remaining personal possessions. Rather than being upset over giving up individual household items, I realized he was providing me an opportunity to clean out my overcrowded shelves and closets.

I sat on the stairs watching him pack the final bits of debris from a failed marriage and asked myself "Why?" Curtis was in an unusually fine and conciliatory mood, filled with goodwill in the afterglow of his marriage vows. I put the question to him.

"Curt, what happened to us?" I had no feelings whatsoever. Now it was a good sign. It showed that my emotional attachment was broken, gone forever.

He never looked up, never stopped wrapping the dishes and placing them in the carton.

"We were just two very different people, Phyllis," he said pleasantly. "We wanted two very different things out of life."

His statement was made without malice or hostility. He was absolutely correct. Had we really understood the extent of our differences from the beginning we would probably never have married. Curtis had wanted me to be something I wasn't, and could never be. I had tried to mold myself to his expectations and in the effort became a satellite appendage. It didn't work. Both of us were unhappy with me.

Curtis finally looked up from his packing.

"Have you made a decision about what you are going to do with your life?" he asked. Although his question appeared to reflect genuine interest, I was uncertain of his motives. I was suspicious of anything he wanted to know about me. Would he use the information to cut off my support payments, or claim that I wasn't spending enough time with my son?

"I have no idea," I replied. I really didn't. I was trying a few things to see if anything panned out. A little corporate free-lance ghostwriting, a potential business partnership publishing newsletters, a full-time job. By postponing any firm decisions I was avoiding the unpleasant fact that I would soon be completely on my own. The safety net was about to be removed.

"You have to take some control over your life, Phyllis," he said again. "Your alimony won't last forever and you cannot expect to come back to me for more support. You have to start thinking about your future."

He was right. I just wasn't ready to move off dead center. He got up to leave. As we said good-bye, I looked straight into his eyes. Nothing. There was nothing left. Good-bye eleven years, I thought. Forever.

As Curtis drove off with his odd mixture of postmarital remains, I felt a terrible sadness come over me. For myself. For Curt.

Nathaniel had remained upstairs for most of the shopping expedition, coming down only to say a brief hello to his father. I found him plumped under the covers, reading Judy Blume's classic tale of divorce, *It's Not the End of the World*. I had purchased the book months earlier and placed it without comment on his bookshelf, and there it had remained, unopened.

"Is that a good book?" I asked.

"It's okay—it's about a divorce," he replied.

"Yes, I know. You've had it a pretty long time."

"I didn't want to read it before this," he confided.

I was pleased. His willingness to read about divorce and talk about our own was a positive sign that the emotional healing process had begun.

"I guess now that Dad's married, you feel you can read the book, huh?" I said, sitting on the edge of his bed.

"Yeah, I guess so." He shrugged off the subject.

I smiled and suggested he get ready for his soccer game.

"I don't want to play on my soccer team," he said. "We always lose."

"Well, you're on an older team," I consoled him. "It's harder, more competitive. You have to work harder and try harder."

No response. Nothing. He just stared at me.

"Look, when I started writing, I wasn't very good," I persisted. "I had to work hard at it, practice every day, keep at it."

"You're still not very good," he said. "You don't have a job yet."

The truth, always the truth from this child.

"Thanks a heap."

"Well, you're not bad," he said, rethinking his criticism. "But you're not as good as William Shakespeare. Hey, what about my copy of *Entrepreneurial Mothers*? You forgot to give me one of your books."

"Take one," I said. "You can have whatever you want."

"No, never mind, I'm not going to read it anyway."

I bent over and kissed him on the cheek. He would accept kisses when we were alone, but never within eyeshot of friends.

"I love you, Mom," he said.

"I love you, too, Natty."

"I love you more than anything in the whole wide world."

"That's what you used to say when you were little," I told him.

"You're a great mom," he said. "I'm glad you're mine."

"Thanks," I replied. "You're a great kid. I'm glad you're mine."

The mutual admiration society lasted until the end of the weekend. On Monday, with only minutes to go before we were to leave the house for the school bus, all the anxieties, frustrations, and tensions of the past two years, his father's marriage, and a new school year erupted at once.

"I can't find my shoes," he cried, as he raced from room to room. "Where are my shoes?"

"I don't know. Look in your room."

We went through the "I can't find" routine every morning. Sometimes it was a jacket. Other times a school book. This day it was shoes. I had told him the night before that I had an early morning appointment and that he would

have to be ready to leave promptly at 7:00 to meet the
school bus at 7:10.

"If you can't find your sneakers, put on your mocca-
sins," I suggested.

"I'm not wearing them. Those are my jacket-and-tie
shoes. I'm not wearing those shoes to school." He was
screaming.

"Nat," I tried to reason with him, "those are summer-
fall shoes. You wear them all the time. Just wear them
today and we'll look for your sneakers when you get home."

He sat down in the middle of the kitchen floor and
refused to get up.

"I'm not going to school," he was screaming and crying.

I stood and looked at him, uncertain whether to yell at
him to get up or to try to reason with him. He was having
a full-blown temper tantrum. I knew he would never pull
this nonsense on Curtis. Sometimes it doesn't pay to be a
mom.

"Somebody stole my shoes," he screamed. I started
laughing. I knew I shouldn't, but it was so ludicrous.

"Nobody stole your shoes," I told him. "You put them
some place and now you can't find them"

That was not what he wanted to hear. He turned
on me.

"You stole my shoes!"

"Why would I want to steal your shoes?"

"Because you want me to wear my dress shoes to school."

"That's ridiculous," I said, trying to calm him down.
"If you would put away your clothes, keep your room
neater, and get up on time, you wouldn't have this problem
every morning."

"That's not true. My room is neat. Somebody stole my
shoes."

I had never seen him so hysterical. I knew there was
much more at stake here than the missing shoes.

"Get in the car," I said sternly. "We're going to miss
the bus."

He wept all the way to the bus stop. I looked at him in the rearview mirror. His face was puffed, his eyes red. Tears gushed down his cheeks. He looked awful and I felt awful. I wavered at the stop sign, considered returning home to search for the missing shoes, and decided not to. Since the beginning of the school semester, he had lost three sweaters, one jacket, and countless sports items. I just couldn't afford the replacements. He was old enough now to assume some responsibility for his belongings. I was also determined not to tolerate this kind of behavior, whatever the trigger. This time I was going to stand firm, no matter how guilty I felt.

"Wipe your eyes," I said, trying to comfort him. "We're almost at the school bus."

"No," he replied belligerently. "I want the kids to see me crying."

"Why?"

"I'm going to tell them that my mom stole my shoes."

I didn't say anything. He continued screaming.

"You go home right now and look for my shoes!" he commanded. "You won't find them. You stole them! I'll go barefoot to school."

He opened the car door and turned around, glaring at me.

"I'm not taking the bus home," he said. "If you want me home you'll have to come and get me."

"I'll see you at the bus stop after school," I snapped, as I watched him mount the steps of the van.

When I got home I found his shoes in the bathroom, lying next to a dirty pair of pants he had left on the floor the previous evening and which I had refused to pick up for him.

I was beside myself with anger and frustration; angry that I had allowed a senseless quarrel to explode into a major confrontation, frustrated that I had sent my son off to school in that state. *How* could I have done this?

We were going to have a talk when he returned. I was going to apologize. He was going to learn that he had to be more careful about his belongings. This kind of flare-up, I vowed, was *not* going to happen again.

Once again Nat beat me to the punch.

"I can't believe I threw such a fit about my shoes," he said as he descended the steps of the school bus. "It was pretty dumb."

We were both on the way to regaining our equilibrium. It would take time, there would be flare-ups, but we were on our way.

My publishing partnership wasn't working. The heady romance of the first few months of the business honeymoon had worn off. My partner was disenchanted with me and I with him. I couldn't concentrate, couldn't produce the promised copy for our first three prototype newsletters. I knew from years of experience that when my writing was strained, the conditions or the subject matter were wrong. I didn't need an expert to tell me that two months to produce sixteen pages of copy indicated a problem somewhere along the line.

My free-lance writing was coming along, but there was no security in *that* field. A little magazine work, a little corporate work—and little fees. I enjoyed my diverse assignments and the executives whose thoughts I turned into words, but I couldn't support myself and my son on enjoyment.

I looked for a full-time job. What I knew was marketing and communications for small businesses. What I didn't know was how radically large corporations had changed since my departure from the traditional work world eight years earlier. Technical specialists were in demand. Computer experts. Engineers. I was none of these, nor did I hold any semblance of qualifications in these fields. Even word processing had not yet come to Phyllis Ellsworth. If anyone had had workplace experience, it was me—I had dabbled in everything, but now I was completely out of touch and totally ill-equipped to re-enter corporate America in the 1980s.

An unexpected February snowstorm which left me stranded at the summit of my own Swiss Alps provided the setting for my future fantasies. Huddled under an electric blanket in my bed one afternoon, I was aimlessly watching the snow drift from the sky and mentally assessing, "What next?" It felt like the scene in *The Graduate* where Dustin Hoffman floats in his parents' swimming pool and ponders his future.

I pondered for hours. I had to move off dead center. With Nathaniel building a snow fort outside and no one else around, I began to talk to myself, carrying on a conversation as if a confidante were helping me work through a difficult problem. I played both roles, shifting my voice and gestures to reflect the two participants.

"So, Phyllis, don't you think it's about time you did something with your life?" I began. "You've been divorced for four months now. It's two and a half years since you separated."

"I thought I was doing something," I answered. "Nothing seems to be working out."

"Why not?" I had expected my other self to come up with lightningbolt ideas, not ask self-assessment questions. I thought a while before answering.

"Number one, I don't want to sit in a room and write lengthy newsletters every month," I said. "I need some social interaction.

"Number two, I am not ready for *any* relationship—business or personal."

"Okay, that's fair enough," I said, encouraging the other voice to continue. "Anything else?"

"Number three, I'm out of touch with corporate America.

"Number four, free-lance work is little more than a subsistence income.

"And number five, in every one of these I don't have any financial control over my life, and without financial control I am back where I was in my marriage!"

Aha! Now that was an interesting series of revelations.

I was trying to organize my life without a firm grasp of my own needs, desires, and expectations. Maybe I was making progress.

I was interrupted by a telephone call.

"I figured you'd be snowbound," said the voice on the other end. "It's time to come down from the Alps. I've got a house I want you to look at. Your appointment is set for Saturday at three."

The caller was a friend who also happened to be a real estate agent in a nearby community. She had been working on me to move closer to "civilization" since the early days of my marriage. Her cajoling was nothing new. We had had this conversation many, many times.

"I'm not ready for a move," I laughed. "I have to come to terms with my career first. Actually, you caught me in the middle of a 'What am I going to do with my life?' reverie."

"Good, maybe a move is in order," she said. "C'mon over and take a look. There's lots happening here. If you can get off that mountain, I'll take you to lunch."

Real estate agents, even friends, were all the same, I thought. Pushing, always pushing, always the perfect deal. I went anyway.

The house was small, in disrepair, and overpriced.

"You dragged me out on the coldest day of the year to see this?" I screeched.

"Yes," she said emphatically. "You can afford it, it's right in town, and it's zoned commercial. You can rent space for small professional offices. This area is the boom town of the eighties. Where else could you find in-town property with three parking spaces across the street from the New York City bus line? You can even rent the parking spaces for $35 a month."

I shook my head at her enthusiastic pitch. She was not selling me a complete load of garbage. Natty attended school here and I was aware of the area's burgeoning growth and development, but this house was more than a handyman's special. It needed a complete overhaul.

"I'll get back to you," I said, kissing her lightly on the cheek. "Thanks for lunch."

All the way home I laughed at her arguments. I threw the listing sheets on the kitchen counter with a batch of mail, inserted a movie into the VCR, and crawled back under my electric blanket. Hours later I emerged to brew a cup of coffee. As I waited for the coffee to drip, I glanced at the listing sheet once again. Three words caught my eye.

*Zoned Neighborhood Business.*

What exactly did that mean? Could I have a business on the premises? What kind? Of all the ideas I had explored in the past few months, the only one that held any continuing appeal was my own business. I really did want a venture of my own. Could I pull it off? Did I have the right stuff? Nothing I had touched in years seemed to succeed. I had failed in my job searches, in my partnership, in my marriage. Why did I think I could succeed now?

My mind never settled down that evening. As I tossed and turned in my bed, I started to mentally fill in the jagged pieces of the puzzle which comprised my life. By the time I telephoned my friend at ten the next morning, the puzzle was almost complete.

"Could you check the zoning in that house and get back to me?" I instructed her. "Tell me what I can do and what zoned neighborhood business means. I also want to know what's happening in the area."

"The only thing you can't do is raise sheep and pigs," she chuckled as she returned my call later that morning. "The neighborhood is sound. It hasn't peaked yet. You may have a decent investment if you decide to move on this property."

I had no source of income other than my alimony payments, which were scheduled to end in two years. I had the equity from the inn and my house. I could use most of it—roughly $13,000—as a down payment for the house, but once again I would be left without a cushion. I could sell my house, but that would take time. I hesitated only a moment.

"All right! Put in a bid for me! Let's negotiate," I said exuberantly.

My friend was perplexed over my sudden interest in the house, but she said nothing. The property was put under contract to me within twenty-four hours. I couldn't believe I had bought a house. I also didn't stop to consult anyone or think about the possible fallout if my house didn't sell. At long last I was following my instincts, which were revved up and running in high gear.

Now, how to put the house to optimum use? Huddled once again under my electric blanket, I began to list alternatives on a legal pad. What did I like to do? What skills did I possess? How could I make use of my writing skills and people orientation? What were my priorities? I had acquired an incredibly desirable location for a business virtually overnight. Should I rent out the space to others? No! I was going to start a business myself. I just didn't know what kind of business it would be.

I glanced up at my bookshelf and spotted my book—*Entrepreneurial Mothers*. Now I was going to have the chance to really be one. A business based on something entrepreneurial and involving communications would be perfect, I thought.

*Flash! Bang! Boom!* A lightningbolt of inspiration racked my body. A vision of my future was laid out before me. The vehicle? A public relations company for privately owned firms. The name: Entrepreneurial Communications.

The concept was so right, so obvious, I could not understand why it hadn't occurred to me earlier. My spark of inspiration rekindled my initiative. My adrenalin began to take over.

"Marsha, can you set up a business for me in addition to this house deal?" I was out of bed and on the phone with the attorney I had met only a few days earlier and retained to represent me as the buyer of the house. We met the following day.

"I want my company name registered and protected immediately," I instructed. "First Connecticut, then the other New England and mid-Atlantic states."

She was looking at me as if I were not quite all there. A few days ago I had bought a house virtually on the spur of the moment. Now I was starting a business. We were seated at her kitchen table with her two toddlers playing musical pots and pans at our feet as we spoke. The setting seemed perfectly in keeping with the tenor of my request.

"We should probably have Federal registration as well," she responded. I barely knew the woman, but she was instinctively following my thoughts. She was on my case. I knew there was a reason why I had instantly taken to her.

"Go home and do up a business plan," she said. "I'll get to work."

While she worked on the legalities of the start-up, I worked on my business plan, my business cards and stationery, and my clients. I called every one of my corporate accounts and told them of my plans to incorporate. Since I was now a businesswoman, I boldly suggested, I would need to know if they would commit a specified amount of work to me over the course of the coming year. Every company with whom I had a free-lance relationship signed a retainer agreement. Some small, some not so small, but I now had a basis for my business. I felt free, alive, and excited—and I never gave a second thought as to whether I could carry off the financial end of the venture.

I was elbow-deep in financial projections when I received a surprise phone call from a beau from my pre-marital Washington years who was passing through the area. He was now a successful attorney in the nation's capital and was here to meet with a client starting a high-tech firm. He had a few hours to kill before a late afternoon appointment. How about lunch?

Great, I thought, a little rehashing of old times. I could do with some of that. Besides, I was starving.

We exchanged gossip, tidbits about spouses and families, and talked about work.

"You were always so ambitious," he reminded me. "What happened?"

"What happened," I said, "was that I got married." I still had my ambition. It had just been delayed in fully flowering.

Before long I found myself telling him about my new business. Instead of being amused, he was deeply interested.

"I think you can do it," he said, calling for the check. "When you're ready for investors, send me a copy of your business plan."

I thanked him, and we exchanged pecks on each other's cheeks and agreed that lunch had been fun. I went back to my papers. He continued on to his meeting.

Three days later I received a check from him made out to "Entrepreneurial Communications, Inc." for $15,000. "Corporate Equity" was its notation.

"Send me the stock and the financials when your business plan is completed," said the one-line letter accompanying the cash. "You can do it."

The check was not a gift. It was an unconditional investment, but it was definitely an investment. My backer was a businessman who expected a return on his money and he had faith that I would deliver a good value for his dollars. I was ecstatic. If he had this kind of faith in me, I thought, perhaps others would as well.

For the first time in years I felt good. Really good. And confident. I knew this was right, absolutely right for me.

I also knew I had to break the news to Curtis about my impending move. I wanted him to hear from me that I was moving, and that since we would be less than thirty miles away, our custody arrangements would essentially remain the same. I was not ready for another courtroom confrontation.

I decided to tell him during one of his pickup times for Nat. As he waited for Nathaniel to clean up his room before leaving, I made Curtis a cup of coffee. Even that was a breakthrough in our postmarital relationship.

"Have you decided how you're going to support yourself?" he asked. "Have you found a job yet?"

"I'm starting my own business." I was surprised he had heard nothing about my efforts from anyone. After all, we did live in a small community where everyone's business was common knowledge.

Curtis's response was polite but discouraging.

"Do you have any clients?" he asked, dubiously. I laughed, shook my head, and decided not to tell him that I did. That, I wanted him to hear through the grapevine. I giggled wickedly at my secret knowledge.

Well, I couldn't expect miracles overnight! Curtis never did take my ambitions or abilities seriously. But now we had both gotten what we wanted. I couldn't complain.

With my house on the market, my business in place, my child in good spirits, and my relationship with Jackie and Curtis on an even keel, I could sit back and relax. I was, in my son's terminology, finally "functional."

Of course, it wasn't all that easy. Two months zipped past. March, April, then May. Memorial Day weekend. Still no buyers for the house. I needed $73,000 for my settlement on my new house, which now was only six weeks away. My impulsive business decision was turning into an irrational act.

"We're not questioning whether it's a good investment or not," said my father during an early morning holiday phone call, "nor whether your business is a sound idea. We're questioning why you didn't ask either of us for advice."

My dad was relaying his concerns and those of my brother. I was crying hysterically. I didn't want to hear his concerns. I wanted someone to offer me $73,000.

"I'm going to lose the house, I'm going to lose the business, I'm going to lose everything," I sobbed. "Two years of learning to stand on my own two feet again—all down the drain."

I hadn't asked his advice because I wanted to prove to

myself that I was self-sufficient. This is what my quest had brought me. Maybe Curtis was right not to take me seriously as a businesswoman.

"Look," my father said, "don't let your brother know we discussed this, but he'll bail you out if you really get hung up. He just wants you to stew awhile."

I had had enough stewing. Two more weeks passed. Still no buyer. Briefcase and business plan in hand, I went to see my banker, outlining my needs for a loan and my plans for the future. This was the same banker who had watched me sign away my financial responsibility for my now-defunct restaurant at the inn.

"No problem," he said. "You can have the money. Your house will sell. We'll write it as a swing loan."

As for my business?

"I think you can do it," he said.

I left the bank, incredulous that the loan process had been so easy and amazed at how I was perceived by others. For years I had undervalued myself and underestimated my abilities. I *was* going to do it, I was sure.

Rather than sit around worrying about the sale of my house and my impending move, I dug into my business activities.

I was attending a meeting with one of my clients. We were listening to a third businessman suggest ways of increasing our companys' visibility, when the man to my left said, "I think what you need to do is become more active in local business organizations. There's a meeting of the Connecticut Small Business Development Association tomorrow night. You should go."

He was right. I arranged to meet my host at his home, from where we would leave my car in his driveway and then proceed to the office complex where the meeting was being held. I knew he was single and didn't want to take the chance of being stranded.

"Always take your own car. That way you can leave," had proven to be valued words of advice.

At the meeting my host was pleasant, knowledgeable, and cordial. He introduced me to several potential clients, and we worked the room, exchanging business cards and networking information with several men and women in ancillary fields. It was fun to be back on the boards again. I appreciated the invitation and the business opportunities the evening had presented.

We left around eight P.M.

"I am famished," he said. "Do you have to get home right away or can we stop for something to eat?"

"I'm hungry, too," I replied. "How about the Sandpiper?"

"Good choice," he said. The Sandpiper was a fish house overlooking Long Island Sound. As we waited for a table we sat on the pier overlooking the water, and talked business and future plans. I told him about my cash shortfall on the house.

"You have to come up with how much?" he said incredulously. He looked at me for what seemed hours and then broke into a huge grin. "When you decide you want something you jump in with both feet, don't you?"

I nodded. "Pretty stupid, huh?"

"No, not at all," he said softly and seriously. "It shows you're willing to take a risk on something you believe in. I think that's a good quality to have. Have you talked to your banker yet?"

I assured him that I had, laid out my options, and listened to his suggestions. I was speaking to someone who was treating me as an equal, with respect and sincerity.

"Do you find me intimidating?" I asked him. It certainly was not a question that should have been introduced into a business discussion, but I was curious. I still wasn't rid of my old insecurities. I also felt he would give me an honest answer.

"Hell, no," he answered, standing up and taking my hand as he rose. "I think you're an exciting woman."

Goosebumps tingled my spine. Never had I been told

that before. I attributed it to my hair color. Now I was convinced blondes had more fun.

We chatted incessantly during the hour-long ride home. He was the first man I had met on my own. Direct access. A social equal, straight and not a flake. There were still a few normal-type men around, I was delighted to learn. As we pulled into his driveway I noticed the dashboard clock read 2:04 A.M. I moved to open the car door, he moved to kiss me. His move outmaneuvered my move.

"I really must go," I said demurely, thinking how glad I was to have driven my own car. "I have to get home and walk the dog."

"What dog?" he said. "You didn't say anything about a dog."

"I know, but it's late and she's been alone for hours. I really must go. Don't worry, I'll drive myself home."

Such a great defense, I was thinking. The car and the dog. Every single woman should learn that trick.

I felt his hand on my neck as he pulled me closer, his lips nibbling mine, his hands tenderly stroking my arms and hair.

"Why don't you follow me home?" I heard myself saying. I was shocked at my brazenness. Never, ever had I come on like this before.

"I'd planned to," he said.

It was nearly noon when I awoke. My bedmate had disappeared. I imagined he had let himself out at some point. I had never heard him stir. I felt no guilt, no remorse. The evening had been fifteen hours of sustained pleasure-related business.

"Hi." I heard a male voice and raised my head.

"The dog had to be walked," he said. "I let her out."

The new man had learned the old dog tricks.

"You were sleeping so soundly," he said. "I didn't want to wake you. I have to go to work. Don't get up. I'll call you soon."

I watched him close the door and stride toward his car. He was confident, capable, and a gentleman. I liked him and I liked his style, and he liked me for what I was, not what I could become.

I had no illusions that we already had a relationship. Maybe we would get to know each other. Maybe not. Either way, I thought. What was going to happen now, I didn't know. I would just take it one step at a time. So far it was okay.

July 3 burst open with radiant sunshine. I had twelve days before settlement and my $73,000 had to be on the table. It was also my fortieth birthday.

Nathaniel had decided that the best way to celebrate was for me to take him and his best friend to a baseball game. He was spending more time with me lately, after rewriting his custody arrangement with his father. Curtis, to my surprise and delight, had agreed to the revised plan. Who knows, I thought, maybe the situation will be revised later—and I'd be the parent on the other end. Just so Natty was comfortable and happy.

"The Yankees are playing the Blue Jays, Mom," he pleaded. "They're going to have fireworks, too."

Why not, I thought. A little touch of Americana would be good for all of us. Baseball, fireworks, and kids on my fortieth birthday. It said something about my priorities.

An hour before we had to leave, my local real estate agent called to say that my house was sold. We had to be out of the premises within thirty days.

Forty-five minutes before we walked out the door, a new client signed a year's contract with Entrepreneurial Communications. A second, calling minutes later, committed for six months.

Minutes later my gentleman friend called to "touch base."

I heaved several sighs of relief.

The boys and I had a wonderful evening at the ball

game, even though the home team lost. Fifty-six thousand people celebrated my birthday along with the nation's.

The weather was going to be fine at forty. I just knew it. As I watched the fireworks display, I couldn't help but think what a perfect way it was to celebrate. We all had what we wanted. Curtis had Jackie and the lifestyle he coveted. Natty had the best of both families. As for me, I had my child, my business, and my self-esteem. Maybe, someday, I thought, I would also have a love of my own.

Until then, I'm still driving my own car and still going home to walk the dog. That hasn't changed. What *has* changed is the way I think about my future. I do a lot of heavy thinking these days. Heavy thinking about building a sound financial base, about the need to be a self-sufficient woman in a turbulent world, and about living in a skin and a style that's right for me rather than rearranging my needs and desires around those of someone else.

Of course I still do some heavy thinking about my nights at Arturo's. I think about chicken parmesans and French Onion soup and the ever-present smell of marinara sauce and about how I resolved to put those nights with its kitchen scents and secrets behind me forever.

Unfortunately, it's not so easy. My new home, you see, is two doors away from the local pizzeria and the aroma of marinara sauce wafts through my windows from early morning till late at night. For me, maybe there will always be an Arturo's.

One other thing. The chef drives a Mercedes. Maybe my nights at Arturo's hold some hidden lessons for my future. From marinara sauce to a Mercedes, maybe? Why not? Anything's possible.

Spenser taught me that!

# AFTERWORD

I have been asked repeatedly since my divorce was finalized whether I felt the struggle was "worth it." Without doing any heavy thinking about the matter I would have to answer unequivocally yes.

Ultimately our settlement was fair to both sides, but had I given in at the beginning, I would have forfeited my rightful share of marital assets, a sound basis for my economic future, and, I am certain, a healthy portion of my self-esteem. I would also, most importantly, have forfeited a slightly more than equal measure of watchful guardedness over my son's future.

Would I do it again? To that I would also answer unequivocally yes. If I had to rewrite the script, however, I would make a few alterations. As I am neither a therapist, clergyman, nor physician, what advice I tender here springs solely from my own experience. Every situation is different. Every marriage is different and every divorce has its own characteristics. With these caveats in mind, I offer the benefits of hindsight.

A long time passes between getting a divorce and getting it together. I completely underestimated the emotional fallout of the divorce trauma, expecting to wrap up the unpleasantness as one might a nasty bit of spring housekeeping by sweeping out the dust, tying up the loose ends, and getting on with the passage of my life into another season. Notwithstanding the practical aspects of the divorce process—the lengthy negotiations, backlog in court schedules, and overloaded time commitments of the legal and psychological professionals involved in our case—the emotional paralysis was overwhelming and totally unexpected.

Weeks and months passed without much semblance of rational thought or action. I have no idea how I spent my time. I do know that my thoughts were either scrambled or frenetic. I was terrified of the future and terrified of taking any action or making any decisions that might move me forward. I have since heard from other women undergoing divorce as well as a range of mental health professionals that this "crisis inertia" is common and to be expected.

Unfortunately, rather than allowing adequate time to pass between the point of separation and the onset of settlement proceedings, many women find themselves impelled into final negotiations by fear—fear of the unknown, fear of financial destitution, and fear of losing their children. Fueled by the very real lack of financial resources and the emotional imbalance of a life and mind in limbo, many women opt to "settle" quickly rather than undertake the more often than not grueling negotiation process. Although this process is emotionally depleting to men as well, men usually do better because of their familiarity with the rules of business. Essentially, divorce is a business deal. *I don't think I can emphasize this enough*. Had I understood this earlier, perhaps some of the emotional fallout would have been less severe.

I also had unrealistic expectations of springing back to full emotional and financial self-sufficiency immediately after the divorce itself was finalized. Two years later, I am just beginning to reach a plateau of independence.

One of my biggest mistakes was not assuming more financial responsibility during my marriage. I was vaguely aware of our financial holdings, but gave over the bulk of the day-to-day decisions regarding money to my spouse. Here, I blame myself totally. My then husband discussed every investment with me and encouraged me to take a greater role in the household finances. I abdicated my responsibility. There was always something more pressing to divert my attention. I know now that taking responsibility for one's finances—present and future—should be put well ahead of other chores and commitments. What I looked at then as tedious—checkbooks, financial statements, banking relationships, and establishment of credit —I see now as essential elements in nurturing a sound financial base. In this day and age, no woman can afford not to take her finances seriously.

I was totally ignorant of the divorce laws until well after I became an unmarried woman. "I never thought it would happen to me" was my mind-set, so I chose to ignore any divorce literature, discussions or "what if" scenarios. Because the divorce laws have changed so dramatically across the nation in recent years, I would urge *every* woman who chooses to marry to place a premium on fully understanding the shifts in these laws and how they affect families.

One thing that should be kept in mind, however, is that procedural and statutory law varies from state to state, and that while some of my references to legal rights in this book are universal in the fifty states, others are not. So you should take care to find out about the specific laws of the state in which you will be getting divorced. The simplest way to do this is to call the individual state bar association and ask for a copy of the state's divorce codes. During the last phase of the writing of *Days Like This*, two books were published documenting in detail the negative consequences to women from the no-fault/equitable distribution aspects of the divorce codes and child custody laws. Lenore Weitzman's *The Divorce Revolution: The Unexpected Social and Economic Consequences for Women and Children in America* and Phyllis Chesler's *Mothers on Trial: The Battle for Children and Custody* are both broad-based, analytically acute studies giving statistical credence to the failure of divorce reforms. I urge those who wish to become better informed about the true inequities of divorce and custody today to read these two very fine works.

Finally, I came to recognize that there is no right and no wrong in divorce. There are only two parties who for whatever reason become unhinged. Nor can one parent unilaterally be seen as "better" than the other. The important factor is the relationship each has with his or her children.

We will never return to the days where one party took the children and the marital assets and the other was set adrift. That is a plus, for those laws were grossly unfair. On the other hand, however, the divorce revolution has tragically backfired, creating an underclass of women and children cruelly unprepared for their new future.

In its effort to rectify past abuses, the legal system has gone haywire. Today's unmarried women have no choice but to resist the reforms that have been imposed on them. I chose to resist—and I would choose to resist again—for me, for my child, and for the benefit of our extended family relationships in a society currently so marked by turbulence and change.